THE CHILDREN'S BOOK OF CHRISTMAS STORIES

Various

[ZHINGOORA BOOKS]

PREFACE

Many librarians have felt the need and expressed the desire for a select collection of children's Christmas stories in one volume. This books claims to be just that and nothing more.

Each of the stories has already won the approval of thousands of children, and each is fraught with the true Christmas spirit.

It is hoped that the collection will prove equally acceptable to parents, teachers, and librarians.

Asa Don Dickinson.

CONTENTS

(DETAILED) CONTENTS

(Note.—The stories marked with a star (*) will be most enjoyed by younger children; those marked with a two stars (**) are better suited to older children.)

I. CHRISTMAS AT FEZZIWIG'S WAREHOUSE

CHARLES DICKENS

"Yo Ho! my boys," said Fezziwig. "No more work to-night! Christmas Eve, Dick! Christmas, Ebenezer! Let's have the shutters up!" cried old Fezziwig with a sharp clap of his hands, "before a man can say Jack Robinson...."

"Hilli-ho!" cried old Fezziwig, skipping down from the high desk with wonderful agility. "Clear away, my lads, and let's have lots of room here! Hilli-ho, Dick! Cheer-up, Ebenezer!"

Clear away! There was nothing they wouldn't have cleared away, or couldn't have cleared away with old Fezziwig looking on. It was done in a minute. Every movable was packed off, as if it were dismissed from public life forevermore; the floor was swept and watered, the lamps were trimmed, fuel was heaped upon the fire; and the warehouse was as snug, and warm, and dry, and bright a ballroom as you would desire to see on a winter's night.

In came a fiddler with a music book, and went up to the lofty desk and made an orchestra of it and tuned like fifty stomach-aches. In came Mrs. Fezziwig, one vast substantial smile. In came the three Misses Fezziwig, beaming and lovable. In came the six followers whose hearts they broke. In came all the young men and women employed in the business. In came the housemaid with her cousin the baker. In came the cook with her brother's particular friend the milkman. In came the boy from over the way, who was suspected of not having board enough from his master, trying to hide himself behind the girl from next door but one who was proved to have had her ears pulled by her mistress; in they all came, anyhow and everyhow. Away they all went, twenty couple at once; hands half round and back again the other way; down the middle and up again; round and round in various stages of affectionate grouping, old top couple always turning up in the wrong place; new top couple starting off again, as soon as they got there; all top couples at last, and not a bottom one to help them.

When this result was brought about the fiddler struck up "Sir Roger de Coverley." Then old Fezziwig stood out to dance with Mrs. Fezziwig. Top couple, too, with a good stiff piece of work cut out for them; three or four and twenty pairs of partners; people who were not to be trifled with; people who would dance and had no notion of walking.

But if they had been thrice as many—oh, four times as many—old Fezziwig would have been a match for them, and so would Mrs. Fezziwig. As to her, she was worthy to be his partner in every sense of the term. If that's not high praise, tell me higher and I'll use it. A positive light appeared to issue from Fezziwig's calves. They shone in every part of the dance like moons. You couldn't have predicted at any given time what would become of them next. And when old Fezziwig and Mrs. Fezziwig had gone all through the dance, advance and retire; both hands to your partner, bow and courtesy, corkscrew, thread the needle, and back again to your place; Fezziwig "cut"—cut so deftly that he appeared to wink with his legs, and came upon his feet again with a stagger.

When the clock struck eleven the domestic ball broke up. Mr. and Mrs. Fezziwig took their stations, one on either side of the door, and shaking hands with every person individually, as he or she went out, wished him or her a Merry Christmas!

II. THE FIR-TREE*

*Reprinted by permission of the Houghton-Mifflin Company.

HANS CHRISTIAN ANDERSEN

Out in the woods stood a nice little Fir-tree. The place he had was a very good one; the sun shone on him; as to fresh air, there was enough of that, and round him grew many large-sized comrades, pines as well as firs. But the little Fir wanted so very much to be a grown-up tree.

He did not think of the warm sun and of the fresh air; he did not care for the little cottage children that ran about and prattled when they were in the woods looking for wild strawberries. The children often came with a whole pitcher full of berries, or a long row of them threaded on a straw, and sat down near the young tree and said, "Oh, how pretty he is! what a nice little fir!" But this was what the Tree could not bear to hear.

At the end of a year he had shot up a good deal, and after another year he was another long bit taller; for with fir-trees one can always tell by the shoots how many years old they are.

"Oh, were I but such a high tree as the others are!" sighed he. "Then I should be able to spread out my branches, and with the tops to look into the wide world! Then would the birds build nests among my branches; and when there was a breeze, I could bend with as much stateliness as the others!"

Neither the sunbeams, nor the birds, nor the red clouds, which morning and evening sailed above them, gave the little Tree any pleasure.

In winter, when the snow lay glittering on the ground, a hare would often come leaping along, and jump right over the little Tree. Oh, that made him so angry! But two winters were past, and in the third the tree was so large that the hare was obliged to go round it. "To grow and grow, to get older and be tall," thought the Tree—"that, after all, is the most delightful thing in the world!"

In autumn the wood-cutters always came and felled some of the largest trees. This happened every year; and the young Fir-tree, that had now grown to a very comely size, trembled at the sight; for the magnificent great trees fell to the earth with noise and cracking, the branches were lopped off, and the trees looked long and bare; they were hardly to be recognized; and then they were laid in carts, and the horses dragged them out of the woods.

Where did they go to? What became of them?

In spring, when the Swallows and the Storks came, the Tree asked them, "Don't you know where they have been taken? Have you not met them anywhere?"

The Swallows did not know anything about it; but the Stork looked musing, nodded his head, and said: "Yes, I think I know; I met many ships as I was flying hither from Egypt; on the ships were magnificent masts, and I venture to assert that it was they that smelt so of fir. I may congratulate you, for they lifted themselves on high most majestically!"

"Oh, were I but old enough to fly across the sea! But how does the sea look in reality? What is it like?"

"That would take a long time to explain," said the Stork, and with these words off he went.

"Rejoice in thy growth!" said the Sunbeams, "rejoice in thy vigorous growth, and in the fresh life that moveth within thee!"

And the Wind kissed the Tree, and the Dew wept tears over him; but the Fir understood it not.

When Christmas came, quite young trees were cut down; trees which often were not even as large or of the same age as this Fir-tree, who could never rest, but always wanted to be off. These young trees, and they were always the finest looking, retained their branches; they were laid on carts, and the horses drew them out of the woods.

"Where are they going to?" asked the Fir. "They are not taller than I; there was one indeed that was considerably shorter; and why do they retain all their branches? Whither are they taken?"

"We know! we know!" chirped the Sparrows. "We have peeped in at the windows in the town below! We know whither they are taken! The greatest splendour and the greatest magnificence one can imagine await them. We peeped through the windows, and saw them planted in the middle of the warm room, and ornamented with the most splendid things—with gilded apples, with gingerbread, with toys, and many hundred lights!"

"And then?" asked the Fir-tree, trembling in every bough. "And then? What happens then?"

"We did not see anything more: it was incomparably beautiful."

"I would fain know if I am destined for so glorious a career," cried the Tree, rejoicing. "That is still better than to cross the sea! What a longing do I suffer! Were Christmas but come! I am now tall, and my branches spread like the others that were carried off last year! Oh, were I but already on the cart. Were I in the warm room with all the splendour and magnificence! Yes; then something better, something still grander, will surely follow, or wherefore should they thus ornament me? Something better, something still grander, MUST follow—but what? Oh, how I long, how I suffer! I do not know myself what is the matter with me!"

"Rejoice in our presence!" said the Air and the Sunlight; "rejoice in thy own fresh youth!"

But the Tree did not rejoice at all; he grew and grew, and was green both winter and summer. People that saw him said, "What a fine tree!" and toward Christmas he was one of the first that was cut down. The axe struck deep into the very pith; the tree fell to the earth with a sigh: he felt a pang—it was like a swoon; he could not think of happiness, for he was sorrowful at being separated from his home, from the place where he had sprung up. He knew well that he should never see his dear old comrades, the little bushes and flowers around him, any more; perhaps not even the birds! The departure was not at all agreeable.

The Tree only came to himself when he was unloaded in a courtyard with the other trees, and heard a man say, "That one is splendid! we don't want the others." Then two servants came in rich livery and carried the Fir-tree into a large and splendid drawing-room. Portraits were hanging on the walls, and near the white porcelain stove stood two large Chinese vases with lions on the covers. There, too, were large easy chairs, silken sofas, large tables full of picture-books, and full of toys worth hundreds and hundreds of crowns—at least the children said so. And the Fir-tree was stuck upright in a cask that was filled with sand: but no one could see that it was a cask, for green cloth was hung all around it, and it stood on a large gayly coloured carpet. Oh, how the Tree quivered! What was to happen? The servants, as well as the young ladies, decorated it. On one branch there hung little nets cut out of coloured paper, and each net was filled with sugar-plums; and among the other boughs gilded apples and walnuts were suspended, looking as though they had grown there, and little blue and white tapers were placed among the leaves. Dolls that looked for all the world like men—the Tree had never beheld such before—were seen among the foliage, and at the very top a large star of gold tinsel was fixed. It was really splendid—beyond description splendid.

"This evening!" said they all; "how it will shine this evening!"

"Oh," thought the Tree, "if the evening were but come! If the tapers were but lighted! And then I wonder what will happen! Perhaps the other trees from the forest will come to look at me! Perhaps the sparrows will beat against the window-panes! I wonder if I shall take root here, and winter and summer stand covered with ornaments!"

He knew very much about the matter! but he was so impatient that for sheer longing he got a pain in his back, and this with trees is the same thing as a headache with us.

The candles were now lighted. What brightness! What splendour! The Tree trembled so in every bough that one of the tapers set fire to the foliage. It blazed up splendidly.

"Help! Help!" cried the young ladies, and they quickly put out the fire.

Now the Tree did not even dare tremble. What a state he was in! He was so uneasy lest he should lose something of his splendour, that he was quite bewildered amidst the glare and brightness; when suddenly both folding-doors opened, and a troop of children rushed in as if they would upset the Tree. The older persons followed quietly; the little ones stood quite still. But it was only for a moment; then they shouted so that the whole place reechoed with their rejoicing; they danced round the tree, and one present after the other was pulled off.

"What are they about?" thought the Tree. "What is to happen now?" And the lights burned down to the very branches, and as they burned down they were put out, one after the other, and then the children had permission to plunder the tree. So they fell upon it with such violence that all its branches cracked; if it had not been fixed firmly in the cask, it would certainly have tumbled down.

The children danced about with their beautiful playthings: no one looked at the Tree except the old nurse, who peeped between the branches; but it was only to see if there was a fig or an apple left that had been forgotten.

"A story! a story!" cried the children, drawing a little fat man toward the tree. He seated himself under it, and said: "Now we are in the shade, and the Tree can listen, too. But I shall tell only one story. Now which will you have: that about Ivedy-Avedy, or about Klumpy-Dumpy who tumbled downstairs, and yet after all came to the throne and married the princess?"

"Ivedy-Avedy!" cried some; "Klumpy-Dumpy" cried the others. There was such a bawling and screaming—the Fir-tree alone was silent, and he thought to himself, "Am I not to bawl with the rest?—am I to do nothing whatever?" for he was one of the company, and had done what he had to do.

And the man told about Klumpy-Dumpy that tumbled down, who notwithstanding came to the throne, and at last married the princess. And the children clapped their hands, and cried out, "Oh, go on! Do go on!" They wanted to hear about Ivedy-Avedy, too, but the little man only told them about Klumpy-Dumpy. The Fir-tree stood quite still and absorbed in thought; the birds in the woods had never related the like of this. "Klumpy-Dumpy fell downstairs, and yet he married the princess! Yes! Yes! that's the way of the world!" thought the Fir-tree, and believed it all, because the man who told the story was so good-looking. "Well, well! who knows, perhaps I may fall downstairs, too, and get a princess as wife!" And he looked forward with joy to the morrow, when he hoped to be decked out again with lights, playthings, fruits, and tinsel.

"I won't tremble to-morrow," thought the Fir tree. "I will enjoy to the full all my splendour. To-morrow I shall hear again the story of Klumpy-

Dumpy, and perhaps that of Ivedy-Avedy, too." And the whole night the Tree stood still and in deep thought.

In the morning the servant and the housemaid came in.

"Now, then, the splendour will begin again," thought the Fir. But they dragged him out of the room, and up the stairs into the loft; and here in a dark corner, where no daylight could enter, they left him. "What's the meaning of this?" thought the Tree. "What am I to do here? What shall I hear now, I wonder?" And he leaned against the wall, lost in reverie. Time enough had he, too, for his reflections; for days and nights passed on, and nobody came up; and when at last somebody did come, it was only to put some great trunks in a corner out of the way. There stood the Tree quite hidden; it seemed as if he had been entirely forgotten.

"'Tis now winter out of doors!" thought the Tree. "The earth is hard and covered with snow; men cannot plant me now, and therefore I have been put up here under shelter till the springtime comes! How thoughtful that is! How kind man is, after all! If it only were not so dark here, and so terribly lonely! Not even a hare. And out in the woods it was so pleasant, when the snow was on the ground, and the hare leaped by; yes—even when he jumped over me; but I did not like it then. It is really terribly lonely here!"

"Squeak! squeak!" said a little Mouse at the same moment, peeping out of his hole. And then another little one came. They sniffed about the Fir-tree, and rustled among the branches.

"It is dreadfully cold," said the Mouse. "But for that, it would be delightful here, old Fir, wouldn't it?"

"I am by no means old," said the Fir-tree. "There's many a one considerably older than I am."

"Where do you come from," asked the Mice; "and what can you do?" They were so extremely curious. "Tell us about the most beautiful spot on the earth. Have you never been there? Were you never in the larder, where cheeses lie on the shelves, and hams hang from above; where one dances about on tallow-candles; that place where one enters lean, and comes out again fat and portly?"

"I know no such place," said the Tree, "but I know the woods, where the sun shines, and where the little birds sing." And then he told all about his youth; and the little Mice had never heard the like before; and they listened and said:

"Well, to be sure! How much you have seen! How happy you must have been!"

"I?" said the Fir-tree, thinking over what he had himself related. "Yes, in reality those were happy times." And then he told about Christmas Eve, when he was decked out with cakes and candles.

"Oh," said the little Mice, "how fortunate you have been, old Fir-tree!"

"I am by no means old," said he. "I came from the woods this winter; I am in my prime, and am only rather short for my age."

"What delightful stories you know!" said the Mice: and the next night they came with four other little Mice, who were to hear what the tree recounted; and the more he related, the more plainly he remembered all himself; and it appeared as if those times had really been happy times. "But they may still come—they may still come. Klumpy-Dumpy fell downstairs and yet he got a princess," and he thought at the moment of a nice little Birch-tree growing out in the woods; to the Fir, that would be a real charming princess.

"Who is Klumpy-Dumpy?" asked the Mice. So then the Fir-tree told the whole fairy tale, for he could remember every single word of it; and the little Mice jumped for joy up to the very top of the Tree. Next night two more Mice came, and on Sunday two Rats, even; but they said the stories were not interesting, which vexed the little Mice; and they, too, now began to think them not so very amusing either.

"Do you know only one story?" asked the Rats.

"Only that one," answered the Tree. "I heard it on my happiest evening; but I did not then know how happy I was."

"It is a very stupid story. Don't you know one about bacon and tallow candles? Can't you tell any larder stories?"

"No," said the Tree.

"Then good-bye," said the Rats; and they went home.

At last the little Mice stayed away also; and the Tree sighed: "After all, it was very pleasant when the sleek little Mice sat around me and listened to what I told them. Now that too is over. But I will take good care to enjoy myself when I am brought out again."

But when was that to be? Why, one morning there came a quantity of people and set to work in the loft. The trunks were moved, the Tree was pulled out and thrown—rather hard, it is true—down on the floor, but a man drew him toward the stairs, where the daylight shone.

"Now a merry life will begin again," thought the Tree. He felt the fresh air, the first sunbeam—and now he was out in the courtyard. All passed so quickly, there was so much going on around him, that the Tree quite forgot to look to himself. The court adjoined a garden, and all was in flower; the roses hung so fresh and odorous over the balustrade, the lindens were in blossom, the Swallows flew by, and said, "Quirre-vit! my husband is come!" but it was not the Fir-tree that they meant.

"Now, then, I shall really enjoy life," said he, exultingly, and spread out his branches; but, alas! they were all withered and yellow. It was in a corner that he lay, among weeds and nettles. The golden star of tinsel was still on the top of the Tree, and glittered in the sunshine.

In the courtyard some of the merry children were playing who had danced at Christmas round the Fir-tree, and were so glad at the sight of him. One of the youngest ran and tore off the golden star.

"Only look what is still on the ugly old Christmas tree!" said he, trampling on the branches, so that they all cracked beneath his feet. And the Tree beheld all the beauty of the flowers, and the freshness in the garden; he beheld himself, and wished he had remained in his dark corner in the loft; he thought of his first youth in the woods, of the merry Christmas Eve, and of the little Mice who had listened with so much pleasure to the story of Klumpy-Dumpy.

"'Tis over—'tis past!" said the poor Tree. "Had I but rejoiced when I had reason to do so! But now 'tis past, 'tis past!"

And the gardener's boy chopped the Tree into small pieces; there was a whole heap lying there. The wood flamed up splendidly under the large brewing copper, and it sighed so deeply! Each sigh was like a shot.

The boys played about in the court, and the youngest wore the gold star on his breast which the Tree had had on the happiest evening of his life. However, that was over now—the Tree gone, the story at an end. All, all was over; every tale must end at last.

III. THE CHRISTMAS MASQUERADE*

* From "The Pot of Gold", copyright by Lothrop, Lee & Shepherd Co.

MARY E. WILKINS FREEMAN

On Christmas Eve the Mayor's stately mansion presented a beautiful appearance. There were rows of different coloured wax candles burning in every window, and beyond them one could see the chandeliers of gold and crystal blazing with light. The fiddles were squeaking merrily, and lovely little forms flew past the windows in time to the music.

There were gorgeous carpets laid from the door to the street, and carriages were constantly arriving and fresh guests tripping over them. They were all children. The Mayor was giving a Christmas Masquerade tonight to all the children in the city, the poor as well as the rich. The preparation for this ball had been making an immense sensation for the last three months. Placards had been up in the most conspicuous points in the city, and all the daily newspapers had at least a column devoted to it, headed with "THE MAYOR'S CHRISTMAS MASQUERADE," in very large letters.

The Mayor had promised to defray the expenses of all the poor children whose parents were unable to do so, and the bills for their costumes were directed to be sent in to him.

Of course there was great excitement among the regular costumers of the city, and they all resolved to vie with one another in being the most popular, and the best patronized on this gala occasion. But the placards and the notices had not been out a week before a new Costumer appeared who cast all the others into the shade directly. He set up his shop on the corner of one of the principal streets, and hung up his beautiful costumes in the windows. He was a little fellow, not much bigger than a boy of ten. His cheeks were as red as roses, and he had on a long curling wig as white as snow. He wore a suit of crimson velvet knee-breeches, and a little swallow-tailed coat with beautiful golden buttons. Deep lace ruffles fell over his slender white hands, and he wore elegant knee buckles of glittering stones. He sat on a high stool behind his counter and served his customers himself; he kept no clerk.

It did not take the children long to discover what beautiful things he had, and how superior he was to the other costumers, and they begun to flock to his shop immediately, from the Mayor's daughter to the poor ragpicker's. The children were to select their own costumes; the Mayor had stipulated that. It was to be a children's ball in every sense of the word.

So they decided to be fairies and shepherdesses, and princesses according to their own fancies; and this new Costumer had charming costumes to suit them.

It was noticeable that, for the most part, the children of the rich, who had always had everything they desired, would choose the parts of goose-girls and peasants and such like; and the poor children jumped eagerly at the chance of being princesses or fairies for a few hours in their miserable lives.

When Christmas Eve came and the children flocked into the Mayor's mansion, whether it was owing to the Costumer's art, or their own adaptation to the characters they had chosen, it was wonderful how lifelike their representations were. Those little fairies in their short skirts of silken gauze, in which golden sparkles appeared as they moved with their little funny gossamer wings, like butterflies, looked like real fairies. It did not seem possible, when they floated around to the music, half supported on the tips of their dainty toes, half by their filmy purple wings, their delicate bodies swaying in time, that they could be anything but fairies. It seemed absurd to imagine that they were Johnny

Mullens, the washerwoman's son, and Polly Flinders, the charwoman's little girl, and so on.

The Mayor's daughter, who had chosen the character of a goose-girl, looked so like a true one that one could hardly dream she ever was anything else. She was, ordinarily, a slender, dainty little lady rather tall for her age. She now looked very short and stubbed and brown, just as if she had been accustomed to tend geese in all sorts of weather. It was so with all the others—the Red Riding-hoods, the princesses, the Bo-Peeps and with every one of the characters who came to the Mayor's ball; Red Riding-hood looked round, with big, frightened eyes, all ready to spy the wolf, and carried her little pat of butter and pot of honey gingerly in her basket; Bo-Peep's eyes looked red with weeping for the loss of her sheep; and the princesses swept about so grandly in their splendid brocaded trains, and held their crowned heads so high that people half-believed them to be true princesses.

But there never was anything like the fun at the Mayor's Christmas ball. The fiddlers fiddled and fiddled, and the children danced and danced on the beautiful waxed floors. The Mayor, with his family and a few grand guests, sat on a dais covered with blue velvet at one end of the dancing hall, and watched the sport. They were all delighted. The Mayor's eldest daughter sat in front and clapped her little soft white hands. She was a tall, beautiful young maiden, and wore a white dress, and a little cap woven of blue violets on her yellow hair. Her name was Violetta.

The supper was served at midnight—and such a supper! The mountains of pink and white ices, and the cakes with sugar castles and flower gardens on the tops of them, and the charming shapes of gold and ruby-coloured jellies. There were wonderful bonbons which even the Mayor's daughter did not have every day; and all sorts of fruits, fresh and candied. They had cowslip wine in green glasses, and elderberry wine in red, and they drank each other's health. The glasses held a thimbleful each; the Mayor's wife thought that was all the wine they ought to have. Under each child's plate there was a pretty present and every one had a basket of bonbons and cake to carry home.

At four o'clock the fiddlers put up their fiddles and the children went home; fairies and shepherdesses and pages and princesses all jabbering gleefully about the splendid time they had had.

But in a short time what consternation there was throughout the city. When the proud and fond parents attempted to unbutton their children's dresses, in order to prepare them for bed, not a single costume would come off. The buttons buttoned again as fast as they were unbuttoned; even if they pulled out a pin, in it would slip again in a twinkling; and when a string was untied it tied itself up again into a bowknot. The parents were dreadfully frightened. But the children were so tired out they finally let them go to bed in their fancy costumes and thought perhaps they would come off better in the morning. So Red Riding-hood went to bed in her little red cloak holding fast to her basket full of dainties for her grandmother, and Bo-Peep slept with her crook in her hand.

The children all went to bed readily enough, they were so very tired, even though they had to go in this strange array. All but the fairies—they danced and pirouetted and would not be still.

"We want to swing on the blades of grass," they kept saying, "and play hide and seek in the lily cups, and take a nap between the leaves of the roses."

The poor charwomen and coal-heavers, whose children the fairies were for the most part, stared at them in great distress. They did not know what to do with these radiant, frisky little creatures into which their Johnnys and their Pollys and Betseys were so suddenly transformed. But the fairies went to bed quietly enough when daylight came, and were soon fast asleep.

There was no further trouble till twelve o'clock, when all the children woke up. Then a great wave of alarm spread over the city. Not one of the costumes would come off then. The buttons buttoned as fast as they were unbuttoned; the pins quilted themselves in as fast as they were pulled out; and the strings flew round like lightning and twisted themselves into bow-knots as fast as they were untied.

And that was not the worst of it; every one of the children seemed to have become, in reality, the character which he or she had assumed.

The Mayor's daughter declared she was going to tend her geese out in the pasture, and the shepherdesses sprang out of their little beds of down, throwing aside their silken quilts, and cried that they must go out and watch their sheep. The princesses jumped up from their straw pallets, and wanted to go to court; and all the rest of them likewise. Poor little Red Riding-hood sobbed and sobbed because she couldn't go and carry her basket to her grandmother, and as she didn't have any grandmother she couldn't go, of course, and her parents were very much doubled. It was all so mysterious and dreadful. The news spread very rapidly over the city, and soon a great crowd gathered around the new Costumer's shop for every one thought he must be responsible for all this mischief.

The shop door was locked; but they soon battered it down with stones. When they rushed in the Costumer was not there; he had disappeared with all his wares. Then they did not know what to do. But it was evident that they must do something before long for the state of affairs was growing worse and worse.

The Mayor's little daughter braced her back up against the tapestried wall, and planted her two feet in their thick shoes firmly. "I will go and tend my geese," she kept crying. "I won't eat my breakfast. I won't go out in the park. I won't go to school. I'm going to tend my geese—I will, I will, I will!"

And the princesses trailed their rich trains over the rough unpainted floors in their parents' poor little huts, and held their crowned heads very high and demanded to be taken to court. The princesses were mostly geese-girls when they were their proper selves, and their geese were suffering, and their poor parents did not know what they were going to do and they wrung their hands and wept as they gazed on their gorgeously apparelled children.

Finally the Mayor called a meeting of the Aldermen, and they all assembled in the City Hall. Nearly every one of them had a son or a daughter who was a chimney-sweep, or a little watch-girl, or a shepherdess. They appointed a chairman and they took a great many votes and contrary votes but they did not agree on anything, until every one proposed that they consult the Wise Woman. Then they all held up their hands, and voted to, unanimously.

So the whole board of Aldermen set out, walking by twos, with the Mayor at their head, to consult the Wise Woman. The Aldermen were all very fleshy, and carried gold-headed canes which they swung very high at every step. They held their heads well back, and their chins stiff, and whenever they met common people they sniffed gently. They were very imposing.

The Wise Woman lived in a little hut on the outskirts of the city. She kept a Black Cat, except for her, she was all alone. She was very old, and had brought up a great many children, and she was considered remarkably wise.

But when the Aldermen reached her hut and found her seated by the fire, holding her Black Cat, a new difficulty presented itself. She had always been quite deaf and people had been obliged to scream as loud as they could in order to make her hear; but lately she had grown much deafer, and when the Aldermen attempted to lay the case before her she could not hear a word. In fact, she was so very deaf that she could not distinguish a tone below G-sharp. The Aldermen screamed till they were quite red in the faces, but all to no purpose: none of them could get up to G-sharp of course.

So the Aldermen all went back, swinging their gold-headed canes, and they had another meeting in the City Hall. Then they decided to send the highest Soprano Singer in the church choir to the Wise Woman; she could sing up to G-sharp just as easy as not. So the high Soprano Singer set out for the Wise Woman's in the Mayor's coach, and the Aldermen marched behind, swinging their gold-headed canes.

The High Soprano Singer put her head down close to the Wise Woman's ear, and sung all about the Christmas Masquerade and the dreadful dilemma everybody was in, in G-sharp—she even went higher, sometimes, and the Wise Woman heard every word.

She nodded three times, and every time she nodded she looked wiser.

"Go home, and give 'em a spoonful of castor-oil, all 'round," she piped up; then she took a pinch of snuff, and wouldn't say any more.

So the Aldermen went home, and every one took a district and marched through it, with a servant carrying an immense bowl and spoon, and every child had to take a dose of castor-oil.

But it didn't do a bit of good. The children cried and struggled when they were forced to take the castor-oil; but, two minutes afterward, the chimney-sweeps were crying for their brooms, and the princesses screaming because they couldn't go to court, and the Mayor's daughter, who had been given a double dose, cried louder and more sturdily: "I want to go and tend my geese. I will go and tend my geese."

So the Aldermen took the high Soprano Singer, and they consulted the Wise Woman again. She was taking a nap this time, and the Singer had to sing up to B-flat before she could wake her. Then she was very cross and the Black Cat put up his back and spit at the Aldermen.

"Give 'em a spanking all 'round," she snapped out, "and if that don't work put 'em to bed without their supper."

Then the Aldermen marched back to try that; and all the children in the city were spanked, and when that didn't do any good they were put to bed without any supper. But the next morning when they woke up they were worse than ever.

The Mayor and Aldermen were very indignant, and considered that they had been imposed upon and insulted. So they set out for the Wise Woman again, with the high Soprano Singer.

She sang in G-sharp how the Aldermen and the Mayor considered her an impostor, and did not think she was wise at all, and they wished her to take her Black Cat and move beyond the limits of the city.

She sang it beautifully; it sounded like the very finest Italian opera music.

"Deary me," piped the Wise Woman, when she had finished, "how very grand these gentlemen are." Her Black Cat put up his back and spit.

"Five times one Black Cat are five Black Cats," said the Wise Woman. And directly there were five Black Cats spitting and miauling.

"Five times five Black Cats are twenty-five Black Cats." And then there were twenty-five of the angry little beasts.

"Five times twenty-five Black Cats are one hundred and twenty-five Black Cats," added the Wise Woman with a chuckle.

Then the Mayor and the Aldermen and the high Soprano Singer fled precipitately out the door and back to the city. One hundred and twenty-five Black Cats had seemed to fill the Wise Woman's hut full, and when they all spit and miauled together it was dreadful. The visitors could not wait for her to multiply Black Cats any longer.

As winter wore on and spring came, the condition of things grew more intolerable. Physicians had been consulted, who advised that the children should be allowed to follow their own bents, for fear of injury to their constitutions. So the rich Aldermen's daughters were actually out in the fields herding sheep, and their sons sweeping chimneys or carrying newspapers; and while the poor charwomen's and coal-heavers, children spent their time like princesses and fairies. Such a topsy-turvy state of society was shocking. While the Mayor's little daughter was tending geese out in the meadow like any common goose-girl, her pretty elder sister, Violetta, felt very sad about it and used often to cast about in her mind for some way of relief.

When cherries were ripe in spring, Violetta thought she would ask the Cherry-man about it. She thought the Cherry-man quite wise. He was a very pretty young fellow, and he brought cherries to sell in graceful little straw baskets lined with moss. So she stood in the kitchen door one morning and told him all about the great trouble that had come upon the city. He listened in great astonishment; he had never heard of it before. He lived several miles out in the country.

"How did the Costumer look?" he asked respectfully; he thought Violetta the most beautiful lady on earth.

Then Violetta described the Costumer, and told him of the unavailing attempts that had been made to find him. There were a great many detectives out, constantly at work.

"I know where he is!" said the Cherry-man. "He's up in one of my cherry-trees. He's been living there ever since cherries were ripe, and he won't come down."

Then Violetta ran and told her father in great excitement, and he at once called a meeting of the Aldermen, and in a few hours half the city was on the road to the Cherry-man's.

He had a beautiful orchard of cherry-trees all laden with fruit. And, sure enough in one of the largest, way up amongst the topmost branches, sat the Costumer in his red velvet and short clothes and his diamond knee-buckles. He looked down between the green boughs. "Good-morning, friends!" he shouted.

The Aldermen shook their gold-headed canes at him, and the people danced round the tree in a rage. Then they began to climb. But they soon found that to be impossible. As fast as they touched a hand or foot to a tree, back it flew with a jerk exactly as if the tree pushed it. They tried a ladder, but the ladder fell back the moment it touched the tree, and lay sprawling upon the ground. Finally, they brought axes and thought they could chop the tree down, Costumer and all; but the wood resisted the axes as if it were iron, and only dented them, receiving no impression itself.

Meanwhile, the Costumer sat up in the tree, eating cherries and throwing the stones down. Finally he stood up on a stout branch, and, looking down, addressed the people.

"It's of no use, your trying to accomplish anything in this way," said he; "you'd better parley. I'm willing to come to terms with you, and make everything right on two conditions."

The people grew quiet then, and the Mayor stepped forward as spokesman, "Name your two conditions," said he rather testily. "You own, tacitly, that you are the cause of all this trouble."

"Well" said the Costumer, reaching out for a handful of cherries, "this Christmas Masquerade of yours was a beautiful idea; but you wouldn't do it every year, and your successors might not do it at all. I want those poor children to have a Christmas every year. My first condition is that every poor child in the city hangs its stocking for gifts in the City Hall on every Christmas Eve, and gets it filled, too. I want the resolution filed and put away in the city archives."

"We agree to the first condition!" cried the people with one voice, without waiting for the Mayor and Aldermen.

"The second condition," said the Costumer, "is that this good young Cherry-man here has the Mayor's daughter, Violetta, for his wife. He has been kind to me, letting me live in his cherry-tree and eat his cherries and I want to reward him."

"We consent," cried all the people; but the Mayor, though he was so generous, was a proud man. "I will not consent to the second condition," he cried angrily.

"Very well," replied the Costumer, picking some more cherries, "then your youngest daughter tends geese the rest of her life, that's all."

The Mayor was in great distress; but the thought of his youngest daughter being a goose-girl all her life was too much for him. He gave in at last.

"Now go home and take the costumes off your children," said the Costumer, "and leave me in peace to eat cherries."

Then the people hastened back to the city, and found, to their great delight, that the costumes would come off. The pins stayed out, the buttons stayed unbuttoned, and the strings stayed untied. The children were dressed in their own proper clothes and were their own proper selves once more. The shepherdesses and the chimney-sweeps came home, and were washed and dressed in silks and velvets, and went to embroidering and playing lawn-tennis. And the princesses and the fairies put on their own suitable dresses, and went about their useful employments. There was great rejoicing in every home. Violetta thought she had never been so happy, now that her dear little sister was no longer a goose-girl, but her own dainty little lady-self.

The resolution to provide every poor child in the city with a stocking full of gifts on Christmas was solemnly filed, and deposited in the city archives, and was never broken.

Violetta was married to the Cherry-man, and all the children came to the wedding, and strewed flowers in her path till her feet were quite hidden in them. The Costumer had mysteriously disappeared from the cherry-tree the night before, but he left at the foot some beautiful wedding presents for the bride—a silver service with a pattern of cherries engraved on it, and a set of china with cherries on it, in hand painting, and a white satin robe, embroidered with cherries down the front.

IV. THE SHEPHERDS AND THE ANGELS

ADAPTED FROM THE BIBLE

And there were shepherds in the same country abiding in the field, and keeping watch by night over their flock. And an angel of the Lord stood by them and the glory of the Lord shone round about them: and they were sore afraid. And the angel said unto them, Be not afraid; for, behold, I bring you good tidings of great joy which shall be to all the people: for there is born to you this day in the city of David a Saviour, which is Christ the Lord. And this is the sign unto you; ye shall find a babe wrapped in swaddling clothes, and lying in a manger. And suddenly there was with the angel a multitude of the heavenly host praising God and saying:

Glory to God in the highest,

And on earth peace,

Good will toward men.

And it came to pass, when the angels went away from them into heaven, the shepherds said one to another, Let us now go even unto Bethlehem, and see this thing that is come to pass, which the Lord hath made known unto us. And they came with haste, and found Mary and Joseph and the babe lying in the manger. And when they saw it, they made known concerning the saying which was spoken to them about this child. And all that heard it wondered at the things which were spoken unto them by the shepherds. But Mary kept all these sayings, pondering them in her heart. And the shepherds returned glorifying and praising God for all the things that they had heard and seen, even as it was spoken unto them.

And when eight days were fulfilled his name was called

JESUS

V. THE TELLTALE TILE*

* From "Kristy's Queer Christmas," Houghton, Mifflin & Co., 1904.

OLIVE THORNE MILLER

It begins with a bit of gossip of a neighbour who had come in to see Miss Bennett, and was telling her about a family who had lately moved into the place and were in serious trouble. "And they do say she'll have to go to the poorhouse," she ended.

"To the poorhouse! how dreadful! And the children, too?" and Miss Bennett shuddered.

"Yes; unless somebody'll adopt them, and that's not very likely. Well, I must go," the visitor went on, rising. "I wish I could do something for her, but, with my houseful of children, I've got use for every penny I can rake and scrape."

"I'm sure I have, with only myself," said Miss Bennett, as she closed the door. "I'm sure I have," she repeated to herself as she resumed her knitting; "it's as much as I can do to make ends meet, scrimping as I do, not to speak of laying up a cent for sickness and old age."

"But the poorhouse!" she said again. "I wish I could help her!" and the needles flew in and out, in and out, faster than ever, as she turned this over in her mind. "I might give up something," she said at last, "though I don't know what, unless—unless," she said slowly, thinking of her one luxury, "unless I give up my tea, and it don't seem as if I COULD do that."

Some time the thought worked in her mind, and finally she resolved to make the sacrifice of her only indulgence for six months, and send the

35

money to her suffering neighbour, Mrs. Stanley, though she had never seen her, and she had only heard she was in want.

How much of a sacrifice that was you can hardly guess, you, Kristy, who have so many luxuries.

That evening Mrs. Stanley was surprised by a small gift of money "from a friend," as was said on the envelope containing it.

"Who sent it?" she asked, from the bed where she was lying.

"Miss Bennett told me not to tell," said the boy, unconscious that he had already told.

The next day Miss Bennett sat at the window knitting, as usual—for her constant contribution to the poor fund of the church was a certain number of stockings and mittens—when she saw a young girl coming up to the door of the cottage.

"Who can that be?" she said to herself. "I never saw her before. Come in!" she called; in answer to a knock. The girl entered, and walked up to Miss Bennett.

"Are you Miss Bennett?" she asked.

"Yes," said Miss Bennett with an amused smile.

"Well, I'm Hetty Stanley."

Miss Bennett started, and her colour grew a little brighter.

"I'm glad to see you, Hetty." she said, "won't you sit down?"

"Yes, if you please," said Hetty, taking a chair near her.

"I came to tell you how much we love you for—"

"Oh, don't! don't say any more!" interrupted Miss Bennett; "never mind that! Tell me about your mother and your baby brother."

This was an interesting subject, and they talked earnestly about it. The time passed so quickly that, before she knew it, she had been in the house an hour. When she went away Miss Bennett asked her to come again, a thing she had never been known to do before, for she was not fond of young people in general.

"But, then, Hetty's different," she said to herself, when wondering at her own interest.

"Did you thank kind Miss Bennett?" was her mother's question as Hetty opened the door.

Hetty stopped as if struck, "Why, no! I don't think I did."

"And stayed so long, too? Whatever did you do? I've heard she isn't fond of people generally."

"We talked; and—I think she's ever so nice. She asked me to come again; may I?"

"Of course you may, if she cares to have you. I should be glad to do something to please her."

That visit of Hetty's was the first of a long series. Almost every day she found her way to the lonely cottage, where a visitor rarely came, and a strange intimacy grew up between the old and the young. Hetty learned of her friend to knit, and many an hour they spent knitting while Miss Bennett ransacked her memory for stories to tell. And then, one day, she brought down from a big chest in the garret two of the books she used to have when she was young, and let Hetty look at them.

One was "Thaddeus of Warsaw," and the other "Scottish Chiefs." Poor Hetty had not the dozens of books you have, and these were treasures indeed. She read them to herself, and she read them aloud to Miss Bennett, who, much to her own surprise, found her interest almost as eager as Hetty's.

All this time Christmas was drawing near, and strange, unusual feelings began to stir in Miss Bennett's heart, though generally she did not think much about that happy time. She wanted to make Hetty a happy day. Money she had none, so she went into the garret, where her youthful treasures had long been hidden. From the chest from which she had taken the books she now took a small box of light-coloured wood, with a transferred engraving on the cover. With a sigh—for the sight of it brought up old memories—Miss Bennett lifted the cover by its loop of ribbon, took out a package of old letters, and went downstairs with the box, taking also a few bits of bright silk from a bundle in the chest.

"I can fit it up for a workbox," she said, "and I'm sure Hetty will like it."

For many days after this Miss Bennett had her secret work, which she carefully hid when she saw Hetty coming. Slowly, in this way, she made a pretty needle-book, a tiny pincushion, and an emery bag like a big strawberry. Then from her own scanty stock she added needles, pins, thread, and her only pair of small scissors, scoured to the last extreme of brightness.

One thing only she had to buy—a thimble, and that she bought for a penny, of brass so bright it was quite as handsome as gold.

Very pretty the little box looked when full; in the bottom lay a quilted lining, which had always been there, and upon this the fittings she had made. Besides this, Miss Bennett knit a pair of mittens for each of Hetty's brothers and sisters.

The happiest girl in town on Christmas morning was Hetty Stanley. To begin with, she had the delight of giving the mittens to the children, and when she ran over to tell Miss Bennett how pleased they were, she was surprised by the present of the odd little workbox and its pretty contents.

Christmas was over all too soon, and New Year's, and it was about the middle of January that the time came which, all her life, Miss Bennett had dreaded—the time when she should be helpless. She had not money enough to hire a girl, and so the only thing she could imagine when that day should come was her special horror—the poorhouse.

But that good deed of hers had already borne fruit, and was still bearing. When Hetty came over one day, and found her dear friend lying on the floor as if dead, she was dreadfully frightened, of course, but she ran after the neighbours and the doctor, and bustled about the house as if she belonged to it.

Miss Bennett was not dead—she had a slight stroke of paralysis; and though she was soon better, and would be able to talk, and probably to knit, and possibly to get about the house, she would never be able to live alone and do everything for herself, as she had done.

So the doctor told the neighbours who came in to help, and so Hetty heard, as she listened eagerly for news.

"Of course she can't live here any longer; she'll have to go to a hospital," said one woman.

"Or to the poorhouse, more likely," said another.

"She'll hate that," said the first speaker. "I've heard her shudder over the poorhouse."

"She shall never go there!" declared Hetty, with blazing eyes.

"Hoity-toity! who's to prevent?" asked the second speaker, turning a look of disdain on Hetty.

"I am," was the fearless answer. "I know all Miss Bennett's ways, and I can take care of her, and I will," went on Hetty indignantly; and turning suddenly, she was surprised to find Miss Bennett's eyes fixed on her with an eager, questioning look.

"There! she understands! she's better!" cried Hetty. "Mayn't I stay and take care of you, dear Miss Bennett?" she asked, running up to the bed.

"Yes, you may," interrupted the doctor, seeing the look in his patient's face; "but you mustn't agitate her now. And now, my good women"— turning to the others—"I think she can get along with her young friend here, whom I happen to know is a womanly young girl, and will be attentive and careful."

They took the hint and went away, and the doctor gave directions to Hetty what to do, telling her she must not leave Miss Bennett. So she was now regularly installed as nurse and housekeeper.

Days and weeks rolled by. Miss Bennett was able to be up in her chair, to talk and knit, and to walk about the house, but was not able to be left alone. Indeed, she had a horror of being left alone; she could not bear Hetty out of her sight, and Hetty's mother was very willing to spare her, for she had many mouths to fill.

To provide food for two out of what had been scrimping for one was a problem; but Miss Bennett ate very little, and she did not resume her tea so they managed to get along and not really suffer.

One day Hetty sat by the fire with her precious box on her knee, which she was putting to rights for the twentieth time. The box was empty, and her sharp young eyes noticed a little dust on the silk lining.

"I think I'll take this out and dust it," she said to Miss Bennett, "if you don't mind."

"Do as you like with it," answered Miss Bennett; "it is yours."

So she carefully lifted the silk, which stuck a little.

"Why, here's something under it," she said—"an old paper, and it has writing on."

"Bring it to me," said Miss Bennett; "perhaps it's a letter I have forgotten."

Hetty brought it.

"Why, it's father's writing!" said Miss Bennett, looking closely at the faded paper; "and what can it mean? I never saw it before. It says, 'Look, and ye shall find'—that's a Bible text. And what is this under it? 'A word to the wise is sufficient.' I don't understand—he must have put it there himself, for I never took that lining out—I thought it was fastened. What can it mean?" and she pondered over it long, and all day seemed absent-minded.

After tea, when they sat before the kitchen fire, as they always did, with only the firelight flickering and dancing on the walls while they knitted, or told stories, or talked, she told Hetty about her father: that they had lived comfortably in this house, which he built, and that everybody supposed that he had plenty of money, and would leave enough to take care of his only child, but that when he died suddenly nothing had been found, and nothing ever had been, from that day to this.

"Part of the place I let to John Thompson, Hetty, and that rent is all I have to live on. I don't know what makes me think of old times so to-night."

"I know," said Hetty; "it's that paper, and I know what it reminds me of," she suddenly shouted, in a way very unusual with her. "It's that tile over there," and she jumped up and ran to the side of the fireplace, and put her hand on the tile she meant.

On each side of the fireplace was a row of tiles. They were Bible subjects, and Miss Bennett had often told Hetty the story of each one, and also the stories she used to make up about them when she was young. The one Hetty had her hand on now bore the picture of a woman standing before a closed door, and below her the words of the yellow bit of paper: "Look, and ye shall find."

"I always felt there was something different about that," said Hetty eagerly, "and you know you told me your father talked to you about it— about what to seek in the world when he was gone away, and other things."

"Yes, so he did," said Miss Bennett thoughtfully; "come to think of it, he said a great deal about it, and in a meaning way. I don't understand it," she said slowly, turning it over in her mind.

"I do!" cried Hetty, enthusiastically. "I believe you are to seek here! I believe it's loose!" and she tried to shake it. "It IS loose!" she cried excitedly. "Oh, Miss Bennett, may I take it out?"

Miss Bennett had turned deadly pale. "Yes," she gasped, hardly knowing what she expected, or dared to hope.

A sudden push from Hetty's strong fingers, and the tile slipped out at one side and fell to the floor. Behind it was an opening into the brickwork. Hetty thrust in her hand.

"There's something in there!" she said in an awed tone.

"A light!" said Miss Bennett hoarsely.

There was not a candle in the house, but Hetty seized a brand from the fire, and held it up and looked in.

"It looks like bags—tied up," she cried. "Oh, come here yourself!"

The old woman hobbled over and thrust her hand into the hole, bringing out what was once a bag, but which crumpled to pieces in her hands, and with it—oh, wonder!—a handful of gold pieces, which fell with a jingle on the hearth, and rolled every way.

"My father's money! Oh, Hetty!" was all she could say, and she seized a chair to keep from falling, while Hetty was nearly wild, and talked like a crazy person.

"Oh, goody! goody! now you can have things to eat! and we can have a candle! and you won't have to go to the poorhouse!"

"No, indeed, you dear child!" cried Miss Bennett who had found her voice. "Thanks to you—you blessing!—I shall be comfortable now the rest of my days. And you! oh! I shall never forget you! Through you has everything good come to me."

"Oh, but you have been so good to me, dear Miss Bennett!"

"I should never have guessed it, you precious child! If it had not been for your quickness I should have died and never found it."

"And if you hadn't given me the box, it might have rusted away in that chest."

"Thank God for everything, child! Take money out of my purse and go buy a candle. We need not save it for bread now. Oh, child!" she interrupted herself, "do you know, we shall have everything we want to-morrow. Go! Go! I want to see how much there is."

The candle bought, the gold was taken out and counted, and proved to be more than enough to give Miss Bennett a comfortable income without touching the principal. It was put back, and the tile replaced, as the safest place to keep it till morning, when Miss Bennett intended to put it into a bank.

But though they went to bed, there was not a wink of sleep for Miss Bennett, for planning what she would do. There were a thousand things she wanted to do first. To get clothes for Hetty, to brighten up the old house, to hire a girl to relieve Hetty, so that the dear child should go to school, to train her into a noble woman—all her old ambitions and wishes for herself sprang into life for Hetty. For not a thought of her future life was separate from Hetty.

In a very short time everything was changed in Miss Bennett's cottage. She had publicly adopted Hetty, and announced her as her heir. A girl had been installed in the kitchen, and Hetty, in pretty new clothes, had begun school. Fresh paint inside and out, with many new comforts, made the old house charming and bright. But nothing could change the pleasant and happy relations between the two friends, and a more contented and cheerful household could not be found anywhere.

Happiness is a wonderful doctor and Miss Bennett grew so much better, that she could travel, and when Hetty had finished school days, they saw a little of the world before they settled down to a quiet, useful life.

"Every comfort on earth I owe to you," said Hetty, one day, when Miss Bennett had proposed some new thing to add to her enjoyment.

"Ah, dear Hetty! how much do I owe to you! But for you, I should, no doubt, be at this moment a shivering pauper in that terrible poorhouse, while some one else would be living in this dear old house. And it all comes," she added softly, "of that one unselfish thought, of that one self-denial for others."

VI. LITTLE GIRL'S CHRISTMAS

WINNIFRED E. LINCOLN

It was Christmas Eve, and Little Girl had just hung up her stocking by the fireplace—right where it would be all ready for Santa when he slipped down the chimney. She knew he was coming, because—well, because it was Christmas Eve, and because he always had come to leave gifts for her on all the other Christmas Eves that she could remember, and because she had seen his pictures everywhere down town that afternoon when she was out with Mother.

Still, she wasn't JUST satisfied. 'Way down in her heart she was a little uncertain—you see, when you have never really and truly seen a person with your very own eyes, it's hard to feel as if you exactly believed in him—even though that person always has left beautiful gifts for you every time he has come.

"Oh, he'll come," said Little Girl; "I just know he will be here before morning, but somehow I wish—"

"Well, what do you wish?" said a Tiny Voice close by her—so close that Little Girl fairly jumped when she heard it.

"Why, I wish I could SEE Santa myself. I'd just like to go and see his house and his workshop, and ride in his sleigh, and know Mrs. Santa—'twould be such fun, and then I'd KNOW for sure."

"Why don't you go, then?" said Tiny Voice. "It's easy enough. Just try on these Shoes, and take this Light in your hand, and you'll find your way all right."

So Little Girl looked down on the hearth, and there were two cunning little Shoes side by side, and a little Spark of a Light close to them—just as if they were all made out of one of the glowing coals of the wood-fire. Such cunning Shoes as they were— Little Girl could hardly wait to pull off her slippers and try them on. They looked as if they were too small, but they weren't—they fitted exactly right, and just as Little Girl had put them both on and had taken the Light in her hand, along came a little Breath of Wind, and away she went up the chimney, along with ever so many other little Sparks, past the Soot Fairies, and out into the Open Air, where Jack Frost and the Star Beams were all busy at work making the world look pretty for Christmas.

Away went Little Girl—Two Shoes, Bright Light, and all—higher and higher, until she looked like a wee bit of a star up in the sky. It was the funniest thing, but she seemed to know the way perfectly, and didn't have to stop to make inquiries anywhere. You see it was a straight road all the way, and when one doesn't have to think about turning to the right or the left, it makes things very much easier. Pretty soon Little Girl noticed that there was a bright light all around her—oh, a very bright light—and right away something down in her heart began to make her feel very happy indeed. She didn't know that the Christmas spirits and little Christmas fairies were all around her and even right inside her, because she couldn't see a single one of them, even though her eyes were very bright and could usually see a great deal.

But that was just it, and Little Girl felt as if she wanted to laugh and sing and be glad. It made her remember the Sick Boy who lived next door, and she said to herself that she would carry him one of her prettiest picture-books in the morning, so that he could have something to make him happy all day. By and by, when the bright light all around her had grown very, very much brighter, Little Girl saw a path right in front of her, all straight and trim, leading up a hill to a big, big house with ever and ever so many windows in it. When she had gone just a bit nearer, she saw candles in every window, red and green and yellow ones, and every one burning brightly, so Little Girl knew right away that these were Christmas candles to light her on her journey, and make the way dear for her, and something told her that this was Santa's house, and that pretty soon she would perhaps see Santa himself.

Just as she neared the steps and before she could possibly have had time to ring the bell, the door opened—opened of itself as wide as could be—and there stood—not Santa himself—don't think it—but a funny Little Man with slender little legs and a roly-poly stomach which shook every now and then when he laughed. You would have known right away, just as Little Girl knew, that he was a very happy little man, and you would have guessed right away, too, that the reason he was so roly-poly was because he laughed and chuckled and smiled all the time—for it's only sour, cross folks who are thin and skimpy. Quick as a wink, he pulled off his little peaked red cap, smiled the broadest kind of a smile, and said, "Merry Christmas! Merry Christmas! Come in! Come in!"

So in went Little Girl, holding fast to Little Man's hand, and when she was really inside there was the jolliest, reddest fire all glowing and snapping, and there were Little Man and all his brothers and sisters, who said their names were "Merry Christmas," and "Good Cheer," and ever so many other jolly-sounding things, and there were such a lot of them that Little Girl just knew she never could count them, no matter how long she tried.

All around her were bundles and boxes and piles of toys and games, and Little Girl knew that these were all ready and waiting to be loaded into Santa's big sleigh for his reindeer to whirl them away over cloudtops and snowdrifts to the little people down below who had left their stockings all ready for him. Pretty soon all the little Good Cheer Brothers began to hurry and bustle and carry out the bundles as fast as they could to the steps where Little Girl could hear the jingling bells and the stamping of hoofs. So Little Girl picked up some bundles and skipped along too, for she wanted to help a bit herself—it's no fun whatever at Christmas unless you can help, you know—and there in the yard stood the BIGGEST sleigh that Little Girl had ever seen, and the reindeer were all stamping and prancing and jingling the bells on their harnesses, because they were so eager to be on their way to the Earth once more.

She could hardly wait for Santa to come, and just as she had begun to wonder where he was, the door opened again and out came a whole forest of Christmas trees, at least it looked just as if a whole forest had started out for a walk somewhere, but a second glance showed Little Girl that there were thousands of Christmas sprites, and that each one carried a tree or a big Christmas wreath on his back. Behind them all, she could hear some one laughing loudly, and talking in a big, jovial voice that sounded as if he were good friends with the whole world.

And straightway she knew that Santa himself was coming. Little Girl's heart went pit-a-pat for a minute while she wondered if Santa would notice her, but she didn't have to wonder long, for he spied her at once and said:

"Bless my soul! who's this? and where did you come from?"

Little Girl thought perhaps she might be afraid to answer him, but she wasn't one bit afraid. You see he had such a kind little twinkle in his eyes that she felt happy right away as she replied, "Oh, I'm Little Girl, and I wanted so much to see Santa that I just came, and here I am!"

"Ho, ho, ho, ho, ho!" laughed Santa, "and here you are! Wanted to see Santa, did you, and so you came! Now that's very nice, and it's too bad I'm in such a hurry, for we should like nothing better than to show you about and give you a real good time. But you see it is quarter of twelve now, and I must be on my way at once, else I'll never reach that first chimney-top by midnight. I'd call Mrs. Santa and ask her to get you some supper, but she is busy finishing dolls' clothes which must be done before morning, and I guess we'd better not bother her. Is there anything that you would like, Little Girl?" and good old Santa put his big warm hand on Little Girl's curls and she felt its warmth and kindness clear down to her very heart. You see, my dears, that even though Santa was in such a great hurry, he wasn't too busy to stop and make some one happy for a minute, even if it was some one no bigger than Little Girl.

So she smiled back into Santa's face and said: "Oh, Santa, if I could ONLY ride down to Earth with you behind those splendid reindeer! I'd love to go; won't you PLEASE take me? I'm so small that I won't take up much room on the seat, and I'll keep very still and not bother one bit!"

Then Santa laughed, SUCH a laugh, big and loud and rollicking, and he said, "Wants a ride, does she? Well, well, shall we take her, Little Elves? Shall we take her, Little Fairies? Shall we take her, Good Reindeer?"

And all the Little Elves hopped and skipped and brought Little Girl a sprig of holly; and all the Little Fairies bowed and smiled and brought her a bit of mistletoe; and all the Good Reindeer jingled their bells loudly, which meant, "Oh, yes! let's take her! She's a good Little Girl! Let her ride!" And before Little Girl could even think, she found herself all tucked up in the big fur robes beside Santa, and away they went, right out into the air, over the clouds, through the Milky Way, and right under the very handle of the Big Dipper, on, on, toward the Earthland, whose lights Little Girl began to see twinkling away down below her. Presently she felt the runners scrape upon something, and she knew they must be on some one's roof, and that Santa would slip down some one's chimney in a minute.

How she wanted to go, too! You see if you had never been down a chimney and seen Santa fill up the stockings, you would want to go quite as much as Little Girl did, now, wouldn't you? So, just as Little Girl was wishing as hard as ever she could wish, she heard a Tiny Voice say, "Hold tight to his arm! Hold tight to his arm!" So she held Santa's arm tight and close, and he shouldered his pack, never thinking that it was heavier than usual, and with a bound and a slide, there they were, Santa, Little Girl, pack and all, right in the middle of a room where there was a fireplace and stockings all hung up for Santa to fill.

Just then Santa noticed Little Girl. He had forgotten all about her for a minute, and he was very much surprised to find that she had come, too. "Bless my soul!" he said, "where did you come from, Little Girl? and how in the world can we both get back up that chimney again? It's easy enough to slide down, but it's quite another matter to climb up again!" and Santa looked real worried. But Little Girl was beginning to feel very tired by this time, for she had had a very exciting evening, so she said, "Oh, never mind me, Santa. I've had such a good time, and I'd just as soon stay here a while as not. I believe I'll curl up on his hearth-rug a few minutes and have a little nap, for it looks as warm and cozy as our own hearth-rug at home, and—why, it is our own hearth and it's my own nursery, for there is Teddy Bear in his chair where I leave him every night, and there's Bunny Cat curled up on his cushion in the corner."

And Little Girl turned to thank Santa and say goodbye to him, but either he had gone very quickly, or else she had fallen asleep very quickly—she never could tell which—for the next thing she knew, Daddy was holding her in his arms and was saying, "What is my Little Girl doing here? She must go to bed, for it's Christmas Eve, and old Santa won't come if he thinks there are any little folks about."

But Little Girl knew better than that, and when she began to tell him all about it, and how the Christmas fairies had welcomed her, and how Santa had given her such a fine ride, Daddy laughed and laughed, and said, "You've been dreaming, Little Girl, you've been dreaming."

But Little Girl knew better than that, too, for there on the hearth was the little Black Coal, which had given her Two Shoes and Bright Light, and tight in her hand she held a holly berry which one of the Christmas Sprites had placed there. More than all that, there she was on the hearth-rug herself, just as Santa had left her, and that was the best proof of all.

The trouble was, Daddy himself had never been a Little Girl, so he couldn't tell anything about it, but we know she hadn't been dreaming, now, don't we, my dears?

VII. "A CHRISTMAS MATINEE"*

*This story was first published in the Youth's Companion, vol. 74.

MRS. M.A.L. LANE

It was the day before Christmas in the year 189-. Snow was falling heavily in the streets of Boston, but the crowd of shoppers seemed undiminished. As the storm increased, groups gathered at the corners and in sheltering doorways to wait for belated cars; but the holiday cheer was in the air, and there was no grumbling. Mothers dragging tired children through the slush of the streets; pretty girls hurrying home for the holidays; here and there a harassed-looking man with perhaps a single package which he had taken a whole morning to select—all had the same spirit of tolerant good-humor.

"School Street! School Street!" called the conductor of an electric car. A group of young people at the farther end of the car started to their feet. One of them, a young man wearing a heavy fur-trimmed coat, addressed the conductor angrily.

"I said, 'Music Hall,' didn't I?" he demanded. "Now we've got to walk back in the snow because of your stupidity!"

"Oh, never mind, Frank!" one of the girls interposed. "We ought to have been looking out ourselves! Six of us, and we went by without a thought! It is all Mrs. Tirrell's fault! She shouldn't have been so entertaining!"

The young matron dimpled and blushed. "That's charming of you, Maidie," she said, gathering up her silk skirts as she prepared to step down into the pond before her. "The compliment makes up for the blame. But how it snows!"

"It doesn't matter. We all have gaiters on," returned Maidie Williams, undisturbed.

"Fares, please!" said the conductor stolidly.

Frank Armstrong thrust his gloved hand deep into his pocket with angry vehemence. "There's your money," he said, "and be quick about the change, will you? We've lost time enough!"

The man counted out the change with stiff, red fingers, closed his lips firmly as if to keep back an obvious rejoinder, rang up the six fares with careful accuracy, and gave the signal to go ahead. The car went on into the drifting storm.

Armstrong laughed shortly as he rapidly counted the bits of silver lying in his open palm. He turned instinctively, but two or three cars were already between him and the one he was looking for.

"The fellow must be an imbecile," he said, rejoining the group on the crossing. "He's given me back a dollar and twenty cents, and I handed him a dollar bill."

"Oh, can't you stop him?" cried Maidie Williams, with a backward step into the wet street.

The Harvard junior, who was carrying her umbrella, protested: "What's the use, Miss Williams? He'll make it up before he gets to Scollay Square, you may be sure. Those chaps don't lose anything. Why, the other day, I gave one a quarter and he went off as cool as you please. 'Where's my change?' said I. 'You gave me a nickel,' said he. And there wasn't anybody to swear that I didn't except myself, and I didn't count."

"But that doesn't make any difference," insisted the girl warmly. "Because one conductor was dishonest, we needn't be. I beg your pardon, Frank, but it does seem to me just stealing."

"Oh, come along!" said her cousin, with an easy laugh. "I guess the West End Corporation won't go without their dinners to-morrow. Here, Maidie, here's the ill-gotten fifty cents. I think you ought to treat us all after the concert; still, I won't urge you. I wash my hands of all responsibility. But I do wish you hadn't such an unpleasant conscience."

Maidie flushed under the sting of his cousinly rudeness, but she went on quietly with the rest. It was evident that any attempt to overtake the car was out of the question.

"Did you notice his number, Frank?" she asked, suddenly.

"No, I never thought of it" said Frank, stopping short. "However, I probably shouldn't make any complaint if I had. I shall forget all about it tomorrow. I find it's never safe to let the sun go down on my wrath. It's very likely not to be there the next day."

"I wasn't thinking of making a complaint," said Maidie; but the two young men were enjoying the small joke too much to notice what she said.

The great doorway of Music Hall was just ahead. In a moment the party were within its friendly shelter, stamping off the snow. The girls were adjusting veils and hats with adroit feminine touches; the pretty chaperon was beaming approval upon them, and the young men were taking off their wet overcoats, when Maidie turned again in sudden desperation.

"Mr. Harris," she said, rather faintly, for she did not like to make herself disagreeable, "do you suppose that car comes right back from Scollay Square?"

"What car?" asked Walter Harris, blankly. "Oh, the one we came in? Yes, I suppose it does. They're running all the time, anyway. Why, you are not sick, are you, Miss Williams?"

There was genuine concern in his tone. This girl, with her sweet, vibrant voice, her clear gray eyes, seemed very charming to him. She wasn't beautiful, perhaps, but she was the kind of girl he liked. There was a steady earnestness in the gray eyes that made him think of his mother.

"No," said Maidie, slowly. "I'm all right, thank you. But I wish I could find that man again. I know sometimes they have to make it up if their accounts are wrong, and I couldn't—we couldn't feel very comfortable—"

Frank Armstrong interrupted her. "Maidie," he said, with the studied calmness with which one speaks to an unreasonable child, "you are perfectly absurd. Here it is within five minutes of the time for the concert to begin. It is impossible to tell when that car is coming back. You are making us all very uncomfortable. Mrs. Tirrell, won't you please tell her not to spoil our afternoon?"

"I think he's right, Maidie," said Mrs. Tirrell. "It's very nice of you to feel so sorry for the poor man, but he really was very careless. It was all his own fault. And just think how far he made us walk! My feet are quite damp. We ought to go in directly or we shall all take cold, and I'm sure you wouldn't like that, my dear."

She led the way as she spoke, the two girls and young Armstrong following. Maidie hesitated. It was so easy to go in, to forget everything in the light and warmth and excitement.

"No," said she, very firmly, and as much to herself as to the young man who stood waiting for her. "I must go back and try to make it right. I'm so sorry, Mr. Harris, but if you will tell them—"

"Why, I'm going with you, of course" said the young fellow, impulsively. "If I'd only looked once at the man I'd go alone, but I shouldn't know him from Adam."

Maidie laughed. "Oh, I don't want to lose the whole concert, Mr. Harris, and Frank, has all the tickets. You must go after them and try to make my peace. I'll come just as soon as I can. Don't wait for me, please. If you'll come and look for me here the first number, and not let them scold me too much—" She ended with an imploring little catch in her breath that was almost a sob.

"They sha'n't say a word, Miss Williams!" cried Walter Harris, with honest admiration in his eyes.

But she was gone already, and conscious that further delay was only making matters worse, he went on into the hall.

Meanwhile, the car swung heavily along the wet rails on its way to the turning-point. It was nearly empty now. An old gentleman and his nurse were the only occupants. Jim Stevens, the conductor, had stepped inside the car.

"Too bad I forgot those young people wanted to get off at Music Hall," he was thinking to himself. "I don't see how I came to do it. That chap looked as if he wanted to complain of me, and I don't know as I blame him. I'd have said I was sorry if he hadn't been so sharp with his tongue. I hope he won't complain just now. 'Twould be a pretty bad time for me to get into trouble, with Mary and the baby both sick. I'm too sleepy to be good for much, that's a fact. Sitting up three nights running takes hold of a fellow somehow when he's at work all day. The rent's paid, that's one thing, if it hasn't left me but half a dollar to my name. Hullo!" He was struck by a sudden distinct recollection of the coins he had returned. "Why, I gave him fifty cents too much!"

He glanced up at the dial which indicated the fares and began to count the change in his pocket. He knew exactly how much money he had had at the beginning of the trip. He counted carefully. Then he plunged his hand into the heavy canvas pocket of his coat. Perhaps he had half a dollar there. No, it was empty!

He faced the fact reluctantly. Fifty cents short, ten fares! Gone into the pocket of the young gentleman with the fur collar! The conductor's hand shook as he put the money back in his pocket. It meant—what did it mean? He drew a long breath.

Christmas Eve! A dark dreary little room upstairs in a noisy tenement house. A pale, thin woman on a shabby lounge vainly trying to quiet a fretful child. The child is thin and pale, too, with a hard, racking cough. There is a small fire in the stove, a very small fire; coal is so high. The medicine stands on the shelf. "Medicine won't do much good," the doctor had said; "he needs beef and cream."

Jim's heart sank at the thought. He could almost hear the baby asking; "Isn't papa coming soon? Isn't he, mamma?"

"Poor little kid!" Jim said, softly, under his breath. "And I shan't have a thing to take home to him; nor Mary's violets, either. It'll be the first Christmas that ever happened. I suppose that chap would think it was ridiculous for me to be buying violets. He wouldn't understand what the flowers mean to Mary. Perhaps he didn't notice I gave him too much. That kind don't know how much they have. They just pull it out as if it was newspaper."

The conductor went out into the snow to help the nurse, who was assisting the old gentleman to the ground. Then the car swung on again. Jim turned up the collar of his coat about his ears and stamped his feet. There was the florist's shop where he had meant to buy the violets, and the toy-shop was just around the corner.

A thought flashed across his tired brain. "Plenty of men would do it; they do it every day. Nobody ever would be the poorer for it. This car will be crowded going home. I needn't ring in every fare; nobody could tell. But Mary! She wouldn't touch those violets if she knew. And she'd know. I'd have to tell her. I couldn't keep it from her, she's that quick."

He jumped off to adjust the trolley with a curious sense of unreality. It couldn't be that he was really going home this Christmas Eve with empty hands. Well, they must all suffer together for his carelessness. It was his own fault, but it was hard. And he was so tired!

To his amazement he found his eyes were blurred as he watched the people crowding into the car. What? Was he going to cry like a baby—he, a great burly man of thirty years?

"It's no use," he thought. "I couldn't do it. The first time I gave Mary violets was the night she said she'd marry me. I told her then I'd do my best to make her proud of me. I guess she wouldn't be very proud of a man who could cheat. She'd rather starve than have a ribbon she couldn't pay for."

He rang up a dozen fares with a steady hand. The temptation was over. Six more strokes—then nine without a falter. He even imagined the bell rang more distinctly than usual, even encouragingly. The car stopped. Jim flung the door open with a triumphant sweep of his arm. He felt ready to face the world. But the baby—his arm dropped. It was hard.

He turned to help the young girl who was waiting at the step. Through the whirling snow he saw her eager face, with a quick recognition lighting the steady eyes, and wondered dimly, as he stood with his hand on the signal-strap, where he could have seen her before.

He knew immediately.

"There was a mistake," she said, with a shy tremor in her voice. "You gave us too much change and here it is." She held out to Jim the piece of silver which had given him such an unhappy quarter of an hour.

He took it like one dazed. Would the young lady think he was crazy to care so much about so small a coin? He must say something. "Thank you, miss," he stammered as well as he could. "You see, I thought it was gone—and there's the baby—and it's Christmas Eve—and my wife's sick—and you can't understand—"

It certainly was not remarkable that she couldn't.

"But I do," she said, simply. "I was afraid of that. And I thought perhaps there was a baby, so I brought my Christmas present for her," and something else dropped into Jim's cold hand.

"What you waiting for?" shouted the motorman from the front platform. The girl had disappeared in the snow.

Jim rang the bell to go ahead, and gazed again at the two shining half dollars in his hand.

"I didn't have a chance to tell her," he explained to his wife late in the evening, as he sat in a tiny rocking-chair several sizes too small for him, "that the baby wasn't a her at all, though if I thought he'd grow up into such a lovely one as she is, I don't know but I almost wish he was."

"Poor Jim!" said Mary, with a little laugh as she put up her hand to stroke his rough cheek. "I guess you're tired."

"And I should say," he added, stretching out his long legs toward the few red sparks in the bottom of the grate, "I should say she had tears in her eyes, too, but I was that near crying myself I couldn't be sure."

The little room was sweet with the odour of English violets. Asleep in the bed lay the boy, a toy horse clasped close to his breast.

"Bless her heart!" said Mary, softly.

"Well, Miss Williams," said Walter Harris, as he sprang to meet a snow-covered figure coming swiftly along the sidewalk. "I can see that you found him. You've lost the first number, but they won't scold you—not this time."

The girl turned a radiant face upon him. "Thank you," she said, shaking the snowy crystals from her skirt. "I don't care now if they do. I should have lost more than that if I had stayed."

VIII. TOINETTE AND THE ELVES*

* Published by arrangement with Little, Brown & Co.

SUSAN COOLIDGE

The winter's sun was nearing the horizon's edge. Each moment the tree shadows grew longer in the forest; each moment the crimson light on the upper boughs became more red and bright. It was Christmas Eve, or would be in half an hour, when the sun should be fairly set; but it did not feel like Christmas, for the afternoon was mild and sweet, and the wind in the leafless boughs sang, as it moved about, as though to imitate the vanished birds. Soft trills and whistles, odd little shakes and twitters—it was astonishing what pretty noises the wind made, for it was in good humor, as winds should be on the Blessed Night; all its storm-tones and bass-notes were for the moment laid aside, and gently as though hushing a baby to sleep, it cooed and rustled and brushed to and fro in the leafless woods.

Toinette stood, pitcher in hand, beside the well. "Wishing Well," the people called it, for they believed that if any one standing there bowed to the East, repeated a certain rhyme and wished a wish, the wish would certainly come true. Unluckily, nobody knew exactly what the rhyme should be. Toinette did not; she was wishing that she did, as she stood with her eyes fixed on the bubbling water. How nice it would be! she thought. What beautiful things should be hers, if it were only to wish and to have. She would be beautiful, rich, good—oh, so good. The children should love her dearly, and never be disagreeable. Mother should not work so hard—they should all go back to France—which mother said was si belle. Oh, dear, how nice it would be. Meantime, the sun sank lower, and mother at home was waiting for the water, but Toinette forgot that.

Suddenly she started. A low sound of crying met her ear, and something like a tiny moan. It seemed close by but she saw nothing.

Hastily she filled her pitcher and turned to go. But again the sound came, an unmistakable sob, right under her feet. Toinette stopped short.

"What is the matter?" she called out bravely. "Is anybody there? and if there is, why don't I see you?"

A third sob—and all at once, down on the ground beside her, a tiny figure became visible, so small that Toinette had to kneel and stoop her head to see it plainly. The figure was that of an odd little man. He wore a garb of green bright and glancing as the scales of a beetle. In his mite of a hand was a cap, out of which stuck a long pointed feather. Two specks of tears stood on his cheeks and he fixed on Toinette a glance so sharp and so sad that it made her feel sorry and frightened and confused all at once.

"Why how funny this is!" she said, speaking to herself out loud.

"Not at all," replied the little man, in a voice as dry and crisp as the chirr of a grasshopper. "Anything but funny. I wish you wouldn't use such words. It hurts my feelings, Toinette."

"Do you know my name, then?" cried Toinette, astonished. "That's strange. But what is the matter? Why are you crying so, little man?"

"I'm not a little man. I'm an elf," responded the dry voice; "and I think you'd cry if you had an engagement out to tea, and found yourself spiked on a great bayonet, so that you couldn't move an inch. Look!" He turned a little as he spoke and Toinette saw a long rose-thorn sticking through the back of the green robe. The little man could by no means reach the thorn, and it held him fast prisoner to the place.

"Is that all? I'll take it out for you," she said.

"Be careful—oh, be careful," entreated the little man. "This is my new dress, you know—my Christmas suit, and it's got to last a year. If there is a hole in it, Peascod will tickle me and Bean Blossom tease, till I shall wish myself dead." He stamped with vexation at the thought.

"Now, you mustn't do that," said Toinette, in a motherly tone, "else you'll tear it yourself, you know." She broke off the thorn as she spoke, and gently drew it out. The elf anxiously examined the stuff. A tiny puncture only was visible and his face brightened.

"You're a good child," he said. "I'll do as much for you some day, perhaps."

"I would have come before if I had seen you," remarked Toinette, timidly. "But I didn't see you a bit."

"No, because I had my cap on," cried the elf. He placed it on his head as he spoke, and hey, presto! nobody was there, only a voice which laughed and said: "Well—don't stare so. Lay your finger on me now."

"Oh," said Toinette, with a gasp. "How wonderful. What fun it must be to do that. The children wouldn't see me. I should steal in and surprise them; they would go on talking, and never guess that I was there. I should so like it. Do elves ever lend their caps to anybody? I wish you'd lend me yours. It must be so nice to be invisible."

"Ho," cried the elf, appearing suddenly again. "Lend my cap, indeed! Why it wouldn't stay on the very tip of your ear, it's so small. As for nice, that depends. Sometimes it is, and sometimes it isn't. No, the only way for mortal people to be invisible is to gather the fern-seed and put it in their shoes."

"Gather it? Where? I never saw any seed to the ferns," said Toinette, staring about her.

"Of course not—we elves take care of that," replied the little man. "Nobody finds the fern-seed but ourselves. I'll tell you what, though. You were such a nice child to take out the thorn so cleverly, that I'll give you a little of the seed. Then you can try the fun of being invisible, to your heart's content."

"Will you really? How delightful. May I have it now?"

"Bless me. Do you think I carry my pockets stuffed with it?" said the elf. "Not at all. Go home, say not a word to any one, but leave your bedroom window open to night, and you'll see what you'll see."

He laid his finger on his nose as he spoke, gave a jump like a grasshopper, clapping on his cap as he went, and vanished. Toinette lingered a moment, in hopes that he might come back, then took her pitcher and hurried home. The woods were very dusky by this time; but full of her strange adventures, she did not remember to feel afraid.

"How long you have been," said her mother. "It's late for a little maid like you to be up. You must make better speed another time, my child."

Toinette pouted as she was apt to do when reproved. The children clamoured to know what had kept her, and she spoke pettishly and crossly; so that they too became cross, and presently went away into the outer kitchen to play by themselves. The children were apt to creep away when Toinette came. It made her angry and unhappy at times that they should do so, but she did not realize that it was in great part her own fault, and so did not set herself to mend it.

"Tell me a 'tory," said baby Jeanneton, creeping to her knee a little later. But Toinette's head was full of the elf; she had no time to spare for Jeanneton.

"Oh, not to-night," she replied. "Ask mother to tell you one."

"Mother's busy," said Jeanneton wistfully.

Toinette took no notice and the little one crept away disconsolately.

Bedtime at last. Toinette set the casement open, and lay a long time waiting and watching; then she fell asleep. She waked with a sneeze and jump and sat up in bed. Behold, on the coverlet stood her elfin friend, with a long train of other elves beside him, all clad in the beetle-wing green, and wearing little pointed caps. More were coming in at the window; outside a few were drifting about in the moon rays, which lit their sparkling robes till they glittered like so many fireflies. The odd thing was, that though the caps were on, Toinette could see the elves distinctly and this surprised her so much, that again she thought out loud and said, "How funny."

"You mean about the caps," replied her special elf, who seemed to have the power of reading thought.

"Yes, you can see us to-night, caps and all. Spells lose their value on Christmas Eve, always. Peascod, where is the box? Do you still wish to try the experiment of being invisible, Toinette?"

"Oh, yes—indeed I do."

"Very well; so let it be."

As he spoke he beckoned, and two elves puffing and panting like little men with a heavy load, dragged forward a droll little box about the size of a pumpkin-seed.

One of them lifted the cover.

"Pay the porter, please, ma'am," he said giving Toinette's ear a mischievous tweak with his sharp fingers.

"Hands off, you bad Peascod!" cried Toinette's elf. "This is my girl. She shan't be pinched!" He dealt Peascod a blow with his tiny hand as he spoke and looked so brave and warlike that he seemed at least an inch taller than he had before. Toinette admired him very much; and Peascod slunk away with an abashed giggle muttering that Thistle needn't be so ready with his fist.

Thistle— for thus, it seemed, Toinette's friend was named— dipped his fingers in the box, which was full of fine brown seeds, and shook a handful into each of Toinette's shoes, as they stood, toes together by the bedside.

"Now you have your wish," he said, "and can go about and do what you like, no one seeing. The charm will end at sunset. Make the most of it while you can; but if you want to end it sooner, shake the seeds from the shoes and then you are just as usual."

"Oh, I shan't want to," protested Toinette; "I'm sure I shan't."

"Good-bye," said Thistle, with a mocking little laugh.

"Good-bye, and thank you ever so much," replied Toinette.

"Good-bye, good-bye," replied the other elves, in shrill chorus. They clustered together, as if in consultation; then straight out of the window they flew like a swarm of gauzy-winged bees, and melted into the moonlight. Toinette jumped up and ran to watch them but the little men were gone— not a trace of them was to be seen; so she shut the window, went back to bed and presently in the midst of her amazed and excited thoughts fell asleep.

She waked in the morning, with a queer, doubtful feeling. Had she dreamed, or had it really happened? She put on her best petticoat and laced her blue bodice; for she thought the mother would perhaps take them across the wood to the little chapel for the Christmas service. Her long hair smoothed and tied, her shoes trimly fastened, downstairs she ran. The mother was stirring porridge over the fire. Toinette went close to her, but she did not move or turn her head.

"How late the children are," she said at last, lifting the boiling pot on the hob. Then she went to the stair-foot and called, "Marc, Jeanneton, Pierre, Marie. Breakfast is ready, my children. Toinette—but where, then, is Toinette? She is used to be down long before this."

"Toinette isn't upstairs," said Marie from above.

"Her door is wide open, and she isn't there."

"That is strange," said the mother. "I have been here an hour, and she has not passed this way since." She went to the outer door and called, "Toinette! Toinette!" passing close to Toinette as she did so. And looking straight at her with unseeing eyes. Toinette, half frightened, half pleased, giggled low to herself. She really was invisible, then. How strange it seemed and what fun it was going to be.

The children sat down to breakfast, little Jeanneton, as the youngest, saying grace. The mother distributed the porridge and gave each a spoon but she looked anxious.

"Where can Toinette have gone?" she said to herself. Toinette was conscious-pricked. She was half inclined to dispel the charm on the spot.

But just then she caught a whisper from Pierre to Marc which so surprised her as to put the idea out of her head.

"Perhaps a wolf has eaten her up—a great big wolf like the 'Capuchon Rouge,' you know." This was what Pierre said; and Marc answered unfeelingly:

"If he has, I shall ask mother to let me have her room for my own."

Poor Toinette, her cheeks burned and her eyes filled with tears at this. Didn't the boys love her a bit then? Next she grew angry, and longed to box Marc's ears, only she recollected in time that she was invisible. What a bad boy he was, she thought.

The smoking porridge reminded her that she was hungry; so brushing away the tears she slipped a spoon off the table and whenever she found the chance, dipped it into the bowl for a mouthful. The porridge disappeared rapidly.

"I want some more," said Jeanneton.

"Bless me, how fast you have eaten," said the mother, turning to the bowl.

This made Toinette laugh, which shook her spoon, and a drop of the hot mixture fell right on the tip of Marie's nose as she sat with upturned face waiting her turn for a second helping. Marie gave a little scream.

"What is it?" said the mother.

"Hot water! Right in my face!" sputtered Marie.

"Water!" cried Marc. "It's porridge."

"You spattered with your spoon. Eat more carefully, my child," said the mother, and Toinette laughed again as she heard her. After all, there was some fun in being invisible.

The morning went by. Constantly the mother went to the door, and, shading her eyes with her hand, looked out, in hopes of seeing a little figure come down the wood-path, for she thought perhaps the child went to the spring after water, and fell asleep there. The children played happily, meanwhile. They were used to doing without Toinette and did not seem to miss her, except that now and then baby Jeanneton said: "Poor Toinette gone—not here—all gone."

"Well, what if she has?" said Marc at last looking up from the wooden cup he was carving for Marie's doll. "We can play all the better."

Marc was a bold, outspoken boy, who always told his whole mind about things.

"If she were here," he went on," she'd only scold and interfere. Toinette almost always scolds. I like to have her go away. It makes it pleasanter."

"It is rather pleasanter," admitted Marie, "only I'd like her to be having a nice time somewhere else."

"Bother about Toinette," cried Pierre.

"Let's play 'My godmother has cabbage to sell.'"

I don't think Toinette had ever felt so unhappy in her life, as when she stood by unseen, and heard the children say these words. She had never meant to be unkind to them, but she was quick-tempered, dreamy, wrapped up in herself. She did not like being interrupted by them, it put her out, and she spoke sharply and was cross. She had taken it for granted that the others must love her, by a sort of right, and the knowledge that they did not grieved over very much. Creeping away, she hid herself in the woods. It was a sparkling day, but the sun did not look so bright as usual. Cuddled down under a rosebush, Toinette sat sobbing as if her heart would break at the recollection of the speeches she had overheard.

By and by a little voice within her woke up and began to make itself audible. All of us know this little voice. We call it conscience.

"Jeanneton missed me," she thought. "And, oh, dear! I pushed her away only last night and wouldn't tell her a story. And Marie hoped I was having a pleasant time somewhere. I wish I hadn't slapped Marie last Friday. And I wish I hadn't thrown Marc's ball into the fire that day I was angry with him. How unkind he was to say that—but I wasn't always kind to him. And once I said that I wished a bear would eat Pierre up. That was because he broke my cup. Oh, dear, oh, dear. What a bad girl I've been to them all."

"But you could be better and kinder if you tried, couldn't you?" said the inward voice. "I think you could."

And Toinette clasped her hands tight and said out loud: "I could. Yes—and I will."

The first thing to be done was to get rid of the fern-seed which she now regarded as a hateful thing. She untied her shoes and shook it out in the grass. It dropped and seemed to melt into the air, for it instantly vanished. A mischievous laugh sounded close behind, and a beetle-green coat-tail was visible whisking under a tuft of rushes. But Toinette had had enough of the elves, and, tying her shoes, took the road toward home, running with all her might.

"Where have you been all day, Toinette?" cried the children, as, breathless and panting, she flew in at the gate. But Toinette could not speak. She made slowly for her mother, who stood in the doorway, flung herself into her arms and burst into a passion of tears.

"Ma cherie, what is it, whence hast thou come?" asked the good mother alarmed. She lifted Toinette into her arms as she spoke, and hastened indoors. The other children followed, whispering and peeping, but the mother sent them away, and sitting down by the fire with Toinette in her lap, she rocked and hushed and comforted, as though Toinette had been again a little baby. Gradually the sobs ceased. For a while Toinette lay quiet, with her head on her mother's breast. Then she wiped her wet eyes, put her arms around her mother's neck, and told her all from the very beginning, keeping not a single thing back. The dame listened with alarm.

"Saints protect us," she muttered. Then feeling Toinette's hands and head, "Thou hast a fever," she said. "I will make thee a tisane, my darling, and thou must at once go to bed." Toinette vainly protested; to bed she went and perhaps it was the wisest thing, for the warm drink threw her into a long sound sleep and when she woke she was herself again, bright and well, hungry for dinner, and ready to do her usual tasks.

Herself—but not quite the same Toinette that she had been before. Nobody changes from bad to better in a minute. It takes time for that, time and effort, and a long struggle with evil habits and tempers. But there is sometimes a certain minute or day in which people begin to change, and thus it was with Toinette. The fairy lesson was not lost upon her. She began to fight with herself, to watch her faults and try to conquer them. It was hard work; often she felt discouraged, but she kept on. Week after week and month after month she grew less selfish, kinder, more obliging than she used to be. When she failed and her old fractious temper got the better of her, she was sorry and begged every one's pardon so humbly that they could not but forgive. The mother began to think that the elves really had bewitched her child. As for the children they learned to love Toinette as never before, and came to her with all their pains and pleasures, as children should to a kind older sister. Each fresh proof of this, every kiss from Jeanneton, every confidence from Marc, was a comfort to Toinette, for she never forgot Christmas Day, and felt that no trouble was too much to wipe out that unhappy recollection. "I think they like me better than they did then," she would say; but then the thought came, "Perhaps if I were invisible again, if they did not know I was there, I might hear something to make me feel as badly as I did that morning." These sad thoughts were part of the bitter fruit of the fairy fern-seed.

So with doubts and fears the year went by, and again it was Christmas Eve. Toinette had been asleep some hours when she was roused by a sharp tapping at the window pane. Startled, and only half awake, she sat up in bed and saw by the moonlight a tiny figure outside which she recognized. It was Thistle drumming with his knuckles on the glass.

"Let me in," cried the dry little voice. So Toinette opened the casement, and Thistle flew in and perched as before on the coverlet.

"Merry Christmas, my girl." he said, "and a Happy New Year when it comes. I've brought you a present;" and, dipping into a pouch tied round his waist, he pulled out a handful of something brown. Toinette knew what it was in a moment.

"Oh, no," she cried shrinking back. "Don't give me any fern-seeds. They frighten me. I don't like them."

"Don't be silly," said Thistle, his voice sounding kind this time, and earnest. "It wasn't pleasant being invisible last year, but perhaps this year it will be. Take my advice, and try it. You'll not be sorry."

"Sha'n't I?" said Toinette, brightening. "Very well, then, I will." She leaned out of bed, and watched Thistle strew the fine dustlike grains in each shoe.

"I'll drop in to-morrow night, and just see how you like it," he said. Then, with a nod, he was gone.

The old fear came back when she woke in the morning, and she tied on her shoes with a tremble at her heart. Downstairs she stole. The first thing she saw was a wooden ship standing on her plate. Marc had made the ship, but Toinette had no idea it was for her.

The little ones sat round the table with their eyes on the door, watching till Toinette should come in and be surprised.

"I wish she'd hurry," said Pierre, drumming on his bowl with a spoon.

"We all want Toinette, don't we?" said the mother, smiling as she poured the hot porridge.

"It will be fun to see her stare," declared Marc.

"Toinette is jolly when she stares. Her eyes look big and her cheeks grow pink. Andre Brugen thinks his sister Aline is prettiest, but I don't. Our Toinette is ever so pretty."

"She is ever so nice, too," said Pierre. "She's as good to play with as—as—a boy," finished triumphantly.

"Oh, I wish my Toinette would come," said Jeanneton.

Toinette waited no longer, but sped upstairs with glad tears in her eyes. Two minutes, and down she came again visible this time. Her heart was light as a feather.

"Merry Christmas!" clamoured the children. The ship was presented, Toinette was duly surprised, and so the happy day began.

That night Toinette left the window open, and lay down in her clothes; for she felt, as Thistle had been so kind, she ought to receive him politely. He came at midnight, and with him all the other little men in green.

"Well, how was it?" asked Thistle.

"Oh, I liked it this time," declared Toinette, with shining eyes, "and I thank you so much."

"I'm glad you did," said the elf. "And I'm glad you are thankful, for we want you to do something for us."

"What can it be?" inquired Toinette, wondering.

"You must know," went on Thistle, "that there is no dainty in the world which we elves enjoy like a bowl of fern-seed broth. But it has to be cooked over a real fire, and we dare not go near fire, you know, lest our wings scorch. So we seldom get any fern-seed broth. Now, Toinette, will you make us some?"

"Indeed, I will!" cried Toinette, "only you must tell me how."

"It is very simple," said Peascod; "only seed and honey dew, stirred from left to right with a sprig of fennel. Here's the seed and the fennel, and here's the dew. Be sure and stir from the left; if you don't, it curdles, and the flavour will be spoiled."

Down into the kitchen they went, and Toinette, moving very softly, quickened the fire, set on the smallest bowl she could find, and spread the doll's table with the wooden saucers which Marc had made for Jeanneton to play with. Then she mixed and stirred as the elves bade, and when the soup was done, served it to them smoking hot. How they feasted! No bumblebee, dipping into a flower-cup, ever sipped and twinkled more rapturously than they.

75

When the last drop was eaten, they made ready to go. Each in turn kissed Toinette's hand, and said a word of farewell. Thistle brushed his feathered cap over the doorpost as he passed.

"Be lucky, house," he said, "for you have received and entertained the luck-bringers. And be lucky, Toinette. Good temper is good luck, and sweet words and kind looks and peace in the heart are the fairest of fortunes. See that you never lose them again, my girl." With this, he, too, kissed Toinette's hand, waved his feathered cap, and—whir! they all were gone, while Toinette, covering the fire with ashes and putting aside the little cups, stole up to her bed a happy child.

IX. THE VOYAGE OF THE WEE RED CAP

*Published originally in the Outlook. Reprinted here by arrangement with the author.

RUTH SAWYER DURAND

It was the night of St. Stephen, and Teig sat alone by his fire with naught in his cupboard but a pinch of tea and a bare mixing of meal, and a heart inside of him as soft and warm as the ice on the water-bucket outside the door. The tuft was near burnt on the hearth—a handful of golden cinders left, just; and Teig took to counting them greedily on his fingers.

"There's one, two, three, an' four an' five," he laughed. "Faith, there be more bits o' real gold hid undther the loose clay in the corner."

It was the truth; and it was the scraping and scrooching for the last piece that had left Teig's cupboard bare of a Christmas dinner.

"Gold is betther nor eatin' an' dthrinkin'. An' if ye have naught to give, there'll be naught asked of ye;" and he laughed again.

He was thinking of the neighbours, and the doles of food and piggins of milk that would pass over their thresholds that night to the vagabonds and paupers who were sure to come begging. And on the heels of that thought followed another: who would be giving old Barney his dinner? Barney lived a stone's throw from Teig, alone, in a wee tumbled-in cabin; and for a score of years past Teig had stood on the doorstep every Christmas Eve, and, making a hollow of his two hands, had called across the road:

"Hey, there, Barney, will ye come over for a sup?"

And Barney had reached for his crutches—there being but one leg to him—and had come.

"Faith," said Teig, trying another laugh, "Barney can fast for the once; 'twill be all the same in a month's time." And he fell to thinking of the gold again. A knock came at the door. Teig pulled himself down in his chair where the shadow would cover him, and held his tongue.

"Teig, Teig!" It was the widow O'Donnelly's voice. "If ye are there, open your door. I have not got the pay for the spriggin' this month, an' the childher are needin' food."

But Teig put the leash on his tongue, and never stirred till he heard the tramp of her feet going on to the next cabin. Then he saw to it that the door was tight-barred. Another knock came, and it was a stranger's voice this time:

"The other cabins are filled; not one but has its hearth crowded; will ye take us in—the two of us? The wind bites mortal sharp, not a morsel o' food have ne tasted this day. Masther, will ye take us in?"

But Teig sat on, a-holding his tongue; and the tramp of the strangers' feet passed down the road. Others took their place—small feet, running. It was the miller's wee Cassie, and she called out as she ran by.

"Old Barney's watchin' for ye. Ye'll not be forgettin' him, will ye, Teig?"

And then the child broke into a song, sweet and clear, as she passed down the road:

"Listen all ye, 'tis the Feast o' St. Stephen,

Mind that ye keep it, this holy even.

Open your door an' greet ye the stranger—

For ye mind that the wee Lord had naught but a manger.

   Mhuire as truagh!

"Feed ye the hungry an' rest ye the weary,

This ye must do for the sake of Our Mary.

'Tis well that ye mind—ye who sit by the fire—

That the Lord he was born in a dark and cold byre.

   Mhuire as truagh!"

Teig put his fingers deep in his ears. "A million murdthering curses on them that won't let me be! Can't a man try to keep what is his without bein' pesthered by them that has only idled an' wasted their days?"

And then the strange thing happened: hundreds and hundreds of wee lights began dancing outside the window, making the room bright; the hands of the clock began chasing each other round the dial, and the bolt of the door drew itself out. Slowly, without a creak or a cringe, the door opened, and in there trooped a crowd of the Good People. Their wee green cloaks were folded close about them, and each carried a rush candle.

Teig was filled with a great wonderment, entirely, when he saw the fairies, but when they saw him they laughed.

"We are takin' the loan o' your cabin this night, Teig," said they. "Ye are the only man hereabout with an empty hearth, an' we're needin' one."

Without saying more, they bustled about the room making ready. They lengthened out the table and spread and set it; more of the Good People trooped in, bringing stools and food and drink. The pipers came last, and they sat themselves around the chimney-piece a-blowing their chanters and trying the drones. The feasting began and the pipers played and never had Teig seen such a sight in his life. Suddenly a wee man sang out:

"Clip, clap, clip, clap, I wish I had my wee red cap!" And out of the air there tumbled the neatest cap Teig ever laid his two eyes on. The wee man clapped it on his head, crying:

"I wish I was in Spain!" and—whist—up the chimney he went, and away out of sight.

It happened just as I am telling it. Another wee man called for his cap, and away he went after the first. And then another and another until the room was empty and Teig sat alone again.

"By my soul," said Teig, "I'd like to thravel that way myself! It's a grand savin' of tickets an' baggage; an' ye get to a place before ye've had time to change your mind. Faith there is no harm done if I thry it."

So he sang the fairies' rhyme and out of the air dropped a wee cap for him. For a moment the wonder had him, but the next he was clapping the cap on his head and crying:

"Spain!"

Then—whist—up the chimney he went after the fairies, and before he had time to let out his breath he was standing in the middle of Spain, and strangeness all about him.

He was in a great city. The doorways of the houses were hung with flowers and the air was warm and sweet with the smell of them. Torches burned along the streets, sweetmeat-sellers went about crying their wares, and on the steps of the cathedral crouched a crowd of beggars.

"What's the meanin' o' that?" asked Teig of one of the fairies. "They are waiting for those that are hearing mass. When they come out, they give half of what they have to those that have nothing, so on this night of all the year there shall be no hunger and no cold."

And then far down the street came the sound of a child's voice, singing:

"Listen all ye, 'tis the Feast o' St. Stephen,

Mind that ye keep it, this holy even".

"Curse it!" said Teig; "can a song fly afther ye?"

And then he heard the fairies cry "Holland!" and cried "Holland!" too.

In one leap he was over France, and another over Belgium; and with the third he was standing by long ditches of water frozen fast, and over them glided hundreds upon hundreds of lads and maids. Outside each door stood a wee wooden shoe empty. Teig saw scores of them as he looked down the ditch of a street.

"What is the meanin' o' those shoes? " he asked the fairies.

"Ye poor lad!" answered the wee man next to him; "are ye not knowing anything? This is the Gift Night of the year, when every man gives to his neighbour."

A child came to the window of one of the houses, and in her hand was a lighted candle. She was singing as she put the light down close to the glass, and Teig caught the words:

"Open your door an' greet ye the stranger—

For ye mind that the wee Lord had naught but a manger.

Mhuire as truagh!"

"'Tis the de'il's work!" cried Teig, and he set the red cap more firmly on his head.

"I'm for another country."

I cannot be telling you a half of the adventures Teig had that night, nor half the sights that he saw. But he passed by fields that held sheaves of grain for the birds and doorsteps that held bowls of porridge for the wee creatures. He saw lighted trees, sparkling and heavy with gifts; and he stood outside the churches and watched the crowds pass in, bearing gifts to the Holy Mother and Child.

At last the fairies straightened their caps and cried, "Now for the great hall in the King of England's palace!"

Whist—and away they went, and Teig after them; and the first thing he knew he was in London, not an arm's length from the King's throne. It was a grander sight than he had seen in any other country. The hall was filled entirely with lords and ladies; and the great doors were open for the poor and the homeless to come in and warm themselves by the King's fire and feast from the King's table. And many a hungry soul did the King serve with his own hands.

Those that had anything to give gave it in return. It might be a bit of music played on a harp or a pipe, or it might be a dance or a song; but more often it was a wish, just, for good luck and safekeeping.

Teig was so taken up with the watching that he never heard the fairies when they wished themselves on; moreover, he never saw the wee girl that was fed, and went laughing away. But he heard a bit of her song as she passed through the door:

"Feed ye the hungry an' rest ye the weary, This ye must do for the sake of Our Mary."

Then the anger had Teig. "I'll stop your pestherin' tongue, once an' for all time!" and, catching the cap from his head, he threw it after her. No sooner was the cap gone than every soul in the hall saw him. The next moment they were about him, catching at his coat and crying:

"Where is he from, what does he here? Bring him before the King!" And Teig was dragged along by a hundred hands to the throne where the King sat.

"He was stealing food," cried one.

"He was robbing the King's jewels," cried another.

"He looks evil," cried a third. "Kill him!"

And in a moment all the voices took it up and the hall rang with: "Aye, kill him, kill him!"

Teig's legs took to trembling, and fear put the leash on his tongue; but after a long silence he managed to whisper:

"I have done evil to no one—no one!"

"Maybe," said the King; "but have ye done good? Come, tell us, have ye given aught to any one this night? If ye have, we will pardon ye."

Not a word could Teig say—fear tightened the leash—for he was knowing full well there was no good to him that night.

"Then ye must die," said the King. "Will ye try hanging or beheading?"

"Hanging, please, your Majesty," said Teig.

The guards came rushing up and carried him off.

But as he was crossing the threshold of the hall a thought sprang at him and held him.

"Your Majesty," he called after him, "will ye grant me a last request?"

"I will," said the King.

"Thank ye. There's a wee red cap that I'm mortal fond of, and I lost it a while ago; if I could be hung with it on, I would hang a deal more comfortable."

The cap was found and brought to Teig.

"Clip, clap, clip, clap, for my wee red cap, I wish I was home," he sang.

Up and over the heads of the dumfounded guard he flew, and—whist—and away out of sight. When he opened his eyes again, he was sitting close by his own hearth, with the fire burnt low. The hands of the clock were still, the bolt was fixed firm in the door. The fairies' lights were gone, and the only bright thing was the candle burning in old Barney's cabin across the road.

A running of feet sounded outside, and then the snatch of a song

"'Tis well that ye mind—ye who sit by the fire—

That the Lord he was born in a dark and cold byre.

Mhuire as traugh!"

"Wait ye, whoever ye are!" and Teig was away to the corner, digging fast at the loose clay, as a terrier digs at a bone. He filled his hands full of the shining gold, then hurried to the door, unbarring it.

The miller's wee Cassie stood there, peering at him out of the darkness.

"Take those to the widow O'Donnelly, do ye hear? And take the rest to the store. Ye tell Jamie to bring up all that he has that is eatable an' dhrinkable; and to the neighbours ye say, 'Teig's keepin' the feast this night.' Hurry now!"

Teig stopped a moment on the threshold until the tramp of her feet had died away; then he made a hollow of his two hands and called across the road:

"Hey there, Barney, will ye come over for a sup?"

X. A STORY OF THE CHRIST-CHILD*

*Reprinted by permission of the author from her collection, "Christmastide," published by the Chicago Kindergarten College.

A German legend for Christmas Eve as told by

ELIZABETH HARKISON

Once upon a time, a long, long time ago, on the night before Christmas, a little child was wandering all alone through the streets of a great city. There were many people on the street, fathers and mothers, sisters and brothers, uncles and aunts, and even gray-haired grandfathers and grandmothers, all of whom were hurrying home with bundles of presents for each other and for their little ones. Fine carriages rolled by, express wagons rattled past, even old carts were pressed into service, and all things seemed in a hurry and glad with expectation of the coming Christmas morning.

From some of the windows bright lights were already beginning to stream until it was almost as bright as day. But the little child seemed to have no home, and wandered about listlessly from street to street. No one took any notice of him except perhaps Jack Frost, who bit his bare toes and made the ends of his fingers tingle. The north wind, too, seemed to notice the child, for it blew against him and pierced his ragged garments through and through, causing him to shiver with cold. Home after home he passed, looking with longing eyes through the windows, in upon the glad, happy children, most of whom were helping to trim the Christmas trees for the coming morrow.

"Surely," said the child to himself, "where there is so must gladness and happiness, some of it may be for me." So with timid steps he approached a large and handsome house. Through the windows, he could see a tall and stately Christmas tree already lighted. Many presents hung upon it. Its green boughs were trimmed with gold and silver ornaments. Slowly he climbed up the broad steps and gently rapped at the door. It was opened by a large man-servant. He had a kindly face, although his voice was deep and gruff. He looked at the little child for a moment, then sadly shook his head and said, "Go down off the steps. There is no room here for such as you." He looked sorry as he spoke; possibly he remembered his own little ones at home, and was glad that they were not out in this cold and bitter night. Through the open door a bright light shone, and the warm air, filled with fragrance of the Christmas pine, rushed out from the inner room and greeted the little wanderer with a kiss. As the child turned back into the cold and darkness, he wondered why the footman had spoken thus, for surely, thought he, those little children would love to have another companion join them in their joyous Christmas festival. But the little children inside did not even know that he had knocked at the door.

The street grew colder and darker as the child passed on. He went sadly forward, saying to himself, "Is there no one in all this great city who will share the Christmas with me?" Farther and farther down the street he wandered, to where the homes were not so large and beautiful. There seemed to be little children inside of nearly all the houses. They were dancing and frolicking about. Christmas trees could be seen in nearly every window, with beautiful dolls and trumpets and picture-books and balls and tops and other dainty toys hung upon them. In one window the child noticed a little lamb made of soft white wool. Around its neck was tied a red ribbon. It had evidently been hung on the tree for one of the children. The little stranger stopped before this window and looked long and earnestly at the beautiful things inside, but most of all was he drawn toward the white lamb. At last creeping up to the window-pane, he gently tapped upon it. A little girl came to the window and looked out into the dark street where the snow had now begun to fall. She saw the child, but she only frowned and shook her head and said, "Go away and come some other time. We are too busy to take care of you now." Back into the dark, cold streets he turned again. The wind was whirling past him and seemed to say, "Hurry on, hurry on, we have no time to stop. 'Tis Christmas Eve and everybody is in a hurry to-night."

Again and again the little child rapped softly at door or window-pane. At each place he was refused admission. One mother feared he might have some ugly disease which her darlings would catch; another father said he had only enough for his own children and none to spare for beggars. Still another told him to go home where he belonged, and not to trouble other folks.

The hours passed; later grew the night, and colder grew the wind, and darker seemed the street. Farther and farther the little one wandered. There was scarcely any one left upon the street by this time, and the few who remained did not seem to see the child, when suddenly ahead of him there appeared a bright, single ray of light. It shone through the darkness into the child's eyes. He looked up smilingly and said, "I will go where the small light beckons, perhaps they will share their Christmas with me."

Hurrying past all the other houses, he soon reached the end of the street and went straight up to the window from which the light was streaming. It was a poor, little, low house, but the child cared not for that. The light seemed still to call him in. From what do you suppose the light came? Nothing but a tallow candle which had been placed in an old cup with a broken handle, in the window, as a glad token of Christmas Eve. There was neither curtain nor shade to the small, square window and as the little child looked in he saw standing upon a neat wooden table a branch of a Christmas tree. The room was plainly furnished but it was very clean. Near the fireplace sat a lovely faced mother with a little two-year-old on her knee and an older child beside her. The two children were looking into their mother's face and listening to a story. She must have been telling them a Christmas story, I think. A few bright coals were burning in the fireplace, and all seemed light and warm within.

The little wanderer crept closer and closer to the window-pane. So sweet was the mother's face, so loving seemed the little children, that at last he took courage and tapped gently, very gently on the door. The mother stopped talking, the little children looked up. "What was that, mother?" asked the little girl at her side. "I think it was some one tapping on the door," replied the mother. "Run as quickly as you can and open it, dear, for it is a bitter cold night to keep any one waiting in this storm." "Oh, mother, I think it was the bough of the tree tapping against the window-pane," said the little girl. "Do please go on with our story." Again the little wanderer tapped upon the door. "My child, my child," exclaimed the mother, rising, "that certainly was a rap on the door. Run quickly and open it. No one must be left out in the cold on our beautiful Christmas Eve."

The child ran to the door and threw it wide open. The mother saw the ragged stranger standing without, cold and shivering, with bare head and almost bare feet. She held out both hands and drew him into the warm, bright room. "You poor, dear child," was all she said, and putting her arms around him, she drew him close to her breast. "He is very cold, my children," she exclaimed. "We must warm him." "And," added the little girl, "we must love him and give him some of our Christmas, too." "Yes," said the mother, "but first let us warm him—"

The mother sat down by the fire with the little child on her lap, and her own little ones warmed his half-frozen hands in theirs. The mother smoothed his tangled curls, and, bending low over his head, kissed the child's face. She gathered the three little ones in her arms and the candle and the fire light shone over them. For a moment the room was very still. By and by the little girl said softly, to her mother, "May we not light the Christmas tree, and let him see how beautiful it looks?" "Yes," said the mother. With that she seated the child on a low stool beside the fire, and went herself to fetch the few simple ornaments which from year to year she had saved for her children's Christmas tree. They were soon so busy that they did not notice the room had filled with a strange and brilliant light. They turned and looked at the spot where the little wanderer sat. His ragged clothes had changed to garments white and beautiful; his tangled curls seemed like a halo of golden light about his head; but most glorious of all was his face, which shone with a light so dazzling that they could scarcely look upon it.

In silent wonder they gazed at the child. Their little room seemed to grow larger and larger, until it was as wide as the whole world, the roof of their low house seemed to expand and rise, until it reached to the sky.

With a sweet and gentle smile the wonderful child looked upon them for a moment, and then slowly rose and floated through the air, above the treetops, beyond the church spire, higher even than the clouds themselves, until he appeared to them to be a shining star in the sky above. At last he disappeared from sight. The astonished children turned in hushed awe to their mother, and said in a whisper, "Oh, mother, it was the Christ-Child, was it not?" And the mother answered in a low tone, "Yes."

And it is said, dear children, that each Christmas Eve the little Christ-Child wanders through some town or village, and those who receive him and take him into their homes and hearts have given to them this marvellous vision which is denied to others.

XI. JIMMY SCARECROW'S CHRISTMAS

MARY E. WILKINS FREEMAN

Jimmy Scarecrow led a sad life in the winter. Jimmy's greatest grief was his lack of occupation. He liked to be useful, and in winter he was absolutely of no use at all.

He wondered how many such miserable winters he would have to endure. He was a young Scarecrow, and this was his first one. He was strongly made, and although his wooden joints creaked a little when the wind blew he did not grow in the least rickety. Every morning, when the wintry sun peered like a hard yellow eye across the dry corn-stubble, Jimmy felt sad, but at Christmas time his heart nearly broke.

On Christmas Eve Santa Claus came in his sledge heaped high with presents, urging his team of reindeer across the field. He was on his way to the farmhouse where Betsey lived with her Aunt Hannah.

Betsey was a very good little girl with very smooth yellow curls, and she had a great many presents. Santa Claus had a large wax doll-baby for her on his arm, tucked up against the fur collar of his coat. He was afraid to trust it in the pack, lest it get broken.

When poor Jimmy Scarecrow saw Santa Claus his heart gave a great leap. "Santa Claus! Here I am!" he cried out, but Santa Claus did not hear him.

"Santa Claus, please give me a little present. I was good all summer and kept the crows out of the corn," pleaded the poor Scarecrow in his choking voice, but Santa Claus passed by with a merry halloo and a great clamour of bells.

Then Jimmy Scarecrow stood in the corn-stubble and shook with sobs until his joints creaked. "I am of no use in the world, and everybody has forgotten me," he moaned. But he was mistaken.

The next morning Betsey sat at the window holding her Christmas doll-baby, and she looked out at Jimmy Scarecrow standing alone in the field amidst the corn-stubble.

"Aunt Hannah?" said she. Aunt Hannah was making a crazy patchwork quilt, and she frowned hard at a triangular piece of red silk and circular piece of pink, wondering how to fit them together. "Well?" said she.

"Did Santa Claus bring the Scarecrow any Christmas present?"

"No, of course he didn't."

"Why not?"

"Because he's a Scarecrow. Don't ask silly questions."

"I wouldn't like to be treated so, if I was a Scarecrow," said Betsey, but her Aunt Hannah did not hear her. She was busy cutting a triangular snip out of the round piece of pink silk so the piece of red silk could be feather-stitched into it.

It was snowing hard out of doors, and the north wind blew. The Scarecrow's poor old coat got whiter and whiter with snow. Sometimes he almost vanished in the thick white storm. Aunt Hannah worked until the middle of the afternoon on her crazy quilt. Then she got up and spread it out over the sofa with an air of pride.

"There," said she, "that's done, and that makes the eighth. I've got one for every bed in the house, and I've given four away. I'd give this away if I knew of anybody that wanted it."

Aunt Hannah put on her hood and shawl, and drew some blue yarn stockings on over her shoes, and set out through the snow to carry a slice of plum-pudding to her sister Susan, who lived down the road. Half an hour after Aunt Hannah had gone Betsey put her little red plaid shawl over her head, and ran across the field to Jimmy Scarecrow. She carried her new doll-baby smuggled up under her shawl.

"Wish you Merry Christmas!" she said to Jimmy Scarecrow.

"Wish you the same," said Jimmy, but his voice was choked with sobs, and was also muffled, for his old hat had slipped down to his chin. Betsey looked pitifully at the old hat fringed with icicles, like frozen tears, and the old snow-laden coat. "I've brought you a Christmas present," said she, and with that she tucked her doll-baby inside Jimmy Scarecrow's coat, sticking its tiny feet into a pocket.

"Thank you," said Jimmy Scarecrow faintly.

"You're welcome," said she. "Keep her under your overcoat, so the snow won't wet her, and she won't catch cold, she's delicate."

"Yes, I will," said Jimmy Scarecrow, and he tried hard to bring one of his stiff, outstretched arms around to clasp the doll-baby.

"Don't you feel cold in that old summer coat?" asked Betsey.

"If I had a little exercise, I should be warm," he replied. But he shivered, and the wind whistled through his rags.

"You wait a minute," said Betsey, and was off across the field.

Jimmy Scarecrow stood in the corn-stubble, with the doll-baby under his coat and waited, and soon Betsey was back again with Aunt Hannah's crazy quilt trailing in the snow behind her.

"Here," said she, "here is something to keep you warm," and she folded the crazy quilt around the Scarecrow and pinned it.

"Aunt Hannah wants to give it away if anybody wants it," she explained. "She's got so many crazy quilts in the house now she doesn't know what to do with them. Good-bye—be sure you keep the doll-baby covered up." And with that she ran cross the field, and left Jimmy Scarecrow alone with the crazy quilt and the doll-baby.

The bright flash of colours under Jimmy's hat-brim dazzled his eyes, and he felt a little alarmed. "I hope this quilt is harmless if it IS crazy," he said. But the quilt was warm, and he dismissed his fears. Soon the doll-baby whimpered, but he creaked his joints a little, and that amused it, and he heard it cooing inside his coat.

Jimmy Scarecrow had never felt so happy in his life as he did for an hour or so. But after that the snow began to turn to rain, and the crazy quilt was soaked through and through: and not only that, but his coat and the poor doll-baby. It cried pitifully for a while, and then it was still, and he was afraid it was dead.

It grew very dark, and the rain fell in sheets, the snow melted, and Jimmy Scarecrow stood halfway up his old boots in water. He was saying to himself that the saddest hour of his life had come, when suddenly he again heard Santa Claus' sleigh-bells and his merry voice talking to his reindeer. It was after midnight, Christmas was over, and Santa was hastening home to the North Pole.

"Santa Claus! dear Santa Claus!" cried Jimmy Scarecrow with a great sob, and that time Santa Claus heard him and drew rein.

"Who's there?" he shouted out of the darkness.

"It's only me," replied the Scarecrow.

"Who's me?" shouted Santa Claus.

"Jimmy Scarecrow!"

Santa got out of his sledge and waded up. "Have you been standing here ever since corn was ripe?" he asked pityingly, and Jimmy replied that he had.

"What's that over your shoulders?" Santa Claus continued, holding up his lantern.

"It's a crazy quilt."

"And what are you holding under your coat?"

"The doll-baby that Betsey gave me, and I'm afraid it's dead," poor Jimmy Scarecrow sobbed.

"Nonsense!" cried Santa Claus. "Let me see it!" And with that he pulled the doll-baby out from under the Scarecrow's coat, and patted its back, and shook it a little, and it began to cry, and then to crow. "It's all right," said Santa Claus. "This is the doll-baby I gave Betsey, and it is not at all delicate. It went through the measles, and the chicken-pox, and the mumps, and the whooping-cough, before it left the North Pole. Now get into the sledge, Jimmy Scarecrow, and bring the doll-baby and the crazy quilt. I have never had any quilts that weren't in their right minds at the North Pole, but maybe I can cure this one. Get in!" Santa chirruped to his reindeer, and they drew the sledge up close in a beautiful curve.

"Get in, Jimmy Scarecrow, and come with me to the North Pole!" he cried.

"Please, how long shall I stay?" asked Jimmy Scarecrow.

"Why, you are going to live with me," replied Santa Claus. "I've been looking for a person like you for a long time."

"Are there any crows to scare away at the North Pole? I want to be useful," Jimmy Scarecrow said, anxiously.

"No," answered Santa Claus, "but I don't want you to scare away crows. I want you to scare away Arctic Explorers. I can keep you in work for a thousand years, and scaring away Arctic Explorers from the North Pole is much more important than scaring away crows from corn. Why, if they found the Pole, there wouldn't be a piece an inch long left in a week's time, and the earth would cave in like an apple without a core! They would whittle it all to pieces, and carry it away in their pockets for souvenirs. Come along; I am in a hurry."

"I will go on two conditions," said Jimmy. "First, I want to make a present to Aunt Hannah and Betsey, next Christmas."

"You shall make them any present you choose. What else?"

"I want some way provided to scare the crows out of the corn next summer, while I am away," said Jimmy.

"That is easily managed," said Santa Claus. "Just wait a minute."

Santa took his stylographic pen out of his pocket, went with his lantern close to one of the fence-posts, and wrote these words upon it:

   NOTICE TO CROWS

Whichever crow shall hereafter hop, fly, or flop into this field during the absence of Jimmy Scarecrow, and therefrom purloin, steal, or abstract corn, shall be instantly, in a twinkling and a trice, turned snow-white, and be ever after a disgrace, a byword and a reproach to his whole race.

      Per order of Santa Claus.

"The corn will be safe now," said Santa Claus, "get in." Jimmy got into the sledge and they flew away over the fields, out of sight, with merry halloos and a great clamour of bells.

The next morning there was much surprise at the farmhouse, when Aunt Hannah and Betsey looked out of the window and the Scarecrow was not in the field holding out his stiff arms over the corn stubble. Betsey had told Aunt Hannah she had given away the crazy quilt and the doll-baby, but had been scolded very little.

"You must not give away anything of yours again without asking permission," said Aunt Hannah. "And you have no right to give anything of mine, even if you know I don't want it. Now both my pretty quilt and your beautiful doll-baby are spoiled."

That was all Aunt Hannah had said. She thought she would send John after the quilt and the doll-baby next morning as soon as it was light.

But Jimmy Scarecrow was gone, and the crazy quilt and the doll-baby with him. John, the servant-man, searched everywhere, but not a trace of them could he find. "They must have all blown away, mum," he said to Aunt Hannah.

"We shall have to have another scarecrow next summer," said she.

But the next summer there was no need of a scarecrow, for not a crow came past the fence-post on which Santa Claus had written his notice to crows. The cornfield was never so beautiful, and not a single grain was stolen by a crow, and everybody wondered at it, for they could not read the crow-language in which Santa had written.

"It is a great mystery to me why the crows don't come into our cornfield, when there is no scarecrow," said Aunt Hannah.

But she had a still greater mystery to solve when Christmas came round again. Then she and Betsey had each a strange present. They found them in the sitting-room on Christmas morning. Aunt Hannah's present was her old crazy quilt, remodelled, with every piece cut square and true, and matched exactly to its neighbour.

"Why, it's my old crazy quilt, but it isn't crazy now!" cried Aunt Hannah, and her very spectacles seemed to glisten with amazement.

Betsey's present was her doll-baby of the Christmas before; but the doll was a year older. She had grown an inch, and could walk and say, "mamma," and "how do?" She was changed a good deal, but Betsey knew her at once. "It's my doll-baby!" she cried, and snatched her up and kissed her.

But neither Aunt Hannah nor Betsey ever knew that the quilt and the doll were Jimmy Scarecrow's Christmas presents to them.

XII. WHY THE CHIMES RANG*

RAYMOND MC ALDEN

There was once in a faraway country where few people have ever travelled, a wonderful church. It stood on a high hill in the midst of a great city; and every Sunday, as well as on sacred days like Christmas, thousands of people climbed the hill to its great archways, looking like lines of ants all moving in the same direction.

When you came to the building itself, you found stone columns and dark passages, and a grand entrance leading to the main room of the church. This room was so long that one standing at the doorway could scarcely see to the other end, where the choir stood by the marble altar. In the farthest corner was the organ; and this organ was so loud, that sometimes when it played, the people for miles around would close their shutters and prepare for a great thunderstorm. Altogether, no such church as this was ever seen before, especially when it was lighted up for some festival, and crowded with people, young and old. But the strangest thing about the whole building was the wonderful chime of bells.

At one corner of the church was a great gray tower, with ivy growing over it as far up as one could see. I say as far as one could see, because the tower was quite great enough to fit the great church, and it rose so far into the sky that it was only in very fair weather that any one claimed to be able to see the top. Even then one could not be certain that it was in sight. Up, and up, and up climbed the stones and the ivy; and as the men who built the church had been dead for hundreds of years, every one had forgotten how high the tower was supposed to be.

Now all the people knew that at the top of the tower was a chime of Christmas bells. They had hung there ever since the church had been built, and were the most beautiful bells in the world. Some thought it was because a great musician had cast them and arranged them in their place; others said it was because of the great height, which reached up where the air was clearest and purest; however that might be no one who had ever heard the chimes denied that they were the sweetest in the world. Some described them as sounding like angels far up in the sky; others as sounding like strange winds singing through the trees.

But the fact was that no one had heard them for years and years. There was an old man living not far from the church who said that his mother had spoken of hearing them when she was a little girl, and he was the only one who was sure of as much as that. They were Christmas chimes, you see, and were not meant to be played by men or on common days. It was the custom on Christmas Eve for all the people to bring to the church their offerings to the Christ-Child; and when the greatest and best offering was laid on the altar there used to come sounding through the music of the choir the Christmas chimes far up in the tower. Some said that the wind rang them, and others, that they were so high that the angels could set them swinging. But for many long years they had never been heard. It was said that people had been growing less careful of their gifts for the Christ-Child, and that no offering was brought great enough to deserve the music of the chimes.

Every Christmas Eve the rich people still crowded to the altar, each one trying to bring some better gift than any other, without giving anything that he wanted for himself, and the church was crowded with those who thought that perhaps the wonderful bells might be heard again. But although the service was splendid, and the offerings plenty, only the roar of the wind could be heard, far up in the stone tower.

Now, a number of miles from the city, in a little country village, where nothing could be seen of the great church but glimpses of the tower when the weather was fine, lived a boy named Pedro, and his little brother. They knew very little about the Christmas chimes, but they had heard of the service in the church on Christmas Eve, and had a secret plan which they had often talked over when by themselves, to go to see the beautiful celebration.

"Nobody can guess, Little Brother," Pedro would say; "all the fine things there are to see and hear; and I have even heard it said that the Christ-Child sometimes comes down to bless the service. What if we could see Him?"

The day before Christmas was bitterly cold, with a few lonely snowflakes flying in the air, and a hard white crust on the ground. Sure enough Pedro and Little Brother were able to slip quietly away early in the afternoon; and although the walking was hard in the frosty air, before nightfall they had trudged so far, hand in hand, that they saw the lights of the big city just ahead of them. Indeed they were about to enter one of the great gates in the wall that surrounded it, when they saw something dark on the snow near their path, and stepped aside to look at it.

It was a poor woman, who had fallen just outside the city, too sick and tired to get in where she might have found shelter. The soft snow made of a drift a sort of pillow for her, and she would soon be so sound asleep, in the wintry air, that no one could ever waken her again. All this Pedro saw in a moment and he knelt down beside her and tried to rouse her, even tugging at her arm a little, as though he would have tried to carry her away. He turned her face toward him, so that he could rub some of the snow on it, and when he had looked at her silently a moment he stood up again, and said:

"It's no use, Little Brother. You will have to go on alone."

"Alone?" cried Little Brother. "And you not see the Christmas festival?"

"No," said Pedro, and he could not keep back a bit of a choking sound in his throat. "See this poor woman. Her face looks like the Madonna in the chapel window, and she will freeze to death if nobody cares for her. Every one has gone to the church now, but when you come back you can bring some one to help her. I will rub her to keep her from freezing, and perhaps get her to eat the bun that is left in my pocket."

"But I cannot bear to leave you, and go on alone," said Little Brother.

"Both of us need not miss the service," said Pedro, "and it had better be I than you. You can easily find your way to church; and you must see and hear everything twice, Little Brother—once for you and once for me. I am sure the Christ-Child must know how I should love to come with you and worship Him; and oh! if you get a chance, Little Brother, to slip up to the altar without getting in any one's way, take this little silver piece of mine, and lay it down for my offering, when no one is looking. Do not forget where you have left me, and forgive me for not going with you."

In this way he hurried Little Brother off to the city and winked hard to keep back the tears, as he heard the crunching footsteps sounding farther and farther away in the twilight. It was pretty hard to lose the music and splendour of the Christmas celebration that he had been planning for so long, and spend the time instead in that lonely place in the snow.

The great church was a wonderful place that night. Every one said that it had never looked so bright and beautiful before. When the organ played and the thousands of people sang, the walls shook with the sound, and little Pedro, away outside the city wall, felt the earth tremble around them.

At the close of the service came the procession with the offerings to be laid on the altar. Rich men and great men marched proudly up to lay down their gifts to the Christ-Child. Some brought wonderful jewels, some baskets of gold so heavy that they could scarcely carry them down the aisle. A great writer laid down a book that he had been making for years and years. And last of all walked the king of the country, hoping with all the rest to win for himself the chime of the Christmas bells. There went a great murmur through the church as the people saw the king take from his head the royal crown, all set with precious stones, and lay it gleaming on the altar, as his offering to the Holy Child. "Surely," every one said, "we shall hear the bells now, for nothing like this has ever happened before."

But still only the cold old wind was heard in the tower and the people shook their heads; and some of them said, as they had before, that they never really believed the story of the chimes, and doubted if they ever rang at all.

The procession was over, and the choir began the closing hymn. Suddenly the organist stopped playing; and every one looked at the old minister, who was standing by the altar, holding up his hand for silence. Not a sound could be heard from any one in the church, but as all the people strained their ears to listen, there came softly, but distinctly, swinging through the air, the sound of the chimes in the tower. So far away, and yet so clear the music seemed—so much sweeter were the notes than anything that had been heard before, rising and falling away up there in the sky, that the people in the church sat for a moment as still as though something held each of them by the shoulders. Then they all stood up together and stared straight at the altar, to see what great gift had awakened the long silent bells.

But all that the nearest of them saw was the childish figure of Little Brother, who had crept softly down the aisle when no one was looking, and had laid Pedro's little piece of silver on the altar.

XIII. THE BIRDS' CHRISTMAS

From "In the Child's World," by Emilie Poulssen, Milton Bradley Co. Publishers. Used by permission.

F. E. MANN

Founded on fact.

"Chickadee-dee-dee-dee! Chickadee-dee-dee-dee! Chicka—" "Cheerup, cheerup, chee-chee! Cheerup, cheerup, chee-chee!" "Ter-ra-lee, ter-ra-lee, ter-ra-lee!"

"Rap-atap-atap-atap!" went the woodpecker; "Mrs. Chickadee may speak first."

"Friends," began Mrs. Chickadee, "why do you suppose I called you together?"

"Because it's the day before Christmas," twittered Snow Bunting. "And you're going to give a Christmas party," chirped the Robin. "And you want us all to come!" said Downy Woodpecker. "Hurrah! Three cheers for Mrs. Chickadee!"

"Hush!" said Mrs. Chickadee, "and I'll tell you all about it. To-morrow IS Christmas Day, but I don't want to give a party."

"Chee, chee, chee!" cried Robin Rusty-breast; "chee, chee, chee!"

"Just listen to my little plan," said Mrs. Chickadee, "for, indeed, I want you all to help. How many remember Thistle Goldfinch—the happy little fellow who floated over the meadows through the summer and fall?"

"Cheerup, chee-chee, cheerup, chee-chee, I do," sang the Robin; "how he loved to sway on thistletops!"

"Yes," said Downy Woodpecker, "and didn't he sing? All about blue skies, and sunshine and happy days, with his 'Swee-e-et sweet-sweet-sweet-a-twitter-witter-witter-witter-wee-twea!'"

"Ter-ra-lee, ter-ra-lee," said Snow Bunting. "We've all heard of Thistle Goldfinch, but what can he have to do with your Christmas party? He's away down South now, and wouldn't care if you gave a dozen parties."

"Oh, but he isn't; he's right in these very woods!"

"Why, you don't mean—"

"Indeed I do mean it, every single word. Yesterday I was flitting about among the trees, peeking at a dead branch here, and a bit of moss there, and before I knew it I found myself away over at the other side of the woods! 'Chickadee-dee-dee, chickadee-dee-dee!' I sang, as I turned my bill toward home. Just then I heard the saddest little voice pipe out: 'Dear-ie me! Dear-ie me!' and there on the sunny side of a branch perched a lonesome bit of yellowish down. I went up to see what it was, and found dear little Thistle Goldfinch! He was very glad to see me, and soon told his short story. Through the summer Papa and Mamma Goldfinch and all the brothers and sisters had a fine time, singing together, fluttering over thistletops, or floating through the balmy air. But when 'little Jack Frost walked through the trees,' Papa Goldfinch said: 'It is high time we went South!' All were ready but Thistle; he wanted to stay through the winter, and begged so hard that Papa Goldfinch soberly said: 'Try it, my son, but do find a warm place to stay in at night.' Then off they flew, and Thistle was alone. For a while he was happy. The sun shone warm through the middle of the day, and there were fields and meadows full of seeds. You all remember how sweetly he sang for us then. But by and by the cold North Wind came whistling through the trees, and chilly Thistle woke up one gray morning to find the air full of whirling snowflakes He didn't mind the light snows, golden-rod and some high grasses were too tall to be easily covered, and he got seeds from them. But now that the heavy snows have come, the poor little fellow is almost starved, and if he doesn't have a warm place to sleep in these cold nights, he'll surely die!"

Mrs. Chickadee paused a minute. The birds were so still one could hear the pine trees whisper. Then she went on: "I comforted the poor little fellow as best I could, and showed him where to find a few seeds; then I flew home, for it was bedtime. I tucked my head under my wing to keep it warm, and thought, and thought, and thought; and here's my plan:

"We Chickadees have a nice warm home here in the spruce trees, with their thick, heavy boughs to shut out the snow and cold. There is plenty of room, so Thistle could sleep here all winter. We would let him perch on a branch, when we Chickadees would nestle around him until he was as warm as in the lovely summer time. These cones are so full of seeds that we could spare him a good many; and I think that you Robins might let him come over to your pines some day and share your seeds. Downy Woodpecker must keep his eyes open as he hammers the trees, and if he spies a supply of seeds he will let us know at once. Snow Bunting is only a visitor, so I don't expect him to help, but I wanted him to hear my plan with the rest of you. Now you WILL try, won't you, EVERY ONE?"

"Cheerup, cheerup, ter-ra-lee! Indeed we'll try; let's begin right away! Don't wait until to-morrow; who'll go and find Thistle?"

"I will," chirped Robin Rusty-breast, and off he flew to the place which Mrs. Chickadee had told of, at the other side of the wood. There, sure enough, he found Thistle Goldfinch sighing: "Dear-ie me! dear-ie me! The winter is so cold and I'm here all alone!" "Cheerup, chee-chee!" piped the Robin:

"Cheerup, cheerup, I'm here!

I'm here and I mean to stay.

What if the winter is drear—

Cheerup, cheerup, anyway!"

"But the snow is so deep," said Thistle, and the Robin replied:

"Soon the snows'll be over and gone,

Run and rippled away;

What's the use of looking forlorn?

Cheerup, cheerup, I say!"

Then he told Thistle all their plans, and wasn't Thistle surprised? Why, he just couldn't believe a word of it till they reached Mrs. Chickadee's and she said it was all true. They fed him and warmed him, then settled themselves for a good night's rest.

Christmas morning they were chirping gaily, and Thistle was trying to remember the happy song he sang in the summer time, when there came a whirr of wings as Snow Bunting flew down.

"Ter-ra-lee, ter-ra-lee, ter-ra-lee," said he, "can you fly a little way?"

"Oh, yes," replied Thistle. "I THINK I could fly a LONG way."

"Come on, then," said Snow Bunting. "Every one who wants a Christmas dinner, follow me!" That was every word he would say, so what could they do but follow?

Soon they came to the edge of the wood, and then to a farmhouse. Snow Bunting flew straight up to the piazza, and there stood a dear little girl in a warm hood and cloak, with a pail of bird-seed on her arm, and a dish of bread crumbs in her hand. As they flew down, she said:

"And here are some more birdies who have come for a Christmas dinner. Of course you shall have some, you dear little things!" and she laughed merrily to see them dive for the crumbs.

After they had finished eating, Elsie (that was the little girl's name) said: "Now, little birds, it is going to be a cold winter, you would better come here every day to get your dinner. I'll always be glad to see you."

"Cheerup chee-chee, cheerup chee-chee! thank you, thank you," cried the Robins. "Ter-ra-lee, ter-ra-lee, ter-ra-lee! thank you, thank you!" twittered Snow Bunting.

"Chick-a-dee-dee-dee-dee, chick-a-dee-dee-dee-dee, chick-a-dee-dee-dee-dee-dee! how kind you are!" sang the Chickadees.

And Thistle Goldfinch? Yes, he remembered his summer song, for he sang as they flew away:

"Swee-e-et-sweet-sweet-sweet-a-twitter-witter-witter-witter—wee-twea!"

notes.—l. The Robin's song is from "Bird Talks," by Mrs. A.D.T. Whitney. 2. The fact upon which this story is based—that is of the other birds adopting and warming the solitary Thistle Goldfinch—was observed near Northampton, Mass., where robins and other migratory birds sometimes spend the winter in the thick pine woods.

XIV. THE LITTLE SISTER'S VACATION*

* This story was first published in the Youth's Companion, vol. 77.

WINIFRED M. KIRKLAND

It was to be a glorious Christmas at Doctor Brower's. All "the children"—
little Peggy and her mother always spoke of the grown-up ones as "the
children"—were coming home. Mabel was coming from Ohio with her big
husband and her two babies, Minna and little Robin, the year-old
grandson whom the home family had never seen; Hazen was coming all
the way from the Johns Hopkins Medical School, and Arna was coming
home from her teaching in New York. It was a trial to Peggy that
vacation did not begin until the very day before Christmas, and then
continued only one niggardly week. After school hours she had helped
her mother in the Christmas preparations every day until she crept into
bed at night with aching arms and tired feet, to lie there tossing about,
whether from weariness or glad excitement she did not know.

"Not so hard, daughter," the doctor said to her once.

"Oh, papa," protested her mother, "when we're so busy, and Peggy is so
handy!"

"Not so hard," he repeated, with his eyes on fifteen-year-old Peggy's
delicate face, as, wearing her braids pinned up on her head and a pinafore
down to her toes, she stoned raisins and blanched almonds, rolled bread
crumbs and beat eggs, dusted and polished and made ready for the
children.

Finally, after a day of flying about, helping with the many last thing,
Peggy let down her braids and put on her new crimson shirtwaist, and
stood with her mother in the front doorway, for it was Christmas Eve at

last, and the station 'bus was rattling up with the first homecomers, Arna and Hazen.

Then there were voices ringing up and down the dark street, and there were happy tears in the mother's eyes, and Arna had taken Peggy's face in her two soft-gloved hands and lifted it up and kissed it, and Hazen had swung his little sister up in the air just as of old. Peggy's tired feet were dancing for joy. She was helping Arna take off her things, was carrying her bag upstairs—would have carried Hazen's heavy grip, too, only her father took it from her.

"Set the kettle to boil, Peggy," directed her mother; "then run upstairs and see if Arna wants anything. We'll wait supper till the rest come."

The rest came on the nine o'clock train, such a load of them—the big, bluff brother-in-law, Mabel, plump and laughing, as always, Minna, elfin and bright-eyed, and sleepy Baby Robin. Such hugging, such a hubbub of baby talk! How many things there seemed to be to do for those precious babies right away!

Peggy was here and there and everywhere. Everything was in joyous confusion. Supper was to be set on, too. While the rest ate, Peggy sat by, holding Robin, her own little nephew, and managing at the same time to pick up the things—napkin, knife, spoon, bread—that Minna, hilarious with the late hour, flung from her high chair.

It seemed as if they would never be all stowed away for the night. Some of them wanted pitchers of warm water, some of them pitchers of cold, and the alcohol stove must be brought up for heating the baby's milk at night. The house was crowded, too. Peggy had given up her room to Hazen, and slept on a cot in the sewing room with Minna.

The cot had been enlarged by having three chairs piled with pillows, set along the side. But Minna preferred to sleep in the middle of the cot, or else across it, her restless little feet pounding at Peggy's ribs; and Peggy was unused to any bedfellow.

She lay long awake thinking proudly of the children; of Hazen, the tall brother, with his twinkling eyes, his drolleries, his teasing; of graceful Arna who dressed so daintily, talked so cleverly, and had been to college. Arna was going to send Peggy to college, too—it was so good of Arna! But for all Peggy's admiration for Arna, it was Mabel, the eldest sister, who was the more approachable. Mabel did not pretend even to as much learning as Peggy had herself; she was happy-go-lucky and sweet-tempered. Then her husband was a great jolly fellow, with whom it was impossible to be shy, and the babies—there never were such cunning babies, Peggy thought. Just here her niece gave her a particularly vicious kick, and Peggy opposed to her train of admiring thoughts, "But I'm so tired."

It did not seem to Peggy that she had been asleep at all when she was waked with a vigorous pounding on her chest and a shrill little voice in her ear:

"Ch'is'mus, Ch'is'mus, Ch'is'mus! It's mornin'! It's Ch'is'mus!"

"Oh, no, it isn't, Minna!" pleaded Peggy, struggling with sleepiness. "It's all dark still."

"Ch'is'mus, Ch'is'mus, Ch'is'mus!" reiterated Minna continuing to pound.

"Hush, dear! You'll wake Aunt Arna, and she's feed after being all day on the chou-chou cars."

"Merry Ch'is'mus, Aunty Arna!" shouted the irrepressible Minna.

"Oh, darling, be quiet! We'll play little pig goes to market. I'll tell you a story, only be quiet a little while."

It took Peggy's utmost effort to keep the little wriggler still for the hour from five to six. Then, however, her shrill, "Merry Ch'is'mus!" roused the household. Protests were of no avail. Minna was the only granddaughter. Dark as it was, people must get up.

Peggy must dress Minna and then hurry down to help get breakfast—not so easy a task with Minna ever at one's heels. The quick-moving sprite seemed to be everywhere—into the sugar-bowl, the cooky jar, the steaming teakettle—before one could turn about. Urged on by the impatient little girl, the grown-ups made short work of breakfast.

After the meal, according to time-honoured Brower custom, they formed in procession, single file, Minna first, then Ben with Baby Robin. They each held aloft a sprig of holly, and they all kept time as they sang, "God rest you, merry gentlemen," in their march from the dining-room to the office. And there they must form in circle about the tree, and dance three times round, singing "The Christmas-tree is an evergreen," before they could touch a single present.

The presents are done up according to custom, packages of every shape and size, but all in white paper and tied with red ribbon, and all marked for somebody with somebody else's best love. They all fall to opening, and the babies' shouts are not the only ones to be heard.

Passers-by smile indulgently at the racket, remembering that all the Browers are home for Christmas, and the Browers were ever a jovial company.

Peggy gazes at her gifts quietly, but with shining eyes—little gold cuff pins from Hazen, just like Arna's; a set of furs from Mabel and Ben; but she likes Arna's gift best of all, a complete set of her favourite author.

113

But much as they would like to linger about the Christmas tree, Peggy
and her mother, at least, must remember that the dishes must be washed
and the beds made, and that the family must get ready for church.
Peggy does not go to church, and nobody dreams how much she wants to
go. She loves the Christmas music. No hymn rings so with joy as:

Jerusalem triumphs, Messiah is king.

The choir sings it only once a year, on the Christmas morning. Besides,
her chum Esther will be at church, and Peggy has been too busy to go to
see her since she came home from boarding-school for the holidays. But
somebody must stay at home, and that somebody who but Peggy?
Somebody must baste the turkey and prepare the vegetables and take
care of the babies.

Peggy is surprised to find how difficult it is to combine dinner-getting
with baby-tending. When she opens the oven-door, there is Minna's head
thrust up under her arm, the inquisitive little nose in great danger by
reason of sputtering gravy.

"Minna," protests Peggy, "you mustn't eat another bit of candy!" and
Minna opens her mouth in a howl, prolonged, but without tears and
without change of colour. Robin joins in, he does not know why. Peggy is
a doting aunt, but an honest one. She is vexed by a growing conviction
that Mabel's babies are sadly spoiled. Peggy is ashamed of herself; surely
she ought to be perfectly happy playing with Minna and Robin. Instead,
she finds that the thing she would like best of all to be doing at this
moment, next to going to church, would be to be lying on her father's
couch in the office, all by herself, reading.

The dinner is a savoury triumph for Peggy and her mother. The gravy
and the mashed potato are entirely of Peggy's workmanship, and Peggy
has had a hand in most of the other dishes, too, as the mother proudly

tells. How that merry party can eat! Peggy is waitress, and it is long before the passing is over, and she can sit down in her own place. She is just as fond of the unusual Christmas good things as are the rest, but somehow, before she is well started at her turkey, it is time for changing plates for dessert, and before she has tasted her nuts and raisins the babies have succumbed to sleepiness, and it is Peggy who must carry them upstairs for their nap—just in the middle of one of Hazen's funniest stories, too.

And all the time the little sister is so ready, so quickly serviceable, that somehow nobody notices—nobody but the doctor. It is he who finds Peggy, half as hour later, all alone in the kitchen. The mother and the older daughters are gathered about the sitting-room hearth, engaged in the dear, delicious talk about the little things that are always left out of letters.

The doctor interrupts them.

"Peggy is all alone," he says.

"But we're having such a good talk," the mother pleads, "and Peggy will be done in no time! Peggy is so handy!"

"Well, girls?" is all the doctor says, with quiet command in his eyes, and Peggy is not left to wash the Christmas dishes all alone. Because she is smiling and her cheeks are bright, her sisters do not notice that her eyes are wet, for Peggy is hotly ashamed of certain thoughts and feelings that she cannot down. She forgets them for a while, however, sitting on the hearth-rug, snuggled against her father's knee in the Christmas twilight.

Yet the troublesome thoughts came back in the evening, when Peggy sat upstairs in the dark with Minna, vainly trying to induce the excited little girl to go to sleep, while bursts of merriment from the family below were always breaking in upon the two in their banishment.

There was another restless night of it with the little niece, and another too early waking. Everybody but Minna was sleepy enough, and breakfast was a protracted meal, to which the "children" came down slowly one by one. Arna did not appear at all, and Peggy carried up to her the daintiest of trays, all of her own preparing. Arna's kiss of thanks was great reward. It was dinner-time before Peggy realized it, and she had hoped to find a quiet hour for her Latin.

The dreadful regent's examination was to come the next week, and Peggy wanted to study for it. She had once thought of asking Arna to help her, but Arna seemed so tired.

In the afternoon Esther came to see her chum, and to take her home with her to spend the night. The babies, fretful with after-Christmas-crossness, were tumbling over their aunt, and sadly interrupting confidences, while Peggy explained that she could not go out that evening. All the family were going to the church sociable, and she must put the babies to bed.

"I think it's mean," Esther broke in. "Isn't it your vacation as well as theirs? Do make that child stop pulling your hair!"

If Esther's words had only not echoed through Peggy's head as they did that night! "But it is so mean of me, so mean of me, to want my own vacation!" sobbed Peggy in the darkness. "I ought just to be glad they're all at home."

Her self-reproach made her readier than ever to wait on them all the next morning. Nobody could make such buckwheat cakes as could Mrs. Brower; nobody could turn them as could Peggy. They were worth coming from New York and Baltimore and Ohio to eat. Peggy stood at the griddle half an hour, an hour, two hours. Her head was aching. Hazen, the latest riser, was joyously calling for more.

At eleven o'clock Peggy realized that she had had no breakfast herself, and that her mother was hurrying her off to investigate the lateness of the butcher. Her head ached more and more, and she seemed strangely slow in her dinner-getting and dish-washing. Her father was away, and there was no one to help in the clearing-up. It was three before she had finished.

Outside the sleigh-bells sounded enticing. It was the first sleighing of the season. Mabel and Ben had been off for a ride, and Arna and Hazen, too. How Peggy longed to be skimming over the snow instead of polishing knives all alone in the kitchen. Sue Cummings came that afternoon to invite Peggy to her party, given in Esther's honour. Sue enumerated six other gatherings that were being given that week in honour of Esther's visit home. Sue seemed to dwell much on the subject. Presently Peggy, with hot cheeks, understood why. Everybody was giving Esther a party, everybody but Peggy herself. Esther's own chum, and all the other girls, were talking about it.

Peggy stood at the door to see Sue out, and watched the sleighs fly by. Out in the sitting-room she heard her mother saying, "Yes, of course we can have waffles for supper. Where's Peggy?" Then Peggy ran away.

In the wintry dusk the doctor came stamping in, shaking the snow from his bearskins. As always, "Where's Peggy?" was his first question.

Peggy was not to be found, they told him. They had been all over the house, calling her. They thought she must have gone out with Sue. The doctor seemed to doubt this. He went through the upstairs rooms, calling her softly. But Peggy was not in any of the bedrooms, or in any of the closets, either. There was still the kitchen attic to be tried.

There came a husky little moan out of its depths, as he whispered, "Daughter!" He groped his way to her, and sitting down on a trunk, folded her into his bearskin coat.

"Now tell father all about it," he said. And it all came out with many sobs—the nights and dawns with Minna, the Latin, the sleighing, Esther's party, breakfast, the weariness, the headache; and last the waffles, which had moved the one unbearable thing.

"And it is so mean of me, so mean of me!" sobbed Peggy. "But, oh, daddy, I do want a vacation!"

"And you shall have one," he answered.

He carried her straight into her own room, laid her down on her own bed, and tumbled Hazen's things into the hall. Then he went downstairs and talked to his family.

Presently the mother came stealing in, bearing a glass of medicine the doctor-father had sent. Then she undressed Peggy and put her to bed as if she had been a baby, and sat by, smoothing her hair, until she fell asleep.

It seemed to Peggy that she had slept a long, long time. The sun was shining bright. Her door opened a crack and Arna peeped in, and seeing her awake, came to the bed and kissed her good morning.

"I'm so sorry, little sister!" she said.

"Sorry for what?" asked the wondering Peggy.

"Because I didn't see," said Arna. "But now I'm going to bring up your breakfast."

"Oh, no!" cried Peggy, sitting up.

"Oh, yes!" said Arna, with quiet authority. It was as dainty cooking as Peggy's own, and Arna sat by to watch her eat.

"You're so good to me, Arna!" said Peggy.

"Not very," answered Arna, dryly. "When you've finished this you must lie up here away from the children and read."

"But who will take care of Minna?" questioned Peggy.

"Minna's mamma," answered a voice from the next room, where Mabel was pounding pillows. She came to the door to look in on Peggy in all her luxury of orange marmalade to eat, Christmas books to read, and Arna to wait upon her.

"I think mothers, not aunts, were meant to look after babies," said Mabel. "I'm so sorry, dear!"

"Oh, I wish you two wouldn't talk like that!" cried Peggy. "I'm so ashamed."

"All right, we'll stop talking," said Mabel quickly, "but we'll remember."

They would not let Peggy lift her hand to any of the work that day. Mabel managed the babies masterfully. Arna moved quietly about, accomplishing wonders.

"But aren't you tired, Arna?" queried Peggy.

"Not a bit of it, and I'll have time to help you with your Caesar before—"

"Before what?" asked Peggy, but got no answer. They had been translating famously, when, in the late afternoon, there came a ring of the doorbell. Peggy found Hazen bowing low, and craving "Mistress Peggy's company." A sleigh and two prancing horses stood at the gate.

It was a glorious drive. Peggy's eyes danced and her laugh rang out at Hazen's drolleries. The world stretched white all about them, and their horses flew on and on like the wind. They rode till dark, then turned back to the village, twinkling with lights.

The Brower house was alight in every window, and there was the sound of many voices in the hall. The door flew open upon a laughing crowd of boys and girls. Peggy, all glowing and rosy with the wind, stood utterly bewildered until Esther rushed forward and hugged and shook her.

"It's a party!" she exclaimed. "One of your mother's waffle suppers! We're all here! Isn't it splendid?"

"But, but, but—" stammered Peggy.

"'But, but, but,'" mimicked Esther. "But this is your vacation, don't you see?"

XV. LITTLE WOLFF'S WOODEN SHOES

A CHRISTMAS STORY BY FRANCOIS COPPEE; ADAPTED AND TRANSLATED BY ALMA J. FOSTER

Once upon a time—so long ago that everybody has forgotten the date—in a city in the north of Europe—with such a hard name that nobody can ever remember it—there was a little seven-year-old boy named Wolff, whose parents were dead, who lived with a cross and stingy old aunt, who never thought of kissing him more than once a year and who sighed deeply whenever she gave him a bowlful of soup.

But the poor little fellow had such a sweet nature that in spite of everything, he loved the old woman, although he was terribly afraid of her and could never look at her ugly old face without shivering.

As this aunt of little Wolff was known to have a house of her own and an old woollen stocking full of gold, she had not dared to send the boy to a charity school; but, in order to get a reduction in the price, she had so wrangled with the master of the school, to which little Wolff finally went, that this bad man, vexed at having a pupil so poorly dressed and paying so little, often punished him unjustly, and even prejudiced his companions against him, so that the three boys, all sons of rich parents, made a drudge and laughing stock of the little fellow.

The poor little one was thus as wretched as a child could be and used to hide himself in corners to weep whenever Christmas time came.

It was the schoolmaster's custom to take all his pupils to the midnight mass on Christmas Eve, and to bring them home again afterward.

Now, as the winter this year was very bitter, and as heavy snow had been falling for several days, all the boys came well bundled up in warm clothes, with fur caps pulled over their ears, padded jackets, gloves and knitted mittens, and strong, thick-soled boots. Only little Wolff presented himself shivering in the poor clothes he used to wear both weekdays and Sundays and having on his feet only thin socks in heavy wooden shoes.

His naughty companions noticing his sad face and awkward appearance, made many jokes at his expense; but the little fellow was so busy blowing on his fingers, and was suffering so much with chilblains, that he took no notice of them. So the band of youngsters, walking two and two behind the master, started for the church.

It was pleasant in the church which was brilliant with lighted candles; and the boys excited by the warmth took advantage of the music of the choir and the organ to chatter among themselves in low tones. They bragged about the fun that was awaiting them at home. The mayor's son had seen, just before starting off, an immense goose ready stuffed and dressed for cooking. At the alderman's home there was a little pine-tree with branches laden down with oranges, sweets, and toys. And the lawyer's cook had put on her cap with such care as she never thought of taking unless she was expecting something very good!

Then they talked, too, of all that the Christ-Child was going to bring them, of all he was going to put in their shoes which, you might be sure, they would take good care to leave in the chimney place before going to bed; and the eyes of these little urchins, as lively as a cage of mice, were sparkling in advance over the joy they would have when they awoke in the morning and saw the pink bag full of sugar-plums, the little lead soldiers ranged in companies in their boxes, the menageries smelling of varnished wood, and the magnificent jumping-jacks in purple and tinsel.

Alas! Little Wolff knew by experience that his old miser of an aunt would send him to bed supperless, but, with childlike faith and certain of having been, all the year, as good and industrious as possible, he hoped that the Christ-Child would not forget him, and so he, too, planned to place his wooden shoes in good time in the fireplace.

Midnight mass over, the worshippers departed, eager for their fun, and the band of pupils always walking two and two, and following the teacher, left the church.

Now, in the porch and seated on a stone bench set in the niche of a painted arch, a child was sleeping—a child in a white woollen garment, but with his little feet bare, in spite of the cold. He was not a beggar, for his garment was white and new, and near him on the floor was a bundle of carpenter's tools.

In the clear light of the stars, his face, with its closed eyes, shone with an expression of divine sweetness, and his long, curling, blond locks seemed to form a halo about his brow. But his little child's feet, made blue by the cold of this bitter December night, were pitiful to see!

The boys so well clothed for the winter weather passed by quite indifferent to the unknown child; several of them, sons of the notables of the town, however, cast on the vagabond looks in which could be read all the scorn of the rich for the poor, of the well-fed for the hungry.

But little Wolff, coming last out of the church, stopped, deeply touched, before the beautiful sleeping child.

"Oh, dear!" said the little fellow to himself, "this is frightful! This poor little one has no shoes and stockings in this bad weather—and, what is still worse, he has not even a wooden shoe to leave near him to-night while he sleeps, into which the little Christ-Child can put something good to soothe his misery."

And carried away by his loving heart, Wolff drew the wooden shoe from his right foot, laid it down before the sleeping child, and, as best he could, sometimes hopping, sometimes limping with his sock wet by the snow, he went home to his aunt.

"Look at the good-for-nothing!" cried the old woman, full of wrath at the sight of the shoeless boy. "What have you done with your shoe, you little villain?"

Little Wolff did not know how to lie, so, although trembling with terror when he saw the rage of the old shrew, he tried to relate his adventure.

But the miserly old creature only burst into a frightful fit of laughter.

"Aha! So my young gentleman strips himself for the beggars. Aha! My young gentleman breaks his pair of shoes for a bare-foot! Here is something new, forsooth. Very well, since it is this way, I shall put the only shoe that is left into the chimney-place, and I'll answer for it that the Christ-Child will put in something to-night to beat you with in the morning! And you will have only a crust of bread and water to-morrow. And we shall see if the next time, you will be giving your shoes to the first vagabond that happens along."

And the wicked woman having boxed the ears of the poor little fellow, made him climb up into the loft where he had his wretched cubbyhole.

Desolate, the child went to bed in the dark and soon fell asleep, but his pillow was wet with tears.

But behold! the next morning when the old woman, awakened early by the cold, went downstairs—oh, wonder of wonders—she saw the big chimney filled with shining toys, bags of magnificent bonbons, and riches of every sort, and standing out in front of all this treasure, was the right wooden shoe which the boy had given to the little vagabond, yes, and beside it, the one which she had placed in the chimney to hold the bunch of switches.

As little Wolff, attracted by the cries of his aunt, stood in an ecstasy of childish delight before the splendid Christmas gifts, shouts of laughter were heard outside. The woman and child ran out to see what all this meant, and behold! all the gossips of the town were standing around the public fountain. What could have happened? Oh, a most ridiculous and extraordinary thing! The children of the richest men in the town, whom their parents had planned to surprise with the most beautiful presents had found only switches in their shoes!

Then the old woman and the child thinking of all the riches in their chimney were filled with fear. But suddenly they saw the priest appear, his countenance full of astonishment. Just above the bench placed near the door of the church, in the very spot where, the night before, a child in a white garment and with bare feet, in spite of the cold, had rested his lovely head, the priest had found a circlet of gold imbedded in the old stones.

Then, they all crossed themselves devoutly, perceiving that this beautiful sleeping child with the carpenter's tools had been Jesus of Nazareth himself, who had come back for one hour just as he had been when he used to work in the home of his parents; and reverently they bowed before this miracle, which the good God had done to reward the faith and the love of a little child.

XVI. CHRISTMAS IN THE ALLEY*

* From "Kristy's Queer Christmas," Houghton, Mifflin & Co., 1904.

OLIVE THORNE MILLER

"I declare for 't, to-morrow is Christmas Day an' I clean forgot all about it," said old Ann, the washerwoman, pausing in her work and holding the flatiron suspended in the air.

"Much good it'll do us," growled a discontented voice from the coarse bed in the corner.

"We haven't much extra, to be sure," answered Ann cheerfully, bringing the iron down onto the shirt-bosom before her, "but at least we've enough to eat, and a good fire, and that's more'n some have, not a thousand miles from here either."

"We might have plenty more," said the fretful voice, "if you didn't think so much more of strangers than you do of your own folk's comfort, keeping a houseful of beggars, as if you was a lady!"

"Now, John," replied Ann, taking another iron from the fire, "you're not half so bad as you pretend. You wouldn't have me turn them poor creatures into the streets to freeze, now, would you?"

"It's none of our business to pay rent for them," grumbled John. "Every one for himself, I say, these hard times. If they can't pay you'd ought to send 'em off; there's plenty as can."

"They'd pay quick enough if they could get work," said Ann. "They're good honest fellows, every one, and paid me regular as long as they had a cent. But when hundreds are out o' work in the city, what can they do?"

"That's none o' your business, you can turn 'em out!" growled John.

"And leave the poor children to freeze as well as starve?" said Ann. "Who'd ever take 'em in without money, I'd like to know? No, John," bringing her iron down as though she meant it, "I'm glad I'm well enough to wash and iron, and pay my rent, and so long as I can do that, and keep the hunger away from you and the child, I'll never turn the poor souls out, leastways, not in this freezing winter weather."

"An' here's Christmas," the old man went on whiningly, "an' not a penny to spend, an' I needin' another blanket so bad, with my rhumatiz, an' haven't had a drop of tea for I don't know how long!"

"I know it," said Ann, never mentioning that she too had been without tea, and not only that, but with small allowance of food of any kind, "and I'm desperate sorry I can't get a bit of something for Katey. The child never missed a little something in her stocking before."

"Yes," John struck in, "much you care for your flesh an' blood. The child ha'n't had a thing this winter."

"That's true enough," said Ann, with a sigh, "an' it's the hardest thing of all that I've had to keep her out o' school when she was doing so beautiful."

"An' her feet all on the ground," growled John.

"I know her shoes is bad," said Ann, hanging the shirt up on a line that stretched across the room, and was already nearly full of freshly ironed clothes, "but they're better than the Parker children's."

"What's that to us?" almost shouted the weak old man, shaking his fist at her in his rage.

"Well, keep your temper, old man," said Ann. "I'm sorry it goes so hard with you, but as long as I can stand on my feet, I sha'n't turn anybody out to freeze, that's certain."

"How much'll you get for them?" said the miserable old man, after a few moments' silence, indicating by his hand the clean clothes on the line.

"Two dollars," said Ann, "and half of it must go to help make up next month's rent. I've got a good bit to make up yet, and only a week to do it in, and I sha'n't have another cent till day after to-morrow."

"Well, I wish you'd manage to buy me a little tea," whined the old man; "seems as if that would go right to the spot, and warm up my old bones a bit."

"I'll try," said Ann, revolving in her mind how she could save a few pennies from her indispensable purchases to get tea and sugar, for without sugar he would not touch it.

Wearied with his unusual exertion, the old man now dropped off to sleep, and Ann went softly about, folding and piling the clothes into a big basket already half full. When they were all packed in, and nicely covered with a piece of clean muslin, she took an old shawl and hood from a nail in the corner, put them on, blew out the candle, for it must not burn one moment unnecessarily, and, taking up her basket, went out into the cold winter night, softly closing the door behind her.

The house was on an alley, but as soon as she turned the corner she was in the bright streets, glittering with lamps and gay people. The shop windows were brilliant with Christmas displays, and thousands of warmly dressed buyers were lingering before them, laughing and chatting, and selecting their purchases. Surely it seemed as if there could be no want here.

As quickly as her burden would let her, the old washerwoman passed through the crowd into a broad street and rang the basement bell of a large, showy house.

"Oh, it's the washerwoman!" said a flashy-looking servant who answered the bell; "set the basket right in here. Mrs. Keithe can't look them over to-night. There's company in the parlour—Miss Carry's Christmas party."

"Ask her to please pay me—at least a part," said old Ann hastily. "I don't see how I can do without the money. I counted on it."

"I'll ask her," said the pert young woman, turning to go upstairs; "but it's no use."

Returning in a moment, she delivered the message. "She has no change to-night; you're to come in the morning."

"Dear me!" thought Ann, as she plodded back through the streets, "it'll be even worse than I expected, for there's not a morsel to eat in the house, and not a penny to buy one with. Well—well—the Lord will provide, the Good Book says, but it's mighty dark days, and it's hard to believe."

Entering the house, Ann sat down silently before the expiring fire. She was tired, her bones ached, and she was faint for want of food.

Wearily she rested her head on her hands, and tried to think of some way to get a few cents. She had nothing she could sell or pawn, everything she could do without had gone before, in similar emergencies. After sitting there some time, and revolving plan after plan, only to find them all impossible, she was forced to conclude that they must go supperless to bed.

Her husband grumbled, and Katey—who came in from a neighbour's—cried with hunger, and after they were asleep old Ann crept into bed to keep warm, more disheartened than she had been all winter.

If we could only see a little way ahead! All this time—the darkest the house on the alley had seen—help was on the way to them. A kind-hearted city missionary, visiting one of the unfortunate families living in the upper rooms of old Ann's house, had learned from them of the noble charity of the humble old washerwoman. It was more than princely charity, for she not only denied herself nearly every comfort, but she endured the reproaches of her husband, and the tears of her child.

Telling the story to a party of his friends this Christmas Eve, their hearts were troubled, and they at once emptied their purses into his hands for her. And the gift was at that very moment in the pocket of the missionary, waiting for morning to make her Christmas happy. Christmas morning broke clear and cold. Ann was up early, as usual, made her fire, with the last of her coal, cleared up her two rooms, and, leaving her husband and Katey in bed, was about starting out to try and get her money to provide a breakfast for them. At the door she met the missionary.

"Good-morning, Ann," said he. "I wish you a Merry Christmas."

"Thank you, sir," said Ann cheerfully; "the same to yourself."

"Have you been to breakfast already?" asked the missionary.

"No, sir," said Ann. "I was just going out for it."

"I haven't either," said he, "but I couldn't bear to wait until I had eaten breakfast before I brought you your Christmas present—I suspect you haven't had any yet."

Ann smiled. "Indeed, sir, I haven't had one since I can remember."

"Well, I have one for you. Come in, and I'll tell you about it."

Too much amazed for words, Ann led him into the room. The missionary opened his purse, and handed her a roll of bills.

"Why—what!" she gasped, taking it mechanically.

"Some friends of mine heard of your generous treatment of the poor families upstairs," he went on, "and they send you this, with their respects and best wishes for Christmas. Do just what you please with it— it is wholly yours. No thanks," he went on, as she struggled to speak. "It's not from me. Just enjoy it—that's all. It has done them more good to give than it can you to receive," and before she could speak a word he was gone.

What did the old washerwoman do?

Well, first she fell on her knees and buried her agitated face in the bedclothes. After a while she became aware of a storm of words from her husband, and she got up, subdued as much as possible her agitation, and tried to answer his frantic questions.

"How much did he give you, old stupid?" he screamed; "can't you speak, or are you struck dumb? Wake up! I just wish I could reach you! I'd shake you till your teeth rattled!"

His vicious looks were a sign, it was evident that he only lacked the strength to be as good as his word. Ann roused herself from her stupour and spoke at last.

"I don't know. I'll count it." She unrolled the bills and began.

"O Lord!" she exclaimed excitedly, "here's ten-dollar bills! One, two, three, and a twenty-that makes five—and five are fifty-five—sixty— seventy—eighty—eighty-five—ninety—one hundred—and two and five are seven, and two and one are ten, twenty—twenty-five—one hundred and twenty-five! Why, I'm rich!" she shouted. "Bless the Lord! Oh, this is the glorious Christmas Day! I knew He'd provide. Katey! Katey!" she screamed at the door of the other room, where the child lay asleep. "Merry Christmas to you, darlin'! Now you can have some shoes! and a new dress! and—and—breakfast, and a regular Christmas dinner! Oh! I believe I shall go crazy!"

But she did not. Joy seldom hurts people, and she was brought back to everyday affairs by the querulous voice of her husband.

"Now I will have my tea, an' a new blanket, an' some tobacco—how I have wanted a pipe!" and he went on enumerating his wants while Ann bustled about, putting away most of her money, and once more getting ready to go out.

"I'll run out and get some breakfast," she said, "but don't you tell a soul about the money."

"No! they'll rob us!" shrieked the old man.

"Nonsense! I'll hide it well, but I want to keep it a secret for another reason. Mind, Katey, don't you tell?"

"No!" said Katey, with wide eyes. "But can I truly have a new frock, Mammy, and new shoes—and is it really Christmas?"

"It's really Christmas, darlin'," said Ann, "and you'll see what mammy'll bring home to you, after breakfast."

The luxurious meal of sausages, potatoes, and hot tea was soon smoking on the table, and was eagerly devoured by Katey and her father. But Ann could not eat much. She was absent-minded, and only drank a cup of tea. As soon as breakfast was over, she left Katey to wash the dishes, and started out again.

She walked slowly down the street, revolving a great plan in her mind.

"Let me see," she said to herself. "They shall have a happy day for once. I suppose John'll grumble, but the Lord has sent me this money, and I mean to use part of it to make one good day for them."

Having settled this in her mind, she walked on more quickly, and visited various shops in the neighbourhood. When at last she went home, her big basket was stuffed as full as it could hold, and she carried a bundle besides.

"Here's your tea, John," she said cheerfully, as she unpacked the basket, "a whole pound of it, and sugar, and tobacco, and a new pipe."

"Give me some now," said the old man eagerly; "don't wait to take out the rest of the things."

"And here's a new frock for you, Katey," old Ann went on, after making John happy with his treasures, "a real bright one, and a pair of shoes, and some real woollen stockings; oh! how warm you'll be!"

"Oh, how nice, Mammy!" cried Katey, jumping about. "When will you make my frock?"

"To-morrow," answered the mother, "and you can go to school again."

"Oh, goody!" she began, but her face fell. "If only Molly Parker could go too!"

"You wait and see," answered Ann, with a knowing look. "Who knows what Christmas will bring to Molly Parker?"

"Now here's a nice big roast," the happy woman went on, still unpacking, "and potatoes and turnips and cabbage and bread and butter and coffee and—"

"What in the world! You goin' to give a party?" asked the old man between the puffs, staring at her in wonder.

"I'll tell you just what I am going to do," said Ann firmly, bracing herself for opposition, "and it's as good as done, so you needn't say a word about it. I'm going to have a Christmas dinner, and I'm going to invite every blessed soul in this house to come. They shall be warm and full for once in their lives, please God! And, Katey," she went on breathlessly, before the old man had sufficiently recovered from his astonishment to speak, "go right upstairs now, and invite every one of 'em from the fathers down to Mrs. Parker's baby to come to dinner at three o'clock; we'll have to keep fashionable hours, it's so late now; and mind, Katey, not a word about the money. And hurry back, child, I want you to help me."

To her surprise, the opposition from her husband was less than she expected. The genial tobacco seemed to have quieted his nerves, and even opened his heart. Grateful for this, Ann resolved that his pipe should never lack tobacco while she could work.

But now the cares of dinner absorbed her. The meat and vegetables were prepared, the pudding made, and the long table spread, though she had to borrow every table in the house, and every dish to have enough to go around.

At three o'clock when the guests came in, it was really a very pleasant sight. The bright warm fire, the long table, covered with a substantial, and, to them, a luxurious meal, all smoking hot. John, in his neatly brushed suit, in an armchair at the foot of the table, Ann in a bustle of hurry and welcome, and a plate and a seat for every one.

How the half-starved creatures enjoyed it; how the children stuffed and the parents looked on with a happiness that was very near to tears; how old John actually smiled and urged them to send back their plates again and again, and how Ann, the washerwoman, was the life and soul of it all, I can't half tell.

After dinner, when the poor women lodgers insisted on clearing up, and the poor men sat down by the fire to smoke, for old John actually passed around his beloved tobacco, Ann quietly slipped out for a few minutes, took four large bundles from a closet under the stairs, and disappeared upstairs. She was scarcely missed before she was back again.

Well, of course it was a great day in the house on the alley, and the guests sat long into the twilight before the warm fire, talking of their old homes in the fatherland, the hard winter, and prospects for work in the spring.

When at last they returned to the chilly discomfort of their own rooms, each family found a package containing a new warm dress and pair of shoes for every woman and child in the family.

"And I have enough left," said Ann the washerwoman, to herself, when she was reckoning up the expenses of the day, "to buy my coal and pay my rent till spring, so I can save my old bones a bit. And sure John can't grumble at their staying now, for it's all along of keeping them that I had such a blessed Christmas day at all."

XVII. A CHRISTMAS STAR*

* Published by permission of the American Book Co.

KATHERINE PYLE

"Come now, my dear little stars," said Mother Moon, "and I will tell you the Christmas story."

Every morning for a week before Christmas, Mother Moon used to call all the little stars around her and tell them a story.

It was always the same story, but the stars never wearied of it. It was the story of the Christmas star—the Star of Bethlehem.

When Mother Moon had finished the story the little stars always said: "And the star is shining still, isn't it, Mother Moon, even if we can't see it?"

And Mother Moon would answer: "Yes, my dears, only now it shines for men's hearts instead of their eyes."

Then the stars would bid the Mother Moon good-night and put on their little blue nightcaps and go to bed in the sky chamber; for the stars' bedtime is when people down on the earth are beginning to waken and see that it is morning.

But that particular morning when the little stars said good-night and went quietly away, one golden star still lingered beside Mother Moon.

"What is the matter, my little star?" asked the Mother Moon. "Why don't you go with your little sisters?"

"Oh, Mother Moon," said the golden star. "I am so sad! I wish I could shine for some one's heart like that star of wonder that you tell us about."

"Why, aren't you happy up here in the sky country?" asked Mother Moon.

"Yes, I have been very happy," said the star; "but to-night it seems just as if I must find some heart to shine for."

"Then if that is so," said Mother Moon, "the time has come, my little star, for you to go through the Wonder Entry."

"The Wonder Entry? What is that?" asked the star. But the Mother Moon made no answer.

Rising, she took the little star by the hand and led it to a door that it had never seen before.

The Mother Moon opened the door, and there was a long dark entry; at the far end was shining a little speck of light.

"What is this?" asked the star.

"It is the Wonder Entry; and it is through this that you must go to find the heart where you belong," said the Mother Moon.

Then the little star was afraid.

It longed to go through the entry as it had never longed for anything before; and yet it was afraid and clung to the Mother Moon.

But very gently, almost sadly, the Mother Moon drew her hand away. "Go, my child," she said.

Then, wondering and trembling, the little star stepped into the Wonder Entry, and the door of the sky house closed behind it.

The next thing the star knew it was hanging in a toy shop with a whole row of other stars blue and red and silver. It itself was gold. The shop smelled of evergreen, and was full of Christmas shoppers, men and women and children; but of them all, the star looked at no one but a little boy standing in front of the counter; for as soon as the star saw the child it knew that he was the one to whom it belonged.

The little boy was standing beside a sweet-faced woman in a long black veil and he was not looking at anything in particular.

The star shook and trembled on the string that held it, because it was afraid lest the child would not see it, or lest, if he did, he would not know it as his star.

The lady had a number of toys on the counter before her, and she was saying: "Now I think we have presents for every one: There's the doll for Lou, and the game for Ned, and the music box for May; and then the rocking horse and the sled."

Suddenly the little boy caught her by the arm. "Oh, mother," he said. He had seen the star.

"Well, what is it, darling?" asked the lady.

"Oh, mother, just see that star up there! I wish—oh, I do wish I had it."

"Oh, my dear, we have so many things for the Christmas-tree," said the mother.

"Yes, I know, but I do want the star," said the child.

"Very well," said the mother, smiling; "then we will take that, too."

So the star was taken down from the place where it hung and wrapped up in a piece of paper, and all the while it thrilled with joy, for now it belonged to the little boy.

It was not until the afternoon before Christmas, when the tree was being decorated, that the golden star was unwrapped and taken out from the paper.

"Here is something else," said the sweet-faced lady. "We must hang this on the tree. Paul took such a fancy to it that I had to get it for him. He will never be satisfied unless we hang it on too."

"Oh, yes," said some one else who was helping to decorate the tree; "we will hang it here on the very top."

So the little star hung on the highest branch of the Christmas-tree.

That evening all the candles were lighted on the Christmas-tree, and there were so many that they fairly dazzled the eyes; and the gold and silver balls, the fairies and the glass fruits, shone and twinkled in the light; and high above them all shone the golden star.

At seven o'clock a bell was rung, and then the folding doors of the room where the Christmas-tree stood were thrown open, and a crowd of children came trooping in.

They laughed and shouted and pointed, and all talked together, and after a while there was music, and presents were taken from the tree and given to the children.

How different it all was from the great wide, still sky house!

But the star had never been so happy in all its life; for the little boy was there.

He stood apart from the other children, looking up at the star, with his hands clasped behind him, and he did not seem to care for the toys and the games.

At last it was all over. The lights were put out, the children went home, and the house grew still.

Then the ornaments on the tree began to talk among themselves.

"So that is all over," said a silver ball. "It was very gay this evening—the gayest Christmas I remember."

"Yes," said a glass bunch of grapes; "the best of it is over. Of course people will come to look at us for several days yet, but it won't be like this evening."

"And then I suppose we'll be laid away for another year," said a paper fairy. "Really it seems hardly worth while. Such a few days out of the year and then to be shut up in the dark box again. I almost wish I were a paper doll."

The bunch of grapes was wrong in saying that people would come to look at the Christmas-tree the next few days, for it stood neglected in the library and nobody came near it. Everybody in the house went about very quietly, with anxious faces; for the little boy was ill.

At last, one evening, a woman came into the room with a servant. The woman wore the cap and apron of a nurse.

"That is it," she said, pointing to the golden star. The servant climbed up on some steps and took down the star and put it in the nurse's hand, and she carried it out into the hall and upstairs to a room where the little boy lay.

The sweet-faced lady was sitting by the bed, and as the nurse came in she held out her hand for the star.

"Is this what you wanted, my darling?" she asked, bending over the little boy.

The child nodded and held out his hands for the star; and as he clasped it a wonderful, shining smile came over his face.

The next morning the little boy's room was very still and dark.

The golden piece of paper that had been the star lay on a table beside the bed, its five points very sharp and bright.

But it was not the real star, any more than a person's body is the real person.

The real star was living and shining now in the little boy's heart, and it had gone out with him into a new and more beautiful sky country than it had ever known before—the sky country where the little child angels live, each one carrying in its heart its own particular star.

XVIII. THE QUEEREST CHRISTMAS*

* This story was first published in the Youth's Companion, vol. 83.

GRACE MARGARET GALLAHER

Betty stood at her door, gazing drearily down the long, empty corridor in which the breakfast gong echoed mournfully. All the usual brisk scenes of that hour, groups of girls in Peter Thomson suits or starched shirt-waists, or a pair of energetic ones, red-cheeked and shining-eyed from a run in the snow, had vanished as by the hand of some evil magician. Silent and lonely was the corridor.

"And it's the day before Christmas!" groaned Betty. Two chill little tears hung on her eyelashes.

The night before, in the excitement of getting the girls off with all their trunks and packages intact, she had not realized the homesickness of the deserted school. Now it seemed to pierce her very bones.

"Oh, dear, why did father have to lose his money? 'Twas easy enough last September to decide I wouldn't take the expensive journey home these holidays, and for all of us to promise we wouldn't give each other as much as a Christmas card. But now!" The two chill tears slipped over the edge of her eyelashes. "Well, I know how I'll spend this whole day; I'll come right up here after breakfast and cry and cry and cry!" Somewhat fortified by this cheering resolve, Betty went to breakfast.

Whatever the material joys of that meal might be, it certainly was not "a feast of reason and a flow of soul." Betty, whose sense of humour never perished, even in such a frost, looked round the table at the eight grim-faced girls doomed to a Christmas in school, and quoted mischievously to herself: "On with the dance, let joy be unconfined."

Breakfast bolted, she lagged back to her room, stopping to stare out of the corridor windows.

She saw nothing of the snowy landscape, however. Instead, a picture, the gayest medley of many colours and figures, danced before her eyes: Christmas-trees thumping in through the door, mysterious bundles scurried into dark corners, little brothers and sisters flying about with festoons of mistletoe, scarlet ribbon and holly, everywhere sound and laughter and excitement. The motto of Betty's family was: "Never do to-day what you can put off till to-morrow"; therefore the preparations of a fortnight were always crowded into a day.

The year before, Betty had rushed till her nerves were taut and her temper snapped, had shaken the twins, raged at the housemaid, and had gone to bed at midnight weeping with weariness. But in memory only the joy of the day remained.

"I think I could endure this jail of a school, and not getting one single present, but it breaks my heart not to give one least little thing to any one! Why, who ever heard of such a Christmas!"

"Won't you hunt for that blue—"

"Broken my thread again!"

"Give me those scissors!"

Betty jumped out of her day-dream. She had wandered into "Cork" and the three O'Neills surrounded her, staring.

"I beg your pardon—I heard you—and it was so like home the day before Christmas—"

"Did you hear the heathen rage?" cried Katherine.

"Dolls for Aunt Anne's mission," explained Constance.

"You're so forehanded that all your presents went a week ago, I suppose," Eleanor swept clear a chair. "The clan O'Neill is never forehanded."

"You'd think I was from the number of thumbs I've grown this morning. Oh, misery!" Eleanor jerked a snarl of thread out on the floor.

Betty had never cared for "Cork" but now the hot worried faces of its girls appealed to her. "Let me help. I'm a regular silkworm."

The O'Neills assented with eagerness, and Betty began to sew in a capable, swift way that made the others stare and sigh with relief.

The dolls were many, the O'Neills slow. Betty worked till her feet twitched on the floor; yet she enjoyed the morning, for it held an entirely new sensation, that of helping some one else get ready for Christmas.

"Done!"

"We never should have finished if you hadn't helped! Thank you, Betty Luther, very, VERY much! You're a duck! Let's run to luncheon together, quick."

Somehow the big corridors did not seem half so bleak echoing to those warm O'Neill voices.

"This morning's just spun by, but, oh, this long, dreary afternoon!" sighed Betty, as she wandered into the library. "Oh, me, there goes Alice Johns with her arms loaded with presents to mail, and I can't give a single soul anything!"

"Do you know where 'Quotations for Occasions' has gone?" Betty turned to face pretty Rosamond Howitt, the only senior left behind.

"Gone to be rebound. I heard Miss Dyce say so."

"Oh, dear, I needed it so."

"Could I help? I know a lot of rhymes and tags of proverbs and things like that."

"Oh, if you would help me, I'd be so grateful! Won't you come to my room? You see, I promised a friend in town, who is to have a Christmas dinner, and who's been very kind to me, that I'd paint the place cards and write some quotation appropriate to each guest. I'm shamefully late over it, my own gifts took such a time; but the painting, at least, is done."

Rosamond led the way to her room, and there displayed the cards which she had painted.

"You can't think of my helplessness! If it were a Greek verb now, or a lost and strayed angle—but poetry!"

Betty trotted back and forth between the room and the library, delved into books, and even evolved a verse which she audaciously tagged "old play," in imitation of Sir Walter Scott.

"I think they are really and truly very bright, and I know Mrs. Fernell will be delighted." Rosamond wrapped up the cards carefully. "I can't begin to tell you how you've helped me. It was sweet in you to give me your whole afternoon."

The dinner-bell rang at that moment, and the two went down together.

"Come for a little run; I haven't been out all day," whispered Rosamond, slipping her hand into Betty's as they left the table.

A great round moon swung cold and bright over the pines by the lodge.

"Down the road a bit—just a little way—to the church," suggested Betty.

They stepped out into the silent country road.

"Why, the little mission is as gay as—as Christmas! I wonder why?"

Betty glanced at the bright windows of the small plain church. "Oh, some Christmas-eve doings," she answered.

Some one stepped quickly out from the church door.

"Oh, Miss Vernon, I am relieved! I had begun to fear you could not come."

The girls saw it was the tall old rector, his white hair shining silver bright in the moonbeams.

"We're just two girls from the school, sir," said Rosamond.

"Dear, dear!" His voice was both impatient and distressed. "I hoped you were my organist. We are all ready for our Christmas-eve service, but we can do nothing without the music."

"I can play the organ a little," said Betty. "I'd be glad to help."

"You can? My dear child, how fortunate! But—do you know the service?"

"Yes, sir, it's my church."

No vested choir stood ready to march triumphantly chanting into the choir stalls. Only a few boys and girls waited in the dim old choir loft, where Rosamond seated herself quietly.

Betty's fingers trembled so at first that the music sounded dull and far away; but her courage crept back to her in the silence of the church, and the organ seemed to help her with a brave power of its own. In the dark church only the altar and a great gold star above it shone bright.

Through an open window somewhere behind her she could hear the winter wind rattling the ivy leaves and bending the trees. Yet, somehow, she did not feel lonesome and forsaken this Christmas eve, far away from home, but safe and comforted and sheltered. The voice of the old rector reached her faintly in pauses; habit led her along the service, and the star at the altar held her eyes.

Strange new ideas and emotions flowed in upon her brain. Tears stole softly into her eyes, yet she felt in her heart a sweet glow. Slowly the Christmas picture that had flamed and danced before her all day, painted in the glory of holly and mistletoe and tinsel, faded out, and another shaped itself, solemn and beautiful in the altar light.

"My dear child, I thank you very much!" The old rector held Betty's hand in both his. "I cannot have a Christmas morning service—our people have too much to do to come then—but I was especially anxious that our evening service should have some message, some inspiration for them, and your music has made it so. You have given me great aid. May your Christmas be a blessed one."

"I was glad to play, sir. Thank you!" answered Betty, simply.

"Let's run!" she cried to Rosamond, and they raced back to school.

She fell asleep that night without one smallest tear.

The next morning Betty dressed hastily, and catching up her mandolin, set out into the corridor.

Something swung against her hand as she opened the door. It was a great bunch of holly, glossy green leaves and glowing berries, and hidden in the leaves a card: "Betty, Merry Christmas," was all, but only one girl wrote that dainty hand.

"A winter rose," whispered Betty, happily, and stuck the bunch into the ribbon of her mandolin.

Down the corridor she ran until she faced a closed door. Then, twanging her mandolin, she burst out with all her power into a gay Christmas carol. High and sweet sang her voice in the silent corridor all through the gay carol. Then, sweeter still, it changed into a Christmas hymn. Then from behind the closed doors sounded voices:

"Merry Christmas, Betty Luther!"

Then Constance O'Neill's deep, smooth alto flowed into Betty's soprano; and at the last all nine girls joined in "Adeste Fideles." Christmas morning began with music and laughter.

"This is your place, Betty. You are lord of Christmas morning."

Betty stood, blushing, red as the holly in her hand, before the breakfast table. Miss Hyle, the teacher at the head of the table, had given up her place.

The breakfast was a merry one. After it somebody suggested that they all go skating on the pond.

Betty hesitated and glanced at Miss Hyle and Miss Thrasher, the two sad-looking teachers.

She approached them and said, "Won't you come skating, too?"

Miss Thrasher, hardly older than Betty herself, and pretty in a white frightened way, refused, but almost cheerfully. "I have a Christmas box to open and Christmas letters to write. Thank you very much."

Betty's heart sank as she saw Miss Hyle's face. "Goodness, she's coming!"

Miss Hyle was the most unpopular teacher in school. Neither ill-tempered nor harsh, she was so cold, remote and rigid in face, voice, and manner that the warmest blooded shivered away from her, the least sensitive shrank.

"I have no skates, but I should like to borrow a pair to learn, if I may. I have never tried," she said.

The tragedies of a beginner on skates are to the observers, especially if such be school-girls, subjects for unalloyed mirth. The nine girls choked and turned their backs and even giggled aloud as Miss Hyle went prone, now backward with a whack, now forward in a limp crumple.

But amusement became admiration. Miss Hyle stumbled, fell, laughed merrily, scrambled up, struck out, and skated. Presently she was swinging up the pond in stroke with Betty and Eleanor O'Neill.

"Miss Hyle, you're great!" cried Betty, at the end of the morning. "I've taught dozens and scores to skate, but never anybody like you. You've a genius for skating."

Miss Hyle's blue eyes shot a sudden flash at Betty that made her whole severe face light up. "I've never had a chance to learn—at home there never is any ice—but I have always been athletic."

"Where is your home, Miss Hyle?" asked Betty.

"Cawnpore, India."

"India?" gasped Eleanor. "How delightful! Oh, won't you tell us about it, Miss Hyle?"

So it was that Miss Hyle found herself talking about something besides triangles to girls who really wanted to hear, and so it was that the flash came often into her eyes.

"I have had a happy morning, thank you, Betty—and all." She said it very simply, yet a quick throb of pity and liking beat in Betty's heart.

"How stupid we are about judging people!" she thought. Yet Betty had always prided herself on her character-reading.

"Hurrah, the mail and express are in!" The girls ran excitedly to their rooms.

Betty alone went to hers without interest. "Why, Hilma, what's happened?"

The little round-faced Swedish maid mopped the big tears with her duster, and choked out:

"Nothings, ma'am!"

"Of course there is! You're crying like everything."

Hilma wept aloud. "Christmas Day it is, and mine family and mine friends have party, now, all day."

"Where?"

Hilma jerked her head toward the window.

"Oh, you mean in town? Why can't you go?"

"I work. And never before am I from home Christmas day."

Betty shivered. "Never before am I from home Christmas day," she whispered.

She went close to the girl, very tall and slim and bright beside the dumpy, flaxen Hilma.

"What work do you do?"

"The cook, he cooks the dinner and the supper; I put it on and wait it on the young ladies and wash the dishes. The others all are gone."

Betty laughed suddenly. "Hilma, go put on your best clothes, quick, and go down to your party. I'm going to do your work."

Hilma's eyes rounded with amazement. "The cook, he be mad."

"No, he won't. He won't care whether it's Hilma or Betty, if things get done all right. I know how to wait on table and wash dishes. There's no housekeeper here to object. Run along, Hilma; be back by nine o'clock— and—Merry Christmas!"

Hilma's face beamed through her tears. She was speechless with joy, but she seized Betty's slim brown hand and kissed it loudly.

"What larks!" "Is it a joke?" "Betty, you're the handsomest butler!"

Betty, in a white shirt-waist suit, a jolly red bow pinned on her white apron, and a little cap cocked on her dark hair, waved them to their seats at the holly-decked table.

"Merry Christmas! Merry Christmas!"

"Nobody is ill, Betty?" Rosamond asked, anxiously.

"If I had three guesses, I should use every one that our maid wanted to go into town for the day, and Betty took her place." It was Miss Hyle's calm voice.

Betty blushed. It was her turn now to flash back a glance; and those two sparks kindled the fire of friendship.

It was a jolly Christmas dinner, with the "butler" eating with the family.

"And now the dishes!" thought Betty. It must be admitted the "washing up" after a Christmas dinner of twelve is not a subject for much joy.

"I propose we all help Betty wash the dishes!" cried Rosamond Howitt.

Out in the kitchen every one laughed and talked and got in the way, and had a good time; and if the milk pitcher was knocked on the floor and the pudding bowl emptied in Betty's lap—why, it was all "Merry Christmas."

After that they all skated again. When they came in, little Miss Thrasher, looking almost gay in a rose-red gown, met them in the corridor.

"I thought it would be fun," she said, shyly, "to have supper in my room. I have a big box from home. I couldn't possible eat all the things myself, and if you'll bring chafing-dishes and spoons, and those things, I'll cook it, and we can sit round my open fire."

Miss Thrasher's room was homelike, with its fire of white-birch and its easy chairs, and Miss Thrasher herself proved to be a pleasant hostess.

After supper Miss Hyle told a tale of India, Miss Thrasher gave a Rocky Mountain adventure, and the girls contributed ghost and burglar stories till each guest was in a thrill of delightful horror.

"We've had really a fine day!"

"I expected to die of homesickness, but it's been jolly!"

"So did I, but I have actually been happy."

Thus the girls commented as they started for bed.

"I have enjoyed my day," said little Miss Thrasher, "very much."

"Yes, indeed, it's been a merry Christmas." Miss Hyle spoke almost eagerly.

Betty gave a little jump; she realized each one of them was holding her hand and pressing it a little. "Thank you, it's been a lovely evening. Goodnight."

Rosamond had invited Betty to share her roommate's bed, but both girls were too tired and sleepy for any confidence.

"It's been the queerest Christmas!" thought Betty, as she drifted toward sleep. "Why, I haven't given one single soul one single present!"

Yet she smiled, drowsily happy, and then the room seemed to fill with a bright, warm light, and round the bed there danced a great Christmas wreath, made up of the faces of the three O'Neills, and the thin old rector, with his white hair, and pretty Rosamond, and frightened Miss Thrasher and the homesick girls, and lonely Miss Hyle, and tear-dimmed Hilma.

And all the faces smiled and nodded, and called, "Merry Christmas, Betty, Merry Christmas!"

XIX. OLD FATHER CHRISTMAS

J.H. EWING

"The custom of Christmas-trees came from Germany. I can remember when they were first introduced into England, and what wonderful things we thought them. Now, every village school has its tree, and the scholars openly discuss whether the presents have been 'good,' or 'mean,' as compared with other trees in former years. The first one that I ever saw I believed to have come from Good Father Christmas himself; but little boys have grown too wise now to be taken in for their own amusement. They are not excited by secret and mysterious preparations in the back drawing-room; they hardly confess to the thrill—which I feel to this day—when the folding doors are thrown open, and amid the blaze of tapers, mamma, like a Fate, advances with her scissors to give every one what falls to his lot.

"Well, young people, when I was eight years old I had not seen a Christmas-tree, and the first picture of one I ever saw was the picture of that held by Old Father Christmas in my godmother's picture-book."

"'What are those things on the tree?' I asked.

"'Candles,' said my father.

"'No, father, not the candles; the other things?'

"'Those are toys, my son.'

"'Are they ever taken off?'

"'Yes, they are taken off, and given to the children who stand around the tree.'

"Patty and I grasped each other by the hand, and with one voice murmured; 'How kind of Old Father Christmas!'

"By and by I asked, 'How old is Father Christmas?'

"My father laughed, and said, 'One thousand eight hundred and thirty years, child,' which was then the year of our Lord, and thus one thousand eight hundred and thirty years since the first great Christmas Day.

"'He LOOKS very old,' whispered Patty.

"And I, who was, for my age, what Kitty called 'Bible-learned,' said thoughtfully, and with some puzzledness of mind, 'Then he's older than Methuselah.'

"But my father had left the room, and did not hear my difficulty.

"November and December went by, and still the picture-book kept all its charm for Patty and me; and we pondered on and loved Old Father Christmas as children can love and realize a fancy friend. To those who remember the fancies of their childhood I need say no more.

"Christmas week came, Christmas Eve came. My father and mother were mysteriously and unaccountably busy in the parlour (we had only one parlour), and Patty and I were not allowed to go in. We went into the kitchen, but even here was no place of rest for us. Kitty was 'all over the place,' as she phrased it, and cakes, mince pies, and puddings were with her. As she justly observed, 'There was no place there for children and books to sit with their toes in the fire, when a body wanted to be at the oven all along. The cat was enough for HER temper,' she added.

"As to puss, who obstinately refused to take a hint which drove her out into the Christmas frost, she returned again and again with soft steps, and a stupidity that was, I think, affected, to the warm hearth, only to fly at intervals, like a football, before Kitty's hasty slipper.

"We had more sense, or less courage. We bowed to Kitty's behests, and went to the back door.

"Patty and I were hardy children, and accustomed to 'run out' in all weathers, without much extra wrapping up. We put Kitty's shawl over our two heads, and went outside. I rather hoped to see something of Dick, for it was holiday time; but no Dick passed. He was busy helping his father to bore holes in the carved seats of the church, which were to hold sprigs of holly for the morrow—that was the idea of church decoration in my young days. You have improved on your elders there, young people, and I am candid enough to allow it. Still, the sprigs of red and green were better than nothing, and, like your lovely wreaths and pious devices, they made one feel as if the old black wood were bursting into life and leaf again for very Christmas joy; and, if only one knelt carefully, they did not scratch his nose.

"Well, Dick was busy, and not to be seen. We ran across the little yard and looked over the wall at the end to see if we could see anything or anybody. From this point there was a pleasant meadow field sloping prettily away to a little hill about three quarters of a mile distant; which, catching some fine breezes from the moors beyond, was held to be a place of cure for whooping-cough, or kincough, as it was vulgarly called. Up to the top of this Kitty had dragged me, and carried Patty, when we were recovering from the complaint, as I well remember. It was the only 'change of air' we could afford, and I dare say it did as well as if we had gone into badly drained lodgings at the seaside.

"This hill was now covered with snow and stood off against the gray sky. The white fields looked vast and dreary in the dusk. The only gay things to be seen were the berries on the holly hedge, in the little lane—

which, running by the end of our back-yard, led up to the Hall—and the fat robin, that was staring at me. I was looking at the robin, when Patty, who had been peering out of her corner of Kitty's shawl, gave a great jump that dragged the shawl from our heads, and cried:

"'Look!'

"I looked. An old man was coming along the lane. His hair and beard were as white as cotton-wool. He had a face like the sort of apple that keeps well in winter; his coat was old and brown. There was snow about him in patches, and he carried a small fir-tree.

"The same conviction seized upon us both. With one breath, we exclaimed, 'IT'S OLD FATHER CHRISTMAS!'

"I know now that it was only an old man of the place, with whom we did not happen to be acquainted and that he was taking a little fir-tree up to the Hall, to be made into a Christmas-tree. He was a very good-humoured old fellow, and rather deaf, for which he made up by smiling and nodding his head a good deal, and saying, 'aye, aye, to be sure!' at likely intervals.

"As he passed us and met our earnest gaze, he smiled and nodded so earnestly that I was bold enough to cry, 'Good-evening, Father Christmas!'

"'Same to you!' said he, in a high-pitched voice.

"'Then you ARE Father Christmas?' said Patty.

"'And a happy New Year,' was Father Christmas's reply, which rather put me out. But he smiled in such a satisfactory manner that Patty went on, 'You're very old, aren't you?'

"'So I be, miss, so I be,' said Father Christmas, nodding.

"'Father says you're eighteen hundred and thirty years old,' I muttered.

"'Aye, aye, to be sure,' said Father Christmas. 'I'm a long age.'

"A VERY long age, thought I, and I added, 'You're nearly twice as old as Methuselah, you know,' thinking that this might have struck him.

"'Aye, aye,' said Father Christmas; but he did not seem to think anything of it. After a pause he held up the tree, and cried, 'D'ye know what this is, little miss?'

"'A Christmas-tree,' said Patty.

"And the old man smiled and nodded.

"I leant over the wall, and shouted, 'But there are no candles.'

"'By and by,' said Father Christmas, nodding as before. 'When it's dark they'll all be lighted up. That'll be a fine sight!'

"'Toys, too, there'll be, won't there?' said Patty.

"Father Christmas nodded his head. 'And sweeties,' he added, expressively.

"I could feel Patty trembling, and my own heart beat fast. The thought which agitated us both was this: 'Was Father Christmas bringing the tree to us?' But very anxiety, and some modesty also, kept us from asking outright.

"Only when the old man shouldered his tree, and prepared to move on, I cried in despair, 'Oh, are you going?'

"'I'm coming back by and by,' said he.

"'How soon?' cried Patty.

"'About four o'clock,' said the old man smiling. 'I'm only going up yonder.'

"'Up yonder!' This puzzled us. Father Christmas had pointed, but so indefinitely that he might have been pointing to the sky, or the fields, or the little wood at the end of the Squire's grounds. I thought the latter, and suggested to Patty that perhaps he had some place underground like Aladdin's cave, where he got the candles, and all the pretty things for the tree. This idea pleased us both, and we amused ourselves by wondering what Old Father Christmas would choose for us from his stores in that wonderful hole where he dressed his Christmas-trees.

"'I wonder, Patty,' said I, 'why there's no picture of Father Christmas's dog in the book.' For at the old man's heels in the lane there crept a little brown and white spaniel looking very dirty in the snow.

"'Perhaps it's a new dog that he's got to take care of his cave,' said Patty.

"When we went indoors we examined the picture afresh by the dim light from the passage window, but there was no dog there.

"My father passed us at this moment, and patted my head. 'Father,' said I, 'I don't know, but I do think Old Father Christmas is going to bring us a Christmas-tree to-night.'

"'Who's been telling you that?' said my father.

"But he passed on before I could explain that we had seen Father Christmas himself, and had had his word for it that he would return at four o'clock, and that the candles on his tree would be lighted as soon as it was dark.

"We hovered on the outskirts of the rooms till four o'clock came. We sat on the stairs and watched the big clock, which I was just learning to read;

159

and Patty made herself giddy with constantly looking up and counting the four strokes, toward which the hour hand slowly moved. We put our noses into the kitchen now and then, to smell the cakes and get warm, and anon we hung about the parlour door, and were most unjustly accused of trying to peep. What did we care what our mother was doing in the parlour?—we, who had seen Old Father Christmas himself, and were expecting him back again every moment!

"At last the church clock struck. The sounds boomed heavily through the frost, and Patty thought there were four of them. Then, after due choking and whirring, our own clock struck, and we counted the strokes quite clearly—one! two! three! four! Then we got Kitty's shawl once more, and stole out into the backyard. We ran to our old place, and peeped, but could see nothing.

"'We'd better get up on to the wall,' I said; and with some difficulty and distress from rubbing her bare knees against the cold stone, and getting the snow up her sleeves, Patty got on to the coping of the little wall. I was just struggling after her, when something warm and something cold coming suddenly against the bare calves of my legs made me shriek with fright. I came down 'with a run' and bruised my knees, my elbows, and my chin; and the snow that hadn't gone up Patty's sleeves went down my neck. Then I found that the cold thing was a dog's nose and the warm thing was his tongue; and Patty cried from her post of observation, 'It's Father Christmas's dog and he's licking your legs.'

"It really was the dirty little brown and white spaniel, and he persisted in licking me, and jumping on me, and making curious little noises, that must have meant something if one had known his language. I was rather harassed at the moment. My legs were sore, I was a little afraid of the dog, and Patty was very much afraid of sitting on the wall without me.

"'You won't fall,' I said to her. 'Get down, will you?' I said to the dog.

"'Humpty Dumpty fell off a wall,' said Patty.

"'Bow! wow!' said the dog.

"I pulled Patty down, and the dog tried to pull me down; but when my little sister was on her feet, to my relief, he transferred his attentions to her. When he had jumped at her, and licked her several times, he turned around and ran away.

"'He's gone,' said I; 'I'm so glad.'

"But even as I spoke he was back again, crouching at Patty's feet, and glaring at her with eyes the colour of his ears.

"Now, Patty was very fond of animals, and when the dog looked at her she looked at the dog, and then she said to me, 'He wants us to go with him.'

"On which (as if he understood our language, though we were ignorant of his) the spaniel sprang away, and went off as hard as he could; and Patty and I went after him, a dim hope crossing my mind—'Perhaps Father Christmas has sent him for us.'

"The idea was rather favoured by the fact he led us up the lane. Only a little way; then he stopped by something lying in the ditch—and once more we cried in the same breath, 'It's Old Father Christmas!'

"Returning from the Hall, the old man had slipped upon a bit of ice, and lay stunned in the snow.

"Patty began to cry. 'I think he's dead!' she sobbed.

"'He is so very old, I don't wonder,' I murmured; 'but perhaps he's not. I'll fetch father.'

"My father and Kitty were soon on the spot. Kitty was as strong as a man; and they carried Father Christmas between them into the kitchen. There he quickly revived.

"I must do Kitty the justice to say that she did not utter a word of complaint at the disturbance of her labours; and that she drew the old man's chair close up to the oven with her own hand. She was so much affected by the behaviour of his dog that she admitted him even to the hearth; on which puss, being acute enough to see how matters stood, lay down with her back so close to the spaniel's that Kitty could not expel one without kicking both.

"For our parts, we felt sadly anxious about the tree; otherwise we could have wished for no better treat than to sit at Kitty's round table taking tea with Father Christmas. Our usual fare of thick bread and treacle was to-night exchanged for a delicious variety of cakes, which were none the worse to us for being 'tasters and wasters'—that is, little bits of dough, or shortbread, put in to try the state of the oven, and certain cakes that had got broken or burnt in the baking.

"Well, there we sat, helping Old Father Christmas to tea and cake, and wondering in our hearts what could have become of the tree.

"Patty and I felt a delicacy in asking Old Father Christmas about the tree. It was not until we had had tea three times round, with tasters and wasters to match, that Patty said very gently: 'It's quite dark now.' And then she heaved a deep sigh.

"Burning anxiety overcame me. I leaned toward Father Christmas, and shouted—I had found out that it was needful to shout—"'I suppose the candles are on the tree now?'

"'Just about putting of 'em on,' said Father Christmas.

"'And the presents, too?' said Patty.

"'Aye, aye, TO be sure,' said Father Christmas, and he smiled delightfully.

"I was thinking what further questions I might venture upon, when he pushed his cup toward Patty saying, 'Since you are so pressing, miss, I'll take another dish.'

"And Kitty, swooping on us from the oven, cried, 'Make yourself at home, sir; there's more where these came from. Make a long arm, Miss Patty, and hand them cakes.'

"So we had to devote ourselves to the duties of the table; and Patty, holding the lid with one hand and pouring with the other, supplied Father Christmas's wants with a heavy heart.

"At last he was satisfied. I said grace, during which he stood, and, indeed, he stood for some time afterward with his eyes shut—I fancy under the impression that I was still speaking. He had just said a fervent 'amen,' and reseated himself, when my father put his head into the kitchen, and made this remarkable statement:

"'Old Father Christmas has sent a tree to the young people.'

"Patty and I uttered a cry of delight, and we forthwith danced round the old man, saying, 'How nice; Oh, how kind of you!' which I think must have bewildered him, but he only smiled and nodded.

"'Come along,' said my father. 'Come, children. Come, Reuben. Come, Kitty.'

"And he went into the parlour, and we all followed him.

"My godmother's picture of a Christmas-tree was very pretty; and the flames of the candles were so naturally done in red and yellow that I always wondered that they did not shine at night. But the picture was nothing to the reality. We had been sitting almost in the dark, for, as Kitty said, 'Firelight was quite enough to burn at meal-times.' And when the parlour door was thrown open, and the tree, with lighted tapers on all the branches, burst upon our view, the blaze was dazzling, and threw such a glory round the little gifts, and the bags of coloured muslin, with acid drops and pink rose drops and comfits inside, as I shall never forget. We all got something; and Patty and I, at any rate, believed that the things came from the stores of Old Father Christmas. We were not undeceived even by his gratefully accepting a bundle of old clothes which had been hastily put together to form his present.

"We were all very happy; even Kitty, I think, though she kept her sleeves rolled up, and seemed rather to grudge enjoying herself (a weak point in some energetic characters). She went back to her oven before the lights were out and the angel on the top of the tree taken down. She locked up her present (a little work-box) at once. She often showed it off afterward, but it was kept in the same bit of tissue paper till she died. Our presents certainly did not last so long!

"The old man died about a week afterward, so we never made his acquaintance as a common personage. When he was buried, his little dog came to us. I suppose he remembered the hospitality he had received. Patty adopted him, and he was very faithful. Puss always looked on him with favour. I hoped during our rambles together in the following summer that he would lead us at last to the cave where Christmas-trees are dressed. But he never did.

"Our parents often spoke of his late master as 'old Reuben,' but children are not easily disabused of a favourite fancy, and in Patty's thoughts and in mine the old man was long gratefully remembered as Old Father Christmas."

XX. A CHRISTMAS CAROL

CHARLES DICKENS

Master Peter, and the two ubiquitous young Cratchits went to fetch the goose, with which they soon returned in high procession.

Such a bustle ensued that you might have thought a goose the rarest of all birds; a feathered phenomenon, to which a black swan was a matter of course—and in truth it was something very like it in that house. Mrs. Cratchit made the gravy (ready beforehand in a little saucepan) hissing hot; Master Peter mashed the potatoes with incredible vigour; Miss Belinda sweetened up the apple-sauce; Martha dusted the hot plates; Bob took Tiny Tim beside him in a tiny corner at the table; the two young Cratchits set chairs for everybody, not forgetting themselves, and mounting guard upon their posts, crammed spoons into their mouths, lest they should shriek for goose before their turn came to be helped. At last the dishes were set on, and grace was said. It was succeeded by a breathless pause, as Mrs. Cratchit, looking slowly all along the carving-knife, prepared to plunge it in the breast; but when she did, and when the long expected gush of stuffing issued forth, one murmur of delight arose all round the board, and even Tiny Tim, excited by the two young Cratchits, beat on the table with the handle of his knife, and feebly cried Hurrah!

There never was such a goose. Bob said he didn't believe there ever was such a goose cooked. Its tenderness and flavour, size and cheapness, were the themes of universal admiration. Eked out by the apple-sauce and mashed potatoes, it was a sufficient dinner for the whole family; indeed, as Mrs. Cratchit said with great delight (surveying one small atom of a bone upon the dish), they hadn't ate it all at last! Yet every one had had enough, and the youngest Cratchits in particular, were steeped in sage and onion to the eyebrows! But now, the plates being changed by Miss

Belinda, Mrs. Cratchit left the room alone—too nervous to bear witnesses—to take the pudding up and bring it in.

Suppose it should not be done enough! Suppose it should break in turning out. Suppose somebody should have got over the wall of the back-yard and stolen it, while they were merry with the goose—a supposition at which the two young Cratchits became livid! All sorts of horrors were supposed.

Hallo! A great deal of steam! The pudding was out of the copper. A smell like a washing-day! That was the cloth. A smell like an eating-house and a pastrycook's next door to each other, with a laundress's next door to that! That was the pudding! In half a minute Mrs. Cratchit entered—flushed, but smiling proudly—with the pudding, like a speckled cannon-ball, so hard and firm, blazing in half of half-a-quartern of ignited brandy, and bedight with Christmas holly stuck into the top.

Oh, a wonderful pudding! Bob Cratchit said, and calmly too, that he regarded it as the greatest success achieved by Mrs. Cratchit since their marriage. Mrs. Cratchit said that now the weight was off her mind, she would confess she had had her doubts about the quantity of flour. Everybody had something to say about it, but nobody said or thought it was at all a small pudding for a large family. It would have been, flat heresy to do so. Any Cratchit would have blushed to hint at such a thing.

At last the dinner was all done, the cloth was cleared, the hearth swept, and the fire made up. The compound in the jug being tasted, and considered perfect, apples and oranges were put upon the table, and a shovel-full of chestnuts on the fire. Then all the Cratchit family drew round the hearth, in what Bob Cratchit called a circle, meaning half a one; and at Bob Cratchit's elbow stood the family display of glasses. Two tumblers, and a custard-cup without a handle.

These held the hot stuff from the jug, however, as well as golden goblets would have done; and Bob served it out with beaming looks, while the chestnuts on the fire sputtered and cracked noisily. Then Bob proposed:

"A Merry Christmas to us all, my dears. God bless us!"

Which all the family re-echoed.

"God bless us every one!" said Tiny Tim, the last of all.

XXI. HOW CHRISTMAS CAME TO THE SANTA MARIA FLATS*

* From "Ickery Ann and Other Girls and Boys," by Elia W. Peattie. Copyright, 1898, by Herbert S. Stone & Co., Duffield & Co., successors.

ELIA W. PEATTIE

There were twenty-six flat children, and none of them had ever been flat children until that year. Previously they had all been home children. and as such had, of course, had beautiful Christmases, in which their relations with Santa Claus had been of the most intimate and personal nature.

Now, owing to their residence in the Santa Maria flats, and the Lease, all was changed. The Lease was a strange forbiddance, a ukase issued by a tyrant, which took from children their natural liberties and rights.

Though, to be sure—as every one of the flat children knew—they were in the greatest kind of luck to be allowed to live at all, and especially were they fortunate past the lot of children to be permitted to live in a flat. There were many flats in the great city, so polished and carved and burnished and be-lackeyed that children were not allowed to enter within the portals, save on visits of ceremony in charge of parents or governesses. And in one flat, where Cecil de Koven le Baron was born—just by accident and without intending any harm—he was evicted, along with his parents, by the time he reached the age where he seemed likely to be graduated from the go-cart. And yet that flat had not nearly so imposing a name as the Santa Maria.

The twenty-six children of the Santa Maria flats belonged to twenty families. All of these twenty families were peculiar, as you might learn any day by interviewing the families concerning one another. But they bore with each other's peculiarities quite cheerfully and spoke in the hall when they met. Sometimes this tolerance would even extend to conversation about the janitor, a thin creature who did the work of five men. The ladies complained that he never smiled.

"I wouldn't so much mind the hot water pipes leaking now and then," the ladies would remark in the vestibule, rustling their skirts to show that they wore silk petticoats, "if only the janitor would smile. But he looks like a cemetery."

"I know it," would be the response. "I told Mr. Wilberforce last night that if he would only get a cheerful janitor I wouldn't mind our having rubber instead of Axminster on the stairs."

"You know we were promised Axminster when we moved in," would be the plaintive response. The ladies would stand together for a moment wrapped in gloomy reflection, and then part.

The kitchen and nurse maids felt on the subject, too.

"If Carl Carlsen would only smile," they used to exclaim in sibilant whispers, as they passed on the way to the laundry. "If he'd come in an' joke while we wus washin'!"

Only Kara Johnson never said anything on the subject because she knew why Carlsen didn't smile, and was sorry for it, and would have made it all right—if it hadn't been for Lars Larsen.

Dear, dear, but this is a digression from the subject of the Lease. That terrible document was held over the heads of the children as the Herodian pronunciamento concerning small boys was over the heads of the Israelites.

It was in the Lease not to run—not to jump—not to yell. It was in the Lease not to sing in the halls, not to call from story to story, not to slide down the banisters. And there were blocks of banisters so smooth and wide and beautiful that the attraction between them and the seats of the little boy's trousers was like the attraction of a magnet for a nail. Yet not a leg, crooked or straight, fat or thin, was ever to be thrown over these polished surfaces!

It was in the Lease, too, that no peddler or agent, or suspicious stranger was to enter the Santa Maria, neither by the front door nor the back. The janitor stood in his uniform at the rear, and the lackey in his uniform at the front, to prevent any such intrusion upon the privacy of the aristocratic Santa Marias. The lackey, who politely directed people, and summoned elevators, and whistled up tubes and rang bells, thus conducting the complex social life of those favoured apartments, was not one to make a mistake, and admit any person not calculated to ornament the front parlours of the flatters.

It was this that worried the children.

For how could such a dear, disorderly, democratic rascal as the children's saint ever hope to gain a pass to that exclusive entrance and get up to the rooms of the flat children?

"You can see for yourself," said Ernest, who lived on the first floor, to Roderick who lived on the fourth, "that if Santa Claus can't get up the front stairs, and can't get up the back stairs, that all he can do is to come down the chimney. And he can't come down the chimney—at least, he can't get out of the fireplace."

"Why not?" asked Roderick, who was busy with an "all-day sucker" and not inclined to take a gloomy view of anything.

"Goosey!" cried Ernest, in great disdain. "I'll show you!" and he led Roderick, with his sucker, right into the best parlour, where the fireplace was, and showed him an awful thing.

Of course, to the ordinary observer, there was nothing awful about the fireplace. Everything in the way of bric-a-brac possessed by the Santa Maria flatters was artistic. It may have been in the Lease that only people with esthetic tastes were to be admitted to the apartments. However that may be, the fireplace, with its vases and pictures and trinkets, was something quite wonderful. Indian incense burned in a mysterious little dish, pictures of purple ladies were hung in odd corners, calendars in letters nobody could read, served to decorate, if not to educate, and glass vases of strange colours and extraordinary shapes stood about filled with roses. None of these things were awful. At least no one would have dared say they were. But what was awful was the formation of the grate. It was not a hospitable place with andirons, where noble logs of wood could be laid for the burning, nor did it have a generous iron basket where honest anthracite could glow away into the nights. Not a bit of it. It held a vertical plate of stuff that looked like dirty cotton wool, on which a tiny blue flame leaped when the gas was turned on and ignited.

"You can see for yourself!" said Ernest tragically.

Roderick could see for himself. There was an inch-wide opening down which the Friend of the Children could squeeze himself, and, as everybody knows, he needs a good deal of room now, for he has grown portly with age, and his pack every year becomes bigger, owing to the ever-increasing number of girls and boys he has to supply

"Gimini!" said Roderick, and dropped his all-day sucker on the old Bokara rug that Ernest's mamma had bought the week before at a fashionable furnishing shop, and which had given the sore throat to all the family, owing to some cunning little germs that had come over with the rug to see what American throats were like.

Oh, me, yes! but Roderick could see! Anybody could see! And a boy could see better than anybody.

"Let's go see the Telephone Boy," said Roderick. This seemed the wisest thing to do. When in doubt, all the children went to the Telephone Boy, who was the most fascinating person, with knowledge of the most wonderful kind and of a nature to throw that of Mrs. Scheherazade quite, quite in the shade—which, considering how long that loquacious lady had been a Shade, is perhaps not surprising.

The Telephone Boy knew the answers to all the conundrums in the world, and a way out of nearly all troubles such as are likely to overtake boys and girls. But now he had no suggestions to offer and could speak no comfortable words.

"He can't git inter de front, an' he can't git inter de back, an' he can't come down no chimney in dis here house, an' I tell yer dose," he said, and shut his mouth grimly, while cold apprehension crept around Ernest's heart and took the sweetness out of Roderick's sucker.

Nevertheless, hope springs eternal, and the boys each and individually asked their fathers—tremendously wise and good men—if they thought there was any hope that Santa Claus would get into the Santa Maria flats, and each of the fathers looked up from his paper and said he'd be blessed if he did!

And the words sunk deep and deep and drew the tears when the doors were closed and the soft black was all about and nobody could laugh because a boy was found crying! The girls cried too—for the awful news was whistled up tubes and whistled down tubes, till all the twenty-six flat children knew about it. The next day it was talked over in the brick court, where the children used to go to shout and race. But on this day there was neither shouting nor racing. There was, instead, a shaking of heads, a surreptitious dropping of tears, a guessing and protesting and lamenting. All the flat mothers congratulated themselves on the fact that their children were becoming so quiet and orderly, and wondered what could have come over them when they noted that they neglected to run after the patrol wagon as it whizzed round the block.

It was decided, after a solemn talk, that every child should go to its own fireplace and investigate. In the event of any fireplace being found with an opening big enough to admit Santa Claus, a note could be left directing him along the halls to the other apartments. A spirit of universal brotherhood had taken possession of the Santa Maria flatters. Misery bound them together. But the investigation proved to be disheartening. The cruel asbestos grates were everywhere. Hope lay strangled!

As time went on, melancholy settled upon the flat children. The parents noted it, and wondered if there could be sewer gas in the apartments. One over-anxious mother called in a physician, who gave the poor little child some medicine which made it quite ill. No one suspected the truth, though the children were often heard to say that it was evident that there was to be no Christmas for them! But then, what more natural for a child to say, thus hoping to win protestations—so the mothers reasoned, and let the remark pass.

The day before Christmas was gray and dismal. There was no wind—indeed, there was a sort of tightness in the air, as if the supply of freshness had given out. People had headaches—even the Telephone Boy was cross—and none of the spirit of the time appeared to enliven the flat children. There appeared to be no stir—no mystery. No whisperings went on in the corners—or at least, so it seemed to the sad babies of the Santa Maria.

"It's as plain as a monkey on a hand-organ," said the Telephone Boy to the attendants at his salon in the basement, "that there ain't to be no Christmas for we—no, not for we!"

Had not Dorothy produced, at this junction, from the folds of her fluffy silken skirts several substantial sticks of gum, there is no saying to what depths of discouragement the flat children would have fallen!

About six o'clock it seemed as if the children would smother for lack of air! It was very peculiar. Even the janitor noticed it. He spoke about it to Kara at the head of the back stairs, and she held her hand so as to let him see the new silver ring on her fourth finger, and he let go of the rope on the elevator on which he was standing and dropped to the bottom of the shaft, so that Kara sent up a wild hallo of alarm. But the janitor emerged as melancholy and unruffled as ever, only looking at his watch to see if it had been stopped by the concussion.

The Telephone Boy, who usually got a bit of something hot sent down to him from one of the tables, owing to the fact that he never ate any meal save breakfast at home, was quite forgotten on this day, and dined off two russet apples, and drew up his belt to stop the ache—for the Telephone Boy was growing very fast indeed, in spite of his poverty, and couldn't seem to stop growing somehow, although he said to himself every day that it was perfectly brutal of him to keep on that way when his mother had so many mouths to feed.

Well, well, the tightness of the air got worse. Every one was cross at dinner and complained of feeling tired afterward, and of wanting to go to bed. For all of that it was not to get to sleep, and the children tossed and tumbled for a long time before they put their little hands in the big, soft shadowy clasp of the Sandman, and trooped away after him to the happy town of sleep.

It seemed to the flat children that they had been asleep but a few moments when there came a terrible burst of wind that shook even that great house to its foundations. Actually, as they sat up in bed and called to their parents or their nurses, their voices seemed smothered with roar. Could it

175

be that the wind was a great wild beast with a hundred tongues which licked at the roof of the building? And how many voices must it have to bellow as it did?

Sounds of falling glass, of breaking shutters, of crashing chimneys greeted their ears—not that they knew what all these sounds meant. They only knew that it seemed as if the end of the world had come. Ernest, miserable as he was, wondered if the Telephone Boy had gotten safely home, or if he were alone in the draughty room in the basement; and Roderick hugged his big brother, who slept with him and said, "Now I lay me," three times running, as fast as ever his tongue would say it.

After a terrible time the wind settled down into a steady howl like a hungry wolf, and the children went to sleep, worn out with fright and conscious that the bedclothes could not keep out the cold.

Dawn came. The children awoke, shivering. They sat up in bed and looked about them—yes, they did, the whole twenty-six of them in their different apartments and their different homes. And what do you suppose they saw—what do you suppose the twenty-six flat children saw as they looked about them?

Why, stockings, stuffed full, and trees hung full, and boxes packed full! Yes, they did! It was Christmas morning, and the bells were ringing, and all the little flat children were laughing, for Santa Claus had come! He had really come! In the wind and wild weather, while the tongues of the wind licked hungrily at the roof, while the wind howled like a hungry wolf, he had crept in somehow and laughing, no doubt, and chuckling, without question, he had filled the stockings and the trees and the boxes! Dear me, dear me, but it was a happy time! It makes me out of breath to think what a happy time it was, and how surprised the flat children were, and how they wondered how it could ever have happened.

But they found out, of course! It happened in the simplest way! Every skylight in the place was blown off and away, and that was how the wind howled so, and how the bedclothes would not keep the children warm, and how Santa Claus got in. The wind corkscrewed down into these holes, and the reckless children with their drums and dolls, their guns and toy dishes, danced around in the maelstrom and sang:

"Here's where Santa Claus came!

This is how he got in—

We should count it a sin

Yes, count it a shame,

If it hurt when he fell on the floor."

Roderick's sister, who was clever for a child of her age, and who had read Monte Cristo ten times, though she was only eleven, wrote this poem, which every one thought very fine.

And of course all the parents thought and said that Santa Claus must have jumped down the skylights. By noon there were other skylights put in, and not a sign left of the way he made his entrance—not that the way mattered a bit, no, not a bit.

Perhaps you think the Telephone Boy didn't get anything! Maybe you imagine that Santa Claus didn't get down that far. But you are mistaken. The shaft below one of the skylights went away to the bottom of the building, and it stands to reason that the old fellow must have fallen way through. At any rate there was a copy of "Tom Sawyer," and a whole plum pudding, and a number of other things, more useful but not so interesting, found down in the chilly basement room. There were, indeed.

In closing it is only proper to mention that Kara Johnson crocheted a white silk four-in-hand necktie for Carl Carlsen, the janitor—and the janitor smiled!

XXII. THE LEGEND OF BABOUSCKA*

*From "The Children's Hour," published by the Milton Bradley Co.

ADAPTED FROM THE RUSSIAN

It was the night the dear Christ-Child came to Bethlehem. In a country far away from Him, an old, old woman named Babouscka sat in her snug little house by her warm fire. The wind was drifting the snow outside and howling down the chimney, but it only made Babouscka's fire burn more brightly.

"How glad I am that I may stay indoors," said Babouscka, holding her hands out to the bright blaze.

But suddenly she heard a loud rap at her door. She opened it and her candle shone on three old men standing outside in the snow. Their beards were as white as the snow, and so long that they reached the ground. Their eyes shone kindly in the light of Babouscka's candle, and their arms were full of precious things—boxes of jewels, and sweet-smelling oils, and ointments.

"We have travelled far, Babouscka," they said, "and we stop to tell you of the Baby Prince born this night in Bethlehem. He comes to rule the world and teach all men to be loving and true. We carry Him gifts. Come with us, Babouscka."

But Babouscka looked at the drifting snow, and then inside at her cozy room and the crackling fire. "It is too late for me to go with you, good sirs," she said, "the weather is too cold." She went inside again and shut the door, and the old men journeyed on to Bethlehem without her. But as Babouscka sat by her fire, rocking, she began to think about the Little Christ-Child, for she loved all babies.

"To-morrow I will go to find Him," she said; "to-morrow, when it is light, and I will carry Him some toys."

So when it was morning Babouscka put on her long cloak and took her staff, and filled her basket with the pretty things a baby would like—gold balls, and wooden toys, and strings of silver cobwebs—and she set out to find the Christ-Child.

But, oh, Babouscka had forgotten to ask the three old men the road to Bethlehem, and they travelled so far through the night that she could not overtake them. Up and down the road she hurried, through woods and fields and towns, saying to whomsoever she met: "I go to find the Christ-Child. Where does He lie? I bring some pretty toys for His sake."

But no one could tell her the way to go, and they all said: "Farther on, Babouscka, farther on." So she travelled on and on and on for years and years—but she never found the little Christ-Child.

They say that old Babouscka is travelling still, looking for Him. When it comes Christmas Eve, and the children are lying fast asleep, Babouscka comes softly through the snowy fields and towns, wrapped in her long cloak and carrying her basket on her arm. With her staff she raps gently at the doors and goes inside and holds her candle close to the little children's faces.

"Is He here?" she asks. "Is the little Christ-Child here?" And then she turns sorrowfully away again, crying: "Farther on, farther on!" But before she leaves she takes a toy from her basket and lays it beside the pillow for a Christmas gift. "For His sake," she says softly, and then hurries on through the years and forever in search of the little Christ-Child.

XXIII. CHRISTMAS IN THE BARN*

* From "In the Child's World," by Emilie Poulsson, Milton Bradley Co., Publishers. Used by permission.

F. ARNSTEIN

Only two more days and Christmas would be here! It had been snowing hard, and Johnny was standing at the window, looking at the soft, white snow which covered the ground half a foot deep. Presently he heard the noise of wheels coming up the road, and a wagon turned in at the gate and came past the window. Johnny was very curious to know what the wagon could be bringing. He pressed his little nose close to the cold window pane, and to his great surprise, saw two large Christmas-trees. Johnny wondered why there were TWO trees, and turned quickly to run and tell mamma all about it; but then remembered that mamma was not at home. She had gone to the city to buy some Christmas presents and would not return until quite late. Johnny began to feel that his toes and fingers had grown quite cold from standing at the window so long; so he drew his own little chair up to the cheerful grate fire and sat there quietly thinking. Pussy, who had been curled up like a little bundle of wool, in the very warmest corner, jumped up, and, going to Johnny, rubbed her head against his knee to attract his attention. He patted her gently and began to talk to her about what was in his thoughts.

He had been puzzling over the TWO trees which had come, and at last had made up his mind about them. "I know now, Pussy," said he, "why there are two trees. This morning when I kissed Papa good-bye at the gate he said he was going to buy one for me, and mamma, who was busy in the house, did not hear him say so; and I am sure she must have bought the other. But what shall we do with two Christmas-trees?"

Pussy jumped into his lap and purred and purred. A plan suddenly flashed into Johnny's mind. "Would you like to have one, Pussy?" Pussy purred more loudly, and it seemed almost as though she had said yes.

"Oh! I will, I will! if mamma will let me. I'll have a Christmas-tree out in the barn for you, Pussy, and for all the pets; and then you'll all be as happy as I shall be with my tree in the parlour."

By this time it had grown quite late. There was a ring at the door-bell; and quick as a flash Johnny ran, with happy, smiling face, to meet papa and mamma and gave them each a loving kiss. During the evening he told them all that he had done that day and also about the two big trees which the man had brought. It was just as Johnny had thought. Papa and mamma had each bought one, and as it was so near Christmas they thought they would not send either of them back. Johnny was very glad of this, and told them of the happy plan he had made and asked if he might have the extra tree. Papa and mamma smiled a little as Johnny explained his plan but they said he might have the tree, and Johnny went to bed feeling very happy.

That night his papa fastened the tree into a block of wood so that it would stand firmly and then set it in the middle of the barn floor. The next day when Johnny had finished his lessons he went to the kitchen, and asked Annie, the cook, if she would save the bones and potato parings and all other leavings from the day's meals and give them to him the following morning. He also begged her to give him several cupfuls of salt and cornmeal, which she did, putting them in paper bags for him. Then she gave him the dishes he asked for—a few chipped ones not good enough to be used at table—and an old wooden bowl. Annie wanted to know what Johnny intended to do with all these things, but he only said: "Wait until to-morrow, then you shall see." He gathered up all the things which the cook had given him and carried them to the barn, placing them on a shelf in one corner, where he was sure no one would touch them and where they would be all ready for him to use the next morning.

Christmas morning came, and, as soon as he could, Johnny hurried out to the barn, where stood the Christmas-tree which he was going to trim for all his pets. The first thing he did was to get a paper bag of oats; this he tied to one of the branches of the tree, for Brownie the mare. Then he made up several bundles of hay and tied these on the other side of the tree, not quite so high up, where White Face, the cow, could reach them; and on the lowest branches some more hay for Spotty, the calf.

Next Johnny hurried to the kitchen to get the things Annie had promised to save for him. She had plenty to give. With his arms and hands full he went back to the barn. He found three "lovely" bones with plenty of meat on them; these he tied together to another branch of the tree, for Rover, his big black dog. Under the tree he placed the big wooden bowl, and filled it well with potato parings, rice, and meat, left from yesterday's dinner; this was the "full and tempting trough" for Piggywig. Near this he placed a bowl of milk for Pussy, on one plate the salt for the pet lamb, and on another the cornmeal for the dear little chickens. On the top of the tree he tied a basket of nuts; these were for his pet squirrel; and I had almost forgotten to tell you of the bunch of carrots tied very low down where soft white Bunny could reach them.

When all was done, Johnny stood off a little way to look at this wonderful Christmas-tree. Clapping his hands with delight, he ran to call papa and mamma and Annie, and they laughed aloud when they saw what he had done. It was the funniest Christmas-tree they had ever seen. They were sure the pets would like the presents Johnny had chosen.

Then there was a busy time in the barn. Papa and mamma and Annie helped about bringing in the animals, and before long, Brownie, White Face, Spotty, Rover, Piggywig, Pussy, Lambkin, the chickens, the squirrel and Bunny, the rabbit, had been led each to his own Christmas breakfast on and under the tree. What a funny sight it was to see them all standing around looking happy and contented, eating and drinking with such an appetite!

While watching them Johnny had another thought, and he ran quickly to the house, and brought out the new trumpet which papa had given him for Christmas. By this time the animals had all finished their breakfast and Johnny gave a little toot on his trumpet as a signal that the tree festival was over. Brownie went, neighing and prancing, to her stall, White Face walked demurely off with a bellow, which Spotty, the calf, running at her heels, tried to imitate; the little lamb skipped bleating away; Piggywig walked off with a grunt; Pussy jumped on the fence with a mew; the squirrel still sat up in the tree cracking her nuts; Bunny hopped to her snug little quarters; while Rover, barking loudly, chased the chickens back to their coop. Such a hubbub of noises! Mamma said it sounded as if they were trying to say "Merry Christmas to you, Johnny! Merry Christmas to all."

XXIV. THE PHILANTHROPIST'S CHRISTMAS*

This story was first published in the Youth's Companion, vol. 82.

JAMES WEBER LINN

"Did you see this committee yesterday, Mr. Mathews?" asked the philanthropist.

His secretary looked up.

"Yes, sir."

"You recommend them then?"

"Yes, sir."

"For fifty thousand?"

"For fifty thousand—yes, sir."

"Their corresponding subscriptions are guaranteed?"

"I went over the list carefully, Mr. Carter. The money is promised, and by responsible people."

"Very well," said the philanthropist. "You may notify them, Mr. Mathews, that my fifty thousand will be available as the bills come in."

"Yes, sir."

Old Mr. Carter laid down the letter he had been reading, and took up another. As he perused it his white eyebrows rose in irritation.

"Mr. Mathews!" he snapped.

"Yes, sir?"

"You are careless, sir!"

"I beg your pardon, Mr. Carter?" questioned the secretary, his face flushing.

The old gentleman tapped impatiently the letter he held in his hand. "Do you pay no attention, Mr. Mathews, to my rule that NO personal letters containing appeals for aid are to reach me? How do you account for this, may I ask?"

"I beg your pardon," said the secretary again. "You will see, Mr. Carter, that that letter is dated three weeks ago. I have had the woman's case carefully investigated. She is undoubtedly of good reputation, and undoubtedly in need; and as she speaks of her father as having associated with you, I thought perhaps you would care to see her letter."

"A thousand worthless fellows associated with me," said the old man, harshly. "In a great factory, Mr. Mathews, a boy works alongside of the men he is put with; he does not pick and choose. I dare say this woman is telling the truth. What of it? You know that I regard my money as a public trust. Were my energy, my concentration, to be wasted by innumerable individual assaults, what would become of them? My fortune would slip through my fingers as unprofitably as sand. You understand, Mr. Mathews? Let me see no more individual letters. You know that Mr. Whittemore has full authority to deal with them. May I trouble you to ring? I am going out."

A man appeared very promptly in answer to the bell.

"Sniffen, my overcoat," said the philanthropist.

"It is 'ere, sir," answered Sniffen, helping the thin old man into the great fur folds.

"There is no word of the dog, I suppose, Sniffen?"

"None, sir. The police was here again yesterday sir, but they said as 'ow—"

"The police!" The words were fierce with scorn. "Eight thousand incompetents!" He turned abruptly and went toward the door, where he halted a moment.

"Mr. Mathews, since that woman's letter did reach me, I suppose I must pay for my carelessness—or yours. Send her—what does she say—four children?—send her a hundred dollars. But, for my sake, send it anonymously. Write her that I pay no attention to such claims." He went out, and Sniffen closed the door behind him.

"Takes losin' the little dog 'ard, don't he?" remarked Sniffen, sadly, to the secretary. "I'm afraid there ain't a chance of findin' 'im now. 'E ain't been stole, nor 'e ain't been found, or they'd 'ave brung him back for the reward. 'E's been knocked on the 'ead, like as not. 'E wasn't much of a dog to look at, you see—just a pup, I'd call 'im. An' after 'e learned that trick of slippin' 'is collar off—well, I fancy Mr. Carter's seen the last of 'im. I do, indeed."

Mr. Carter meanwhile was making his way slowly down the snowy avenue, upon his accustomed walk. The walk, however, was dull to-day, for Skiddles, his little terrier, was not with him to add interest and excitement. Mr. Carter had found Skiddles in the country a year and a half before. Skiddles, then a puppy, was at the time in a most undignified and undesirable position, stuck in a drain tile, and unable either to advance or to retreat. Mr. Carter had shoved him forward, after a heroic struggle, whereupon Skiddles had licked his hand. Something in the little dog's eye, or his action, had induced the rich philanthropist to bargain for him and buy him at a cost of half a dollar. Thereafter

Skiddles became his daily companion, his chief distraction, and finally the apple of his eye.

Skiddles was of no known parentage, hardly of any known breed, but he suited Mr. Carter. What, the millionaire reflected with a proud cynicism, were his own antecedents, if it came to that? But now Skiddles had disappeared.

As Sniffen said, he had learned the trick of slipping free from his collar. One morning the great front doors had been left open for two minutes while the hallway was aired. Skiddles must have slipped down the marble steps unseen, and dodged round the corner. At all events, he had vanished, and although the whole police force of the city had been roused to secure his return, it was aroused in vain. And for three weeks, therefore, a small, straight, white bearded man in a fur overcoat had walked in mournful irritation alone.

He stood upon a corner uncertainly. One way led to the park, and this he usually took; but to-day he did not want to go to the park—it was too reminiscent of Skiddles. He looked the other way. Down there, if one went far enough, lay "slums," and Mr. Carter hated the sight of slums; they always made him miserable and discontented. With all his money and his philanthropy, was there still necessity for such misery in the world? Worse still came the intrusive question at times: Had all his money anything to do with the creation of this misery? He owned no tenements; he paid good wages in every factory; he had given sums such as few men have given in the history of philanthropy. Still—there were the slums. However, the worst slums lay some distance off, and he finally turned his back on the park and walked on.

It was the day before Christmas. You saw it in people's faces; you saw it in the holly wreaths that hung in windows; you saw it, even as you passed the splendid, forbidding houses on the avenue, in the green that here and there banked massive doors; but most of all, you saw it in the shops. Up here the shops were smallish, and chiefly of the provision variety, so there was no bewildering display of gifts; but there were Christmas-trees everywhere, of all sizes. It was astonishing how many people in that neighbourhood seemed to favour the old-fashioned idea of a tree.

Mr. Carter looked at them with his irritation softening. If they made him feel a trifle more lonely, they allowed him to feel also a trifle less responsible—for, after all, it was a fairly happy world.

At this moment he perceived a curious phenomenon a short distance before him—another Christmas-tree, but one which moved, apparently of its own volition, along the sidewalk. As Mr. Carter overtook it, he saw that it was borne, or dragged, rather by a small boy who wore a bright red flannel cap and mittens of the same peculiar material. As Mr. Carter looked down at him, he looked up at Mr. Carter, and spoke cheerfully:

"Goin' my way, mister?"

"Why," said the philanthropist, somewhat taken back, "I WAS!"

"Mind draggin' this a little way?" asked the boy, confidently, "my hands is cold."

"Won't you enjoy it more if you manage to take it home by yourself?"

"Oh, it ain't for me!" said the boy.

"Your employer," said the philanthropist, severely, "is certainly careless if he allows his trees to be delivered in this fashion."

"I ain't deliverin' it, either," said the boy. "This is Bill's tree."

"Who is Bill?"

"He's a feller with a back that's no good."

"Is he your brother?"

"No. Take the tree a little way, will you, while I warm myself?"

The philanthropist accepted the burden—he did not know why. The boy, released, ran forward, jumped up and down, slapped his red flannel mittens on his legs, and then ran back again. After repeating these manoeuvres two or three times, he returned to where the old gentleman stood holding the tree.

"Thanks," he said. "Say, mister, you look like Santa Claus yourself, standin' by the tree, with your fur cap and your coat. I bet you don't have to run to keep warm, hey?" There was high admiration in his look. Suddenly his eyes sparkled with an inspiration.

"Say, mister," he cried, "will you do something for me? Come in to Bill's—he lives only a block from here—and just let him see you. He's only a kid, and he'll think he's seen Santa Claus, sure. We can tell him you're so busy to-morrow you have to go to lots of places to-day. You won't have to give him anything. We're looking out for all that. Bill got hurt in the summer, and he's been in bed ever since. So we are giving him a Christmas—tree and all. He gets a bunch of things—an air gun, and a train that goes around when you wind her up. They're great!"

"You boys are doing this?"

"Well, it's our club at the settlement, and of course Miss Gray thought of it, and she's givin' Bill the train. Come along, mister."

But Mr. Carter declined.

"All right," said the boy. "I guess, what with Pete and all, Bill will have Christmas enough."

"Who is Pete?"

"Bill's dog. He's had him three weeks now—best little pup you ever saw!"

A dog which Bill had had three weeks—and in a neighbourhood not a quarter of a mile from the avenue. It was three weeks since Skiddles had disappeared. That this dog was Skiddles was of course most improbable, and yet the philanthropist was ready to grasp at any clue which might lead to the lost terrier.

"How did Bill get this dog?" he demanded.

"I found him myself. Some kids had tin-canned him, and he came into our entry. He licked my hand, and then sat up on his hind legs. Somebody'd taught him that, you know. I thought right away, 'Here's a dog for Bill!' And I took him over there and fed him, and they kept him in Bill's room two or three days, so he shouldn't get scared again and run off; and now he wouldn't leave Bill for anybody. Of course, he ain't much of a dog, Pete ain't," he added "he's just a pup, but he's mighty friendly!"

"Boy," said Mr. Carter, "I guess I'll just go round and"—he was about to add, "have a look at that dog," but fearful of raising suspicion, he ended—"and see Bill."

The tenements to which the boy led him were of brick, and reasonably clean. Nearly every window showed some sign of Christmas.

The tree-bearer led the way into a dark hall, up one flight—Mr. Carter assisting with the tree—and down another dark hall, to a door, on which he knocked. A woman opened it.

"Here's the tree!" said the boy, in a loud whisper. "Is Bill's door shut?"

Mr. Carter stepped forward out of the darkness. "I beg your pardon, madam," he said. "I met this young man in the street, and he asked me to come here and see a playmate of his who is, I understand, an invalid. But if I am intruding—"

"Come in," said the woman, heartily, throwing the door open. "Bill will be glad to see you, sir."

The philanthropist stepped inside.

The room was decently furnished and clean. There was a sewing machine in the corner, and in both the windows hung wreaths of holly. Between the windows was a cleared space, where evidently the tree, when decorated, was to stand.

"Are all the things here?" eagerly demanded the tree-bearer.

"They're all here, Jimmy," answered Mrs. Bailey. "The candy just came."

"Say," cried the boy, pulling off his red flannel mittens to blow on his fingers, "won't it be great? But now Bill's got to see Santa Claus. I'll just go in and tell him, an' then, when I holler, mister, you come on, and pretend you're Santa Claus." And with incredible celerity the boy opened the door at the opposite end of the room and disappeared.

"Madam," said Mr. Carter, in considerable embarrassment, "I must say one word. I am Mr. Carter, Mr. Allan Carter. You may have heard my name?"

She shook her head. "No, sir."

"I live not far from here on the avenue. Three weeks ago I lost a little dog that I valued very much I have had all the city searched since then, in vain. To-day I met the boy who has just left us. He informed me that three weeks ago he found a dog, which is at present in the possession of your son. I wonder—is it not just possible that this dog may be mine?"

Mrs. Bailey smiled. "I guess not, Mr. Carter. The dog Jimmy found hadn't come off the avenue—not from the look of him. You know there's hundreds and hundreds of dogs without homes, sir. But I will say for this one, he has a kind of a way with him."

"Hark!" said Mr. Carter.

There was a rustling and a snuffing at the door at the far end of the room, a quick scratching of feet. Then:

"Woof! woof! woof!" sharp and clear came happy impatient little barks. The philanthropist's eyes brightened. "Yes," he said, "that is the dog."

"I doubt if it can be, sir," said Mrs. Bailey, deprecatingly.

"Open the door, please," commanded the philanthropist, "and let us see." Mrs. Bailey complied. There was a quick jump, a tumbling rush, and Skiddles, the lost Skiddles, was in the philanthropist's arms. Mrs. Bailey shut the door with a troubled face.

"I see it's your dog, sir," she said, "but I hope you won't be thinking that Jimmy or I—"

"Madam," interrupted Mr. Carter, "I could not be so foolish. On the contrary, I owe you a thousand thanks."

Mrs. Bailey looked more cheerful. "Poor little Billy!" she said. "It'll come hard on him, losing Pete just at Christmas time. But the boys are so good to him, I dare say he'll forget it."

"Who are these boys?" inquired the philanthropist. "Isn't their action—somewhat unusual?"

"It's Miss Gray's club at the settlement, sir," explained Mrs. Bailey. "Every Christmas they do this for somebody. It's not charity; Billy and I don't need charity, or take it. It's just friendliness. They're good boys."

"I see," said the philanthropist. He was still wondering about it, though, when the door opened again, and Jimmy thrust out a face shining with anticipation.

"All ready, mister!" he said. "Bill's waitin' for you!"

"Jimmy," began Mrs. Bailey, about to explain, "the gentleman—"

But the philanthropist held up his hand, interrupting her. "You'll let me see your son, Mrs. Bailey?" he asked, gently.

"Why, certainly, sir."

Mr. Carter put Skiddles down and walked slowly into the inner room. The bed stood with its side toward him. On it lay a small boy of seven, rigid of body, but with his arms free and his face lighted with joy. "Hello, Santa Claus!" he piped, in a voice shrill with excitement.

"Hello, Bill!" answered the philanthropist, sedately.

The boy turned his eyes on Jimmy.

"He knows my name," he said, with glee.

"He knows everybody's name," said Jimmy. "Now you tell him what you want, Bill, and he'll bring it to-morrow.

"How would you like," said the philanthropist, reflectively, "an—an—" he hesitated, it seemed so incongruous with that stiff figure on the bed—"an airgun?"

"I guess yes," said Bill, happily.

"And a train of cars," broke in the impatient Jimmy, "that goes like sixty when you wind her?"

"Hi!" said Bill.

The philanthropist solemnly made notes of this.

"How about," he remarked, inquiringly, "a tree?"

"Honest?" said Bill.

"I think it can be managed," said Santa Claus. He advanced to the bedside.

"I'm glad to have seen you, Bill. You know how busy I am, but I hope—I hope to see you again."

"Not till next year, of course," warned Jimmy.

"Not till then, of course," assented Santa Claus. "And now, good-bye."

"You forgot to ask him if he'd been a good boy," suggested Jimmy.

"I have," said Bill. "I've been fine. You ask mother."

"She gives you—she gives you both a high character," said Santa Claus. "Good-bye again," and so saying he withdrew. Skiddles followed him out. The philanthropist closed the door of the bedroom, and then turned to Mrs. Bailey.

She was regarding him with awestruck eyes.

"Oh, sir," she said, "I know now who you are—the Mr. Carter that gives so much away to people!"

The philanthropist nodded, deprecatingly.

"Just so, Mrs. Bailey," he said. "And there is one gift—or loan rather—which I should like to make to you. I should like to leave the little dog with you till after the holidays. I'm afraid I'll have to claim him then; but if you'll keep him till after Christmas—and let me find, perhaps, another dog for Billy—I shall be much obliged."

Again the door of the bedroom opened, and Jimmy emerged quietly.

"Bill wants the pup," he explained.

"Pete! Pete!" came the piping but happy voice from the inner room.

Skiddles hesitated. Mr. Carter made no sign.

"Pete! Pete!" shrilled the voice again.

Slowly, very slowly, Skiddles turned and went back into the bedroom.

"You see," said Mr. Carter, smiling, "he won't be too unhappy away from me, Mrs. Bailey."

On his way home the philanthropist saw even more evidences of Christmas gaiety along the streets than before. He stepped out briskly, in spite of his sixty-eight years; he even hummed a little tune.

When he reached the house on the avenue he found his secretary still at work.

"Oh, by the way, Mr. Mathews," he said, "did you send that letter to the woman, saying I never paid attention to personal appeals? No? Then write her, please, enclosing my check for two hundred dollars, and wish her a very Merry Christmas in my name, will you? And hereafter will you always let me see such letters as that one—of course after careful investigation? I fancy perhaps I may have been too rigid in the past."

"Certainly, sir," answered the bewildered secretary. He began fumbling excitedly for his note-book.

"I found the little dog," continued the philanthropist. "You will be glad to know that."

"You have found him?" cried the secretary. "Have you got him back, Mr. Carter? Where was he?"

"He was—detained—on Oak Street, I believe," said the philanthropist. "No, I have not got him back yet. I have left him with a young boy till after the holidays."

He settled himself to his papers, for philanthropists must toil even on the twenty-fourth of December, but the secretary shook his head in a daze. "I wonder what's happened?" he said to himself.

XXV. THE FIRST CHRISTMAS-TREE

BY LUCY WHEELOCK

Two little children were sitting by the fire one cold winter's night. All at once they heard a timid knock at the door and one ran to open it.

There, outside in the cold and darkness, stood a child with no shoes upon his feet and clad in thin, ragged garments. He was shivering with cold, and he asked to come in and warm himself.

"Yes, come in," cried both the children. "You shall have our place by the fire. Come in."

They drew the little stranger to their warm seat and shared their supper with him, and gave him their bed, while they slept on a hard bench.

In the night they were awakened by strains of sweet music, and looking out, they saw a band of children in shining garments, approaching the house. They were playing on golden harps and the air was full of melody.

Suddenly the Strange Child stood before them: no longer cold and ragged, but clad in silvery light.

His soft voice said: "I was cold and you took Me in. I was hungry and you fed Me. I was tired and you gave Me your bed. I am the Christ-Child, wandering through the world to bring peace and happiness to all good children. As you have given to Me, so may this tree every year give rich fruit to you."

So saying, He broke a branch from the fir-tree that grew near the door, and He planted it in the ground and disappeared. And the branch grew into a great tree, and every year it bore wonderful fruit for the kind children.

XXVI. THE FIRST NEW ENGLAND CHRISTMAS*

From Stone and Fickett's "Every Day Life in the Colonies;" copyrighted 1905, by D. C. Heath & Co. Used by permission.

G. L. STONE AND M. G. FICKETT

It was a warm and pleasant Saturday—that twenty-third of December, 1620. The winter wind had blown itself away in the storm of the day before, and the air was clear and balmy. The people on board the Mayflower were glad of the pleasant day. It was three long months since they had started from Plymouth, in England, to seek a home across the ocean. Now they had come into a harbour that they named New Plymouth, in the country of New England.

Other people called these voyagers Pilgrims, which means wanderers. A long while before, the Pilgrims had lived in England; later they made their home with the Dutch in Holland; finally they had said goodbye to their friends in Holland and in England, and had sailed away to America.

There were only one hundred and two of the Pilgrims on the Mayflower, but they were brave and strong and full of hope. Now the Mayflower was the only home they had; yet if this weather lasted they might soon have warm log-cabins to live in. This very afternoon the men had gone ashore to cut down the large trees.

The women of the Mayflower were busy, too. Some were spinning, some knitting, some sewing. It was so bright and pleasant that Mistress Rose Standish had taken out her knitting and had gone to sit a little while on deck. She was too weak to face rough weather, and she wanted to enjoy the warm sunshine and the clear salt air. By her side was Mistress Brewster, the minister's wife. Everybody loved Mistress Standish and Mistress Brewster, for neither of them ever spoke unkindly.

The air on deck would have been warm even on a colder day, for in one corner a bright fire was burning. It would seem strange now, would it not, to see a fire on the deck of a vessel? But in those days, when the weather was pleasant, people on shipboard did their cooking on deck.

The Pilgrims had no stoves, and Mistress Carver's maid had built this fire on a large hearth covered with sand. She had hung a great kettle on the crane over the fire, where the onion soup for supper was now simmering slowly.

Near the fire sat a little girl, busily playing and singing to herself. Little Remember Allerton was only six years old, but she liked to be with Hannah, Mistress Carver's maid. This afternoon Remember had been watching Hannah build the fire and make the soup. Now the little girl was playing with the Indian arrowheads her father had brought her the night before. She was singing the words of the old psalm:

"Shout to Jehovah, all the earth, Serve ye Jehovah with gladness; before Him bow with singing mirth."

"Ah, child, methinks the children of Old England are singing different words from those to-day," spoke Hannah at length, with a faraway look in her eyes.

"Why, Hannah? What songs are the little English children singing now?" questioned Remember in surprise.

"It lacks but two days of Christmas, child, and in my old home everybody is singing Merry Christmas songs."

"But thou hast not told me what is Christmas!' persisted the child.

"Ah, me! Thou dost not know, 'tis true. Christmas, Remember, is the birthday of the Christ-Child, of Jesus, whom thou hast learned to love," Hannah answered softly.

"But what makes the English children so happy then? And we are English, thou hast told me, Hannah. Why don't we keep Christmas, too?"

"In sooth we are English, child. But the reason why we do not sing the Christmas carols or play the Christmas games makes a long, long story, Remember. Hannah cannot tell it so that little children will understand. Thou must ask some other, child."

Hannah and the little girl were just then near the two women on the deck, and Remember said:

"Mistress Brewster, Hannah sayeth she knoweth not how to tell why Love and Wrestling and Constance and the others do not sing the Christmas songs or play the Christmas games. But thou wilt tell me wilt thou not?" she added coaxingly.

A sad look came into Mistress Brewster's eyes, and Mistress Standish looked grave, too. No one spoke for a few seconds, until Hannah said almost sharply:

"Why could we not burn a Yule log Monday, and make some meal into little cakes for the children?"

"Nay, Hannah," answered the gentle voice of Mistress Brewster. "Such are but vain shows and not for those of us who believe in holier things. But," she added, with a kind glance at little Remember, "wouldst thou like to know why we have left Old England and do not keep the Christmas Day? Thou canst not understand it all, child, and yet it may do thee no harm to hear the story. It may help thee to be a brave and happy little girl in the midst of our hard life."

"Surely it can do no harm, Mistress Brewster," spoke Rose Standish, gently. "Remember is a little Pilgrim now, and she ought, methinks, to know something of the reason for our wandering. Come here, child, and sit by me, while good Mistress Brewster tells thee how cruel men have made us suffer. Then will I sing thee one of the Christmas carols."

With these words she held out her hands to little Remember, who ran quickly to the side of Mistress Standish, and eagerly waited for the story to begin.

"We have not always lived in Holland, Remember. Most of us were born in England, and England is the best country in the world. 'Tis a land to be proud of, Remember, though some of its rulers have been wicked and cruel.

"Long before you were born, when your mother was a little girl, the English king said that everybody in the land ought to think as he thought, and go to a church like his. He said he would send us away from England if we did not do as he ordered. Now, we could not think as he did on holy matters, and it seemed wrong to us to obey him. So we decided to go to a country where we might worship as we pleased."

"What became of that cruel king, Mistress Brewster?"

"He ruleth England now. But thou must not think too hardly of him. He doth not understand, perhaps. Right will win some day, Remember, though there may be bloody war before peace cometh. And I thank God that we, at least, shall not be called on to live in the midst of the strife," she went on, speaking more to herself than to the little girl.

"We decided to go to Holland, out of the reach of the king. We were not sure whether it was best to move or not, but our hearts were set on God's ways. We trusted Him in whom we believed. Yes," she went on, "and shall we not keep on trusting Him?"

And Rose Standish, remembering the little stock of food that was nearly gone, the disease that had come upon many of their number, and the five who had died that month, answered firmly: "Yes. He who has led us thus far will not leave us now."

They were all silent a few seconds. Presently Remember said: "Then did ye go to Holland, Mistress Brewster?"

"Yes," she said. "Our people all went over to Holland, where the Dutch folk live and the little Dutch children clatter about with their wooden shoes. There thou wast born, Remember, and my own children, and there we lived in love and peace."

"And yet, we were not wholly happy. We could not talk well with the Dutch, and so we could not set right what was wrong among them. 'Twas so hard to earn money that many had to go back to England. And worst of all, Remember, we were afraid that you and little Bartholomew and Mary and Love and Wrestling and all the rest would not grow to be good girls and boys. And so we have come to this new country to teach our children to be pure and noble."

After another silence Remember spoke again: "I thank thee, Mistress Brewster. And I will try to be a good girl. But thou didst not tell me about Christmas after all."

"Nay, child, but now I will. There are long services on that day in every church where the king's friends go. But there are parts of these services which we cannot approve; and so we think it best not to follow the other customs that the king's friends observe on Christmas.

"They trim their houses with mistletoe and holly so that everything looks gay and cheerful. Their other name for the Christmas time is the Yuletide, and the big log that is burned then is called the Yule log. The children like to sit around the hearth in front of the great, blazing Yule log, and listen to stories of long, long ago.

"At Christmas there are great feasts in England, too. No one is allowed to go hungry, for the rich people on the day always send meat and cakes to the poor folk round about.

"But we like to make all our days Christmas days, Remember. We try never to forget God's gifts to us, and they remind us always to be good to other people."

"And the Christmas carols, Mistress Standish? What are they?"

"On Christmas Eve and early on Christmas morning," Rose Standish answered, "little children go about from house to house, singing Christmas songs. 'Tis what I like best in all the Christmas cheer. And I promised to sing thee one, did I not?"

Then Mistress Standish sang in her dear, sweet voice the quaint old English words:

As Joseph was a-walking,

He heard an angel sing:

"This night shall be the birth-time

Of Christ, the heavenly King.

"He neither shall be born

In housen nor in hall,

Nor in the place of Paradise,

But in an ox's stall.

"He neither shall be clothed

In purple nor in pall,

But in the fair white linen

That usen babies all.

"He neither shall be rocked

In silver nor in gold,

But in a wooden manger

That resteth in the mould."

As Joseph was a-walking

There did an angel sing,

And Mary's child at midnight

Was born to be our King.

Then be ye glad, good people,

This night of all the year,

And light ye up your candles,

For His star it shineth clear.

Before the song was over, Hannah had come on deck again, and was listening eagerly. "I thank thee, Mistress Standish," she said, the tears filling her blue eyes. "'Tis long, indeed, since I have heard that song."

"Would it be wrong for me to learn to sing those words, Mistress Standish?" gently questioned the little girl.

"Nay, Remember, I trow not. The song shall be thy Christmas gift."

Then Mistress Standish taught the little girl one verse after another of the sweet old carol, and it was not long before Remember could say it all.

The next day was dull and cold, and on Monday, the twenty-fifth, the sky was still overcast. There was no bright Yule log in the Mayflower, and no holly trimmed the little cabin.

The Pilgrims were true to the faith they loved. They held no special service. They made no gifts.

Instead, they went again to the work of cutting the trees, and no one murmured at his hard lot.

"We went on shore," one man wrote in his diary, "some to fell timber, some to saw, some to rive, and some to carry; so no man rested all that day."

As for little Remember, she spent the day on board the Mayflower. She heard no one speak of England or sigh for the English home across the sea. But she did not forget Mistress Brewster's story; and more than once that day, as she was playing by herself, she fancied that she was in front of some English home, helping the English children sing their Christmas songs. And both Mistress Allerton and Mistress Standish, whom God was soon to call away from their earthly home, felt happier and stronger as they heard the little girl singing:

> He neither shall be born
>
> In housen nor in hall,
>
> Nor in the place of Paradise,
>
> But in an ox's stall.

XXVII. THE CRATCHITS' CHRISTMAS DINNER

(Adapted)

CHARLES DICKENS

Scrooge and the Ghost of Christmas Present stood in the city streets on Christmas morning, where (for the weather was severe) the people made a rough but brisk and not unpleasant kind of music, in scraping the snow from the pavement in front of their dwellings, and from the tops of their houses, whence it was mad delight to the boys to see it come plumping down into the road below, and splitting into artificial little snowstorms.

The house fronts looked black enough, and the windows blacker, contrasting with the smooth white sheet of snow upon the roofs, and with the dirtier snow upon the ground, which last deposit had been ploughed up in deep furrows by the heavy wheels of carts and wagons; furrows that crossed and recrossed each other hundreds of times where the great streets branched off, and made intricate channels, hard to trace, in the thick yellow mud and icy water. The sky was gloomy, and the shortest streets were choked up with a dingy mist, half thawed, half frozen, whose heavier particles descended in a shower of sooty atoms, as if all the chimneys in Great Britain had, by one consent, caught fire, and were blazing away to their dear heart's content. There was nothing very cheerful in the climate or the town, and yet was there an air of cheerfulness abroad that the dearest summer air and brightest summer sun might have endeavoured to diffuse in vain.

For the people who were shovelling away on the housetops were jovial and full of glee, calling out to one another from the parapets, and now and then exchanging a facetious snowball—better-natured missile far than many a wordy jest—laughing heartily if it went right, and not less heartily if it went wrong. The poulterers' shops were still half open, and the fruiterers' were radiant in their glory. There were great, round, potbellied baskets of chestnuts, shaped like the waistcoats of jolly old gentlemen, lolling at the doors, and tumbling out into the street in their apoplectic opulence.

There were ruddy, brown-faced, broad-girthed Spanish onions, shining in the fatness of their growth like Spanish friars, and winking, from their shelves, in wanton slyness at the girls as they went by, and glanced demurely at the hung-up mistletoe. There were pears and apples, clustering high in blooming pyramids; there were bunches of grapes, made, in the shop-keeper's benevolence, to dangle from conspicuous hooks, that people's mouths might water gratis as they passed; there were piles of filberts, mossy and brown, recalling, in their fragrance, ancient walks among the woods, and pleasant shufflings ankle deep through withered leaves; there were Norfolk biffins, squab and swarthy, setting off the yellow of the oranges and lemons, and, in the great compactness of their juicy persons, urgently entreating and beseeching to be carried home in paper bags and eaten after dinner. The very gold and silver fish, set forth among these choice fruits in a bowl, though members of a dull and stagnant-blooded race, appeared to know that there was something going on; and, to a fish, went gasping round and round their little world in slow and passionless excitement.

The grocers'! oh, the grocers'! nearly closed, with perhaps two shutters down, or one; but through those gaps such glimpses! It was not alone that the scales descending on the counter made a merry sound, or that the twine and roller parted company so briskly, or that the canisters were rattled up and down like juggling tricks, or even that the blended scents of tea and coffee were so grateful to the nose, or even that the raisins were so plentiful and rare, the almonds so extremely white, the sticks of cinnamon so long and straight, the other spices so delicious, the candied fruits so caked and spotted with molten sugar as to make the coldest lookers-on feel faint, and subsequently bilious. Nor was it that the figs were moist and pulpy, or that the French plums blushed in modest tartness from their highly decorated boxes, or that everything was good to eat and in its Christmas dress; but the customers were all so hurried and so eager in the hopeful promise of the day that they tumbled up against each other at the door, crashing their wicker baskets wildly, and left their purchases upon the counter, and came running back to fetch them, and committed hundreds of the like mistakes, in the best humour possible; while the grocer and his people were so frank and fresh that the polished hearts with which they fastened their aprons behind might have been their own, worn outside for general inspection, and for Christmas daws to peck at, if they chose.

But soon the steeples called good people all to church and chapel, and away they came, flocking through the streets in their best clothes, and with their gayest faces. And at the same time there emerged from scores of by-streets, lanes, and nameless turnings, innumerable people, carrying their dinners to the bakers' shops. The sight of these poor revellers appeared to interest the Spirit very much, for he stood, with Scrooge beside him, in a baker's doorway, and, taking off the covers as their bearers passed, sprinkled incense on their dinners from his torch. And it was a very uncommon kind of torch, for once or twice when there were angry words between some dinner-carriers who had jostled each other, he shed a few drops of water on them from it, and their good-humour was restored directly. For they said it was a shame to quarrel upon Christmas Day. And so it was! God love it, so it was!

In time the bells ceased, and the bakers were shut up; and yet there was a genial shadowing forth of all these dinners, and the progress of their cooking, in the thawed blotch of wet above each baker's oven, where the pavement smoked as if its stones were cooking too.

"Is there a peculiar flavour in what you sprinkle from your torch?" asked Scrooge.

"There is. My own."

"Would it apply to any kind of dinner on this day?" asked Scrooge.

"To any kindly given. To a poor one most."

"Why to a poor one most?" asked Scrooge.

"Because it needs it most."

They went on, invisible, as they had been before, into the suburbs of the town. It was a remarkable quality of the Ghost (which Scrooge had observed at the baker's) that, notwithstanding his gigantic size, he could accommodate himself to any place with ease; and that he stood beneath a low roof quite as gracefully, and like a supernatural creature, as it was possible he could have done in any lofty hall.

And perhaps it was the pleasure the good Spirit had in showing off this power of his, or else it was his own kind, generous, hearty nature, and his sympathy with all poor men, that led him straight to Scrooge's clerk's; for there he went, and took Scrooge with him, holding to his robe; and on the threshold of the door the Spirit smiled, and stopped to bless Bob Cratchit's dwelling with the sprinklings of his torch. Think of that! Bob had but fifteen "bob" a week himself; he pocketed on Saturdays but fifteen copies of his Christian name; and yet the Ghost of Christmas Present blessed his four-roomed house!

Then up rose Mrs. Cratchit, Cratchit's wife, dressed out but poorly in a twice-turned gown, but brave in ribbons, which are cheap and make a goodly show for sixpence; and she laid the cloth, assisted by Belinda Cratchit, second of her daughters, also brave in ribbons; while Master Peter Cratchit plunged a fork into the saucepan of potatoes, and getting the corners of his monstrous shirt-collar (Bob's private property, conferred upon his son and heir in honour of the day) into his mouth, rejoiced to find himself so gallantly attired, and yearned to show his linen in the fashionable parks. And now two smaller Cratchits, boy and girl, came tearing in, screaming that outside the baker's they had smelt the goose, and known it for their own, and, basking in luxurious thoughts of sage and onion, these young Cratchits danced about the table, and exalted Master Peter Cratchit to the skies, while he (not proud, although his collar nearly choked him) blew the fire, until the slow potatoes, bubbling up, knocked loudly at the saucepan lid to be let out and peeled.

"What has ever got your precious father, then?" said Mrs. Cratchit. "And your brother, Tiny Tim? And Martha warn't as late last Christmas Day by half an hour!"

"Here's Martha, mother!" said a girl, appearing as she spoke.

"Here's Martha, mother!" cried the two young Cratchits. "Hurrah! There's such a goose, Martha!"

"Why, bless your heart alive, my dear, how late you are!" said Mrs. Cratchit, kissing her a dozen times, and taking off her shawl and bonnet for her with officious zeal.

"We'd a deal of work to finish up last night," replied the girl, "and had to clear away this morning, mother!"

"Well, never mind so long as you are come," said Mrs. Cratchit. "Sit ye down before the fire, my dear, and have a warm, Lord bless ye!"

"No, no! There's father coming!" cried the two young Cratchits, who were everywhere at once.

"Hide, Martha, hide!"

So Martha hid herself, and in came little Bob, the father, with at least three feet of comforter, exclusive of the fringe, hanging down before him, and his threadbare clothes darned up and brushed, to look seasonable; and Tiny Tim upon his shoulder. Alas for Tiny Tim, he bore a little crutch, and had his limbs supported by an iron frame!

"Why, where's our Martha?" cried Bob Cratchit, looking around.

"Not coming," said Mrs. Cratchit.

"Not coming?" said Bob, with a sudden declension in his high spirits; for he had been Tim's blood horse all the way from the church, and had come home rampant. "Not coming upon Christmas Day?"

Martha didn't like to see him disappointed, if it were only in joke; so she came out prematurely from behind the closet door, and ran into his arms, while the two young Cratchits hustled Tiny Tim, and bore him off into the wash-house, that he might hear the pudding singing in the copper.

"And how did little Tim behave?" asked Mrs. Cratchit, when she had rallied Bob on his credulity, and Bob had hugged his daughter to his heart's content.

"As good as gold," said Bob, "and better. Somehow he gets thoughtful, sitting by himself so much, and thinks the strangest things you ever heard. He told me, coming home, that he hoped the people saw him in the church, because he was a cripple, and it might be pleasant to them to remember, upon Christmas Day, who made lame beggars walk, and blind men see."

Bob's voice was tremulous when he told them this, and trembled more when he said that Tiny Tim was growing strong and hearty.

His active little crutch was heard upon the floor, and back came Tiny Tim before another word was spoken, escorted by his brother and sister to his stool beside the fire; and while Bob, turning up his cuffs—as if, poor fellow, they were capable of being made more shabby—compounded some hot mixture in a jug with gin and lemons, and stirred it round and round, and put it on the hob to simmer, Master Peter and the two ubiquitous young Cratchits went to fetch the goose, with which they soon returned in high procession.

Such a bustle ensued that you might have thought a goose the rarest of all birds—a feathered phenomenon, to which a black swan was a matter of course—and in truth it was something very like it in that house. Mrs. Cratchit made the gravy (ready beforehand in a little saucepan) hissing hot; Master Peter mashed the potatoes with incredible vigour; Miss Belinda sweetened up the apple-sauce; Martha dusted the hot plates; Bob took Tiny Tim beside him in a tiny corner at the table; the two young Cratchits set chairs for everybody, not forgetting themselves, and, mounting guard upon their posts, crammed spoons into their mouths, lest they should shriek for goose before their turn came to be helped. At last the dishes were set on and grace was said. It was succeeded by a breathless pause, as Mrs. Cratchit, looking slowly all along the carving knife, prepared to plunge it into the breast; but when she did, and when the long expected gush of stuffing issued forth, one murmur of delight arose all round the board, and even Tiny Tim, excited by the two young Cratchits, beat on the table with the handle of his knife, and feebly cried, "Hurrah!"

There never was such a goose. Bob said he didn't believe there ever was such a goose cooked. Its tenderness and flavour, size and cheapness, were the themes of universal admiration. Eked out by apple-sauce and mashed potatoes, it was a sufficient dinner for the whole family; indeed, as Mrs. Cratchit said with great delight (surveying one small atom of a bone upon the dish), they hadn't ate it all at last! Yet every one had had enough, and the youngest Cratchits in particular were steeped in sage and onion to the eyebrows! But now, the plates being changed by Miss

Belinda, Mrs. Cratchit left the room alone—too nervous to bear witnesses—to take the pudding up, and bring it in.

Suppose it should not be done enough? Suppose it should break in turning out? Suppose somebody should have got over the wall of the backyard and stolen it, while they were merry with the goose—a supposition at which the two young Cratchits became livid! All sorts of horrors were supposed.

Hallo! A great deal of steam! The pudding was out of the copper. A smell like a washing-day! That was the cloth. A smell like an eating house and a pastry-cook's next door to each other, with a laundress's next door to that! That was the pudding! In half a minute Mrs. Cratchit entered—flushed, but smiling proudly—with the pudding, like a speckled cannon-ball, so hard and firm, blazing in half of half-a-quartern of ignited brandy, and bedight with Christmas holly stuck into the top.

Oh, a wonderful pudding! Bob Cratchit said, and calmly, too, that he regarded it as the greatest success achieved by Mrs. Cratchit since their marriage. Mrs. Cratchit said that, now the weight was off her mind, she would confess she had her doubts about the quantity of flour. Everybody had something to say about it, but nobody thought or said it was at all a small pudding for a large family. It would have been flat heresy to do so. Any Cratchit would have blushed to hint at such a thing.

At last the dinner was all done, the cloth was cleared, the hearth swept, and the fire made up. The compound in the jug being tasted, and considered perfect, apples and oranges were put upon the table, and a shovelful of chestnuts on the fire. Then all the Cratchit family drew round the hearth in what Bob Cratchit called a circle, meaning half a one; and at Bob Cratchit's elbow stood the family display of glass—two tumblers and a custard-cup without a handle.

These held the hot stuff from the jug, however, as well as golden goblets would have done; and Bob served it out with beaming looks, while the chestnuts on the fire sputtered and cracked noisily. Then Bob proposed:

"A Merry Christmas to us all, my dears. God bless us!"

Which all the family reechoed.

"God bless us every one!" said Tiny Tim, the last of all.

XXVIII. CHRISTMAS IN SEVENTEEN SEVENTY-SIX*

*From "A Last Century Maid and Other Stories for Children," by A.H.W. Lippincott, 1895.

ANNE HOLLINGSWORTH WHARTON

"On Christmas day in Seventy-six,

Our gallant troops with bayonets fixed,

To Trenton marched away."

Children, have any of you ever thought of what little people like you were doing in this country more than a hundred years ago, when the cruel tide of war swept over its bosom? From many homes the fathers were absent, fighting bravely for the liberty which we now enjoy, while the mothers no less valiantly struggled against hardships and discomforts in order to keep a home for their children, whom you only know as your great-grandfathers and great-grandmothers, dignified gentlemen and beautiful ladies, whose painted portraits hang upon the walls in some of your homes. Merry, romping children they were in those far-off times, yet their bright faces must have looked grave sometimes, when they heard the grown people talk of the great things that were happening around them. Some of these little people never forgot the wonderful events of which they heard, and afterward related them to their children and grandchildren, which accounts for some of the interesting stories which you may still hear, if you are good children.

The Christmas story that I have to tell you is about a boy and girl who lived in Bordentown, New Jersey. The father of these children was a soldier in General Washington's army, which was encamped a few miles north of Trenton, on the Pennsylvania side of the Delaware River. Bordentown, as you can see by looking on your map, if you have not hidden them all away for the holidays, is about seven miles south of Trenton, where fifteen hundred Hessians and a troop of British light horse were holding the town. Thus you see that the British, in force, were between Washington's army and Bordentown, besides which there were some British and Hessian troops in the very town. All this seriously interfered with Captain Tracy's going home to eat his Christmas dinner with his wife and children. Kitty and Harry Tracy, who had not lived long enough to see many wars, could not imagine such a thing as Christmas without their father, and had busied themselves for weeks in making everything ready to have a merry time with him. Kitty, who loved to play quite as much as any frolicsome Kitty of to-day, had spent all her spare time in knitting a pair of thick woollen stockings, which seems a wonderful feat for a little girl only eight years old to perform! Can you not see her sitting by the great chimney-place, filled with its roaring, crackling logs, in her quaint, short-waisted dress, knitting away steadily, and puckering up her rosy, dimpled face over the strange twists and turns of that old stocking? I can see her, and I can also hear her sweet voice as she chatters away to her mother about "how 'sprised papa will be to find that his little girl can knit like a grown-up woman," while Harry spreads out on the hearth a goodly store of shellbarks that he has gathered and is keeping for his share of the 'sprise.

"What if he shouldn't come?" asks Harry, suddenly.

"Oh, he'll come! Papa never stays away on Christmas," says Kitty, looking up into her mother's face for an echo to her words. Instead she sees something very like tears in her mother's eyes.

"Oh, mamma, don't you think he'll come?"

"He will come if he possibly can," says Mrs. Tracy; "and if he cannot, we will keep Christmas whenever dear papa does come home."

"It won't be half so nice," said Kitty, "nothing's so nice as REALLY Christmas, and how's Kriss Kringle going to know about it if we change the day?"

"We'll let him come just the same, and if he brings anything for papa we can put it away for him."

This plan, still, seemed a poor one to Miss Kitty, who went to her bed in a sober mood that night, and was heard telling her dear dollie, Martha Washington, that "wars were mis'able, and that when she married she should have a man who kept a candy-shop for a husband, and not a soldier—no, Martha, not even if he's as nice as papa!" As Martha made no objection to this little arrangement, being an obedient child, they were both soon fast asleep. The days of that cold winter of 1776 wore on; so cold it was that the sufferings of the soldiers were great, their bleeding feet often leaving marks on the pure white snow over which they marched. As Christmas drew near there was a feeling among the patriots that some blow was about to be struck; but what it was, and from whence they knew not; and, better than all, the British had no idea that any strong blow could come from Washington's army, weak and out of heart, as they thought, after being chased through Jersey by Cornwallis.

Mrs. Tracy looked anxiously each day for news of the husband and father only a few miles away, yet so separated by the river and the enemy's troops that they seemed like a hundred. Christmas Eve came, but brought with it few rejoicings. The hearts of the people were too sad to be taken up with merrymaking, although the Hessian soldiers in the town, good-natured Germans, who only fought the Americans because they were paid for it, gave themselves up to the feasting and revelry.

"Shall we hang up our stockings?" asked Kitty, in rather a doleful voice.

"Yes," said her mother, "Santa Claus won't forget you, I am sure, although he has been kept pretty busy looking after the soldiers this winter."

"Which side is he on?" asked Harry.

"The right side, of course," said Mrs. Tracy, which was the most sensible answer she could possibly have given. So:

"The stockings were hung by the chimney with care, In hopes that St. Nicholas soon would be there."

Two little rosy faces lay fast asleep upon the pillow when the good old soul came dashing over the roof about one o'clock, and after filling each stocking with red apples, and leaving a cornucopia of sugar-plums for each child, he turned for a moment to look at the sleeping faces, for St. Nicholas has a tender spot in his great big heart for a soldier's children. Then, remembering many other small folks waiting for him all over the land, he sprang up the chimney and was away in a trice.

Santa Claus, in the form of Mrs. Tracy's farmer brother, brought her a splendid turkey; but because the Hessians were uncommonly fond of turkey, it came hidden under a load of wood. Harry was very fond of turkey, too, as well as of all other good things; but when his mother said, "It's such a fine bird, it seems too bad to eat it without father," Harry cried out, "Yes, keep it for papa!" and Kitty, joining in the chorus, the vote was unanimous, and the turkey was hung away to await the return of the good soldier, although it seemed strange, as Kitty told Martha Washington, "to have no papa and no turkey on Christmas Day."

The day passed and night came, cold with a steady fall of rain and sleet. Kitty prayed that her "dear papa might not be out in the storm, and that he might come home and wear his beautiful blue stockings"; "And eat his turkey," said Harry's sleepy voice; after which they were soon in the land of dreams. Toward morning the good people in Bordentown were suddenly aroused by firing in the distance, which became more and more distinct as the day wore on. There was great excitement in the town; men and women gathered together in little groups in the streets to wonder what it was all about, and neighbours came dropping into Mrs. Tracy's parlour, all day long, one after the other, to say what they thought of the firing. In the evening there came a body of Hessians flying into the town, to say that General Washington had surprised the British at Trenton, early that morning, and completely routed them, which so frightened the Hessians in Bordentown that they left without the slightest ceremony.

It was a joyful hour to the good town people when the red-jackets turned their backs on them, thinking every moment that the patriot army would be after them. Indeed, it seemed as if wonders would never cease that day, for while rejoicings were still loud, over the departure of the enemy, there came a knock at Mrs. Tracy's door, and while she was wondering whether she dared open it, it was pushed ajar, and a tall soldier entered. What a scream of delight greeted that soldier, and how Kitty and Harry danced about him and clung to his knees, while Mrs. Tracy drew him toward the warm blaze, and helped him off with his damp cloak!

Cold and tired Captain Tracy was, after a night's march in the streets and a day's fighting; but he was not too weary to smile at the dear faces around him, or to pat Kitty's head when she brought his warm stockings and would put them on the tired feet, herself.

Suddenly there was a sharp, quick bark outside the door. "What's that?" cried Harry.

"Oh, I forgot. Open the door. Here, Fido, Fido!"

Into the room there sprang a beautiful little King Charles spaniel, white, with tan spots, and ears of the longest, softest, and silkiest.

"What a little dear!" exclaimed Kitty; "where did it come from?"

"From the battle of Trenton," said her father. "His poor master was shot. After the red-coats had turned their backs, and I was hurrying along one of the streets where the fight had been the fiercest, I heard a low groan, and, turning, saw a British officer lying among a number of slain. I raised his head; he begged for some water, which I brought him, and bending down my ear I heard him whisper, 'Dying—last battle—say a prayer.' He tried to follow me in the words of a prayer, and then, taking my hand, laid it on something soft and warm, nestling close up to his breast—it was this little dog. The gentleman—for he was a real gentleman—gasped out, 'Take care of my poor Fido; good-night,' and was gone. It was as much as I could do to get the little creature away from his dead master; he clung to him as if he loved him better than life. You'll take care of him, won't you, children? I brought him home to you, for a Christmas present."

"Pretty little Fido," said Kitty, taking the soft, curly creature in her arms; "I think it's the best present in the world, and to-morrow is to be real Christmas, because you are home, papa."

"And we'll eat the turkey," said Harry, "and shellbarks, lots of them, that I saved for you. What a good time we'll have! And oh, papa, don't go to war any more, but stay at home, with mother and Kitty and Fido and me."

"What would become of our country if we should all do that, my little man? It was a good day's work that we did this Christmas, getting the army all across the river so quickly and quietly that we surprised the enemy, and gained a victory, with the loss of few men."

Thus it was that some of the good people of 1776 spent their Christmas, that their children and grandchildren might spend many of them as citizens of a free nation.

XXIX. CHRISTMAS UNDER THE SNOW*

*From "Kristy's Queer Christmas," Houghton, Mifflin & Co., 1904.

OLIVE THORNE MILLER

It was just before Christmas, and Mr. Barnes was starting for the nearest village. The family were out at the door to see him start, and give him the last charges.

"Don't forget the Christmas dinner, papa," said Willie.

"'Specially the chickens for the pie!" put in Nora.

"An' the waisins," piped up little Tot, standing on tiptoe to give papa a good-bye kiss.

"I hate to have you go, George," said Mrs. Barnes anxiously. "It looks to me like a storm."

"Oh, I guess it won't be much," said Mr. Barnes lightly; "and the youngsters must have their Christmas dinner, you know."

"Well," said Mrs. Barnes, "remember this, George: if there is a bad storm don't try to come back. Stay in the village till it is over. We can get along alone for a few days, can't we, Willie?" turning to the boy who was giving the last touches to the harness of old Tim, the horse.

"Oh, yes! Papa, I can take care of mamma," said Willie earnestly.

"And get up the Christmas dinner out of nothing?" asked papa, smiling.

"I don't know," said Willie, hesitating, as he remembered the proposed dinner, in which he felt a deep interest.

"What could you do for the chicken pie?" went on papa with a roguish look in his eye, "or the plum-pudding?"

"Or the waisins?" broke in Tot anxiously.

"Tot has set her heart on the raisins," said papa, tossing the small maiden up higher than his head, and dropping her all laughing on the door-step, "and Tot shall have them sure, if papa can find them in S—. Now good-bye, all! Willie, remember to take care of mamma, and I depend on you to get up a Christmas dinner if I don't get back. Now, wife, don't worry!" were his last words as the faithful old horse started down the road.

Mrs. Barnes turned one more glance to the west, where a low, heavy bank of clouds was slowly rising, and went into the little house to attend to her morning duties.

"Willie," she said, when they were all in the snug little log-cabin in which they lived, "I'm sure there's going to be a storm, and it may be snow. You had better prepare enough wood for two or three days; Nora will help bring it in."

"Me, too!" said grave little Tot.

"Yes, Tot may help too," said mamma.

This simple little home was a busy place, and soon every one was hard at work. It was late in the afternoon before the pile of wood, which had been steadily growing all day, was high enough to satisfy Willie, for now there was no doubt about the coming storm, and it would probably bring snow; no one could guess how much, in that country of heavy storms.

"I wish the village was not so far off, so that papa could get back to-night," said Willie, as he came in with his last load.

Mrs. Barnes glanced out of the window. Broad scattering snowflakes were silently falling; the advance guard, she felt them to be, of a numerous host.

"So do I," she replied anxiously, "or that he did not have to come over that dreadful prairie, where it is so easy to get lost."

"But old Tim knows the way, even in the dark," said Willie proudly. "I believe Tim knows more'n some folks."

"No doubt he does, about the way home," said mamma, "and we won't worry about papa, but have our supper and go to bed. That'll make the time seem short."

The meal was soon eaten and cleared away, the fire carefully covered up on the hearth, and the whole little family quietly in bed. Then the storm, which had been making ready all day, came down upon them in earnest.

The bleak wind howled around the corners, the white flakes by millions and millions came with it, and hurled themselves upon that house. In fact, that poor little cabin alone on the wide prairie seemed to be the object of their sport. They sifted through the cracks in the walls, around the windows, and under the door, and made pretty little drifts on the floor. They piled up against it outside, covered the steps, and then the door, and then the windows, and then the roof, and at last buried it completely out of sight under the soft, white mass.

And all the time the mother and her three children lay snugly covered up in their beds fast asleep, and knew nothing about it.

The night passed away and morning came, but no light broke through the windows of the cabin. Mrs. Barnes woke at the usual time, but finding it still dark and perfectly quiet outside, she concluded that the storm was over, and with a sigh of relief turned over to sleep again. About eight o'clock, however, she could sleep no more, and became wide awake enough to think the darkness strange. At that moment the clock struck, and the truth flashed over her.

Being buried under snow is no uncommon thing on the wide prairies, and since they had wood and cornmeal in plenty, she would not have been much alarmed if her husband had been home. But snow deep enough to bury them must cover up all landmarks, and she knew her husband would not rest till he had found them. To get lost on the trackless prairie was fearfully easy, and to suffer and die almost in sight of home was no unusual thing, and was her one dread in living there.

A few moments she lay quiet in bed, to calm herself and get control of her own anxieties before she spoke to the children.

"Willie," she said at last, "are you awake?"

"Yes, mamma," said Willie; "I've been awake ever so long; isn't it most morning?"

"Willie," said the mother quietly, "we mustn't be frightened, but I think— I'm afraid—we are snowed in."

Willie bounded to his feet and ran to the door. "Don't open it!" said mamma hastily; "the snow may fall in. Light a candle and look out the window."

In a moment the flickering rays of the candle fell upon the window. Willie drew back the curtain. Snow was tightly banked up against it to the top.

"Why, mamma," he exclaimed, "so we are! and how can papa find us? and what shall we do?"

"We must do the best we can," said mamma, in a voice which she tried to make steady, "and trust that it isn't very deep, and that Tim and papa will find us, and dig us out."

By this time the little girls were awake and inclined to be very much frightened, but mamma was calm now, and Willie was brave and hopeful. They all dressed, and Willie started the fire. The smoke refused to rise, but puffed out into the room, and Mrs. Barnes knew that if the chimney were closed they would probably suffocate, if they did not starve or freeze.

The smoke in a few minutes choked them, and, seeing that something must be done, she put the two girls, well wrapped in blankets, into the shed outside the back door, closed the door to keep out the smoke, and then went with Willie to the low attic, where a scuttle door opened onto the roof.

"We must try," she said, "to get it open without letting in too much snow, and see if we can manage to clear the chimney."

"I can reach the chimney from the scuttle with a shovel," said Willie. "I often have with a stick."

After much labour, and several small avalanches of snow, the scuttle was opened far enough for Willie to stand on the top round of the short ladder, and beat a hole through to the light, which was only a foot above. He then shovelled off the top of the chimney, which was ornamented with a big round cushion of snow, and then by beating and shovelling he was able to clear the door, which he opened wide, and Mrs. Barnes came up on the ladder to look out. Dreary indeed was the scene! Nothing but snow as far as the eye could reach, and flakes still falling, though lightly.

The storm was evidently almost over, but the sky was gray and overcast.

They closed the door, went down, and soon had a fire, hoping that the smoke would guide somebody to them.

Breakfast was taken by candle-light, dinner—in time—in the same way, and supper passed with no sound from the outside world.

Many times Willie and mamma went to the scuttle door to see if any one was in sight, but not a shadow broke the broad expanse of white over which toward night the sun shone. Of course there were no signs of the roads, for through so deep snow none could be broken, and until the sun and frost should form a crust on top there was little hope of their being reached.

The second morning broke, and Willie hurried up to his post of lookout the first thing. No person was in sight, but he found a light crust on the snow, and the first thing he noticed was a few half-starved birds trying in vain to pick up something to eat. They looked weak and almost exhausted, and a thought struck Willie.

It was hard to keep up the courage of the little household. Nora had openly lamented that to-night was Christmas Eve, and no Christmas dinner to be had. Tot had grown very tearful about her "waisins," and Mrs. Barnes, though she tried to keep up heart, had become very pale and silent.

Willie, though he felt unbounded faith in papa, and especially in Tim, found it hard to suppress his own complaints when he remembered that Christmas would probably be passed in the same dismal way, with fears for papa added to their own misery.

The wood, too, was getting low, and mamma dared not let the fire go out, as that was the only sign of their existence to anybody; and though she did not speak of it, Willie knew, too, that they had not many candles, and in two days at farthest they would be left in the dark.

The thought that struck Willie pleased him greatly, and he was sure it would cheer up the rest. He made his plans, and went to work to carry them out without saying anything about it.

He brought out of a corner of the attic an old boxtrap he had used in the summer to catch birds and small animals, set it carefully on the snow, and scattered crumbs of corn-bread to attract the birds.

In half an hour he went up again, and found to his delight he had caught bigger game—a poor rabbit which had come from no one knows where over the crust to find food.

This gave Willie a new idea; they could save their Christmas dinner after all; rabbits made very nice pies.

Poor Bunny was quietly laid to rest, and the trap set again. This time another rabbit was caught, perhaps the mate of the first. This was the last of the rabbits, but the next catch was a couple of snowbirds. These Willie carefully placed in a corner of the attic, using the trap for a cage, and giving them plenty of food and water.

When the girls were fast asleep, with tears on their cheeks for the dreadful Christmas they were going to have, Willie told mamma about his plans. Mamma was pale and weak with anxiety, and his news first made her laugh and then cry. But after a few moments given to her long pent-up tears, she felt much better and entered into his plans heartily.

The two captives up in the attic were to be Christmas presents to the girls, and the rabbits were to make the long anticipated pie. As for plum-pudding, of course that couldn't be thought of.

"But don't you think, mamma," said Willie eagerly, "that you could make some sort of a cake out of meal, and wouldn't hickory nuts be good in it? You know I have some left up in the attic, and I might crack them softly up there, and don't you think they would be good?" he concluded anxiously.

"Well, perhaps so," said mamma, anxious to please him and help him in his generous plans. "I can try. If I only had some eggs—but seems to me I have heard that snow beaten into cake would make it light—and there's snow enough, I'm sure," she added with a faint smile, the first Willie had seen for three days.

The smile alone he felt to be a great achievement, and he crept carefully up the ladder, cracked the nuts to the last one, brought them down, and mamma picked the meats out, while he dressed the two rabbits which had come so opportunely to be their Christmas dinner. "Wish you Merry Christmas!" he called out to Nora and Tot when they waked. "See what Santa Claus has brought you!"

Before they had time to remember what a sorry Christmas it was to be, they received their presents, a live bird, for each, a bird that was never to be kept in a cage, but fly about the house till summer came, and then to go away if it wished.

Pets were scarce on the prairie, and the girls were delighted. Nothing papa could have brought them would have given them so much happiness.

They thought no more of the dinner, but hurried to dress themselves and feed the birds, which were quite tame from hunger and weariness. But after a while they saw preparations for dinner, too. Mamma made a crust and lined a deep dish—the chicken pie dish—and then she brought a mysterious something out of the cupboard, all cut up so that it looked as if it might be chicken, and put it in the dish with other things, and then she tucked them all under a thick crust, and set it down in a tin oven before the fire to bake. And that was not all. She got out some more cornmeal, and made a batter, and put in some sugar and something else which she slipped in from a bowl, and which looked in the batter something like raisins; and at the last moment Willie brought her a cup of snow and she hastily beat it into the cake, or pudding, whichever you might call it, while the children laughed at the idea of making a cake out of snow. This went into the same oven and pretty soon it rose up light and showed a beautiful brown crust, while the pie was steaming through little fork holes on top, and sending out most delicious odours.

At the last minute, when the table was set and everything ready to come up, Willie ran up to look out of the scuttle, as he had every hour of daylight since they were buried. In a moment came a wild shout down the ladder.

"They're coming! Hurrah for old Tim!"

Mamma rushed up and looked out, and saw—to be sure—old Tim slowly coming along over the crust, drawing after him a wood sled on which were two men.

"It's papa!" shouted Willie, waving his arms to attract their attention.

"Willie!" came back over the snow in tones of agony. "Is that you? Are all well?"

"All well!" shouted Willie, "and just going to have our Christmas dinner."

"Dinner?" echoed papa, who was now nearer.

"Where is the house, then?"

"Oh, down here!" said Willie, "under the snow; but we're all right, only we mustn't let the plum-pudding spoil."

Looking into the attic, Willie found that mamma had fainted away, and this news brought to her aid papa and the other man, who proved to be a good friend who had come to help.

Tim was tied to the chimney, whose thread of smoke had guided them home, and all went down into the dark room. Mrs. Barnes soon recovered, and while Willie dished up the smoking dinner, stories were told on both sides.

Mr. Barnes had been trying to get through the snow and to find them all the time, but until the last night had made a stiff crust he had been unable to do so. Then Mrs. Barnes told her story, winding up with the account of Willie's Christmas dinner. "And if it hadn't been for his keeping up our hearts I don't know what would have become of us," she said at last.

"Well, my son," said papa, "you did take care of mamma, and get up a dinner out of nothing, sure enough; and now we'll eat the dinner, which I am sure is delicious."

So it proved to be; even the cake, or pudding, which Tot christened snow pudding, was voted very nice, and the hickory nuts as good as raisins. When they had finished, Mr. Barnes brought in his packages, gave Tot and the rest some "sure-enough waisins," and added his Christmas presents to Willie's; but though all were overjoyed, nothing was quite so nice in their eyes as the two live birds.

After dinner the two men and Willie dug out passages from the doors, through the snow, which had wasted a good deal, uncovered the windows, and made a slanting way to his shed for old Tim. Then for two or three days Willie made tunnels and little rooms under the snow, and for two weeks, while the snow lasted, Nora and Tot had fine times in the little snow playhouses.

XXX. MR. BLUFF'S EXPERIENCES OF HOLIDAYS*

* Reprinted by permission of Moffat, Yird & Co., from Christmas. R.H. Schauffler, Editor.

OLIVER BELL BUNCE

"I hate holidays," said Bachelor Bluff to me, with some little irritation, on a Christmas a few years ago. Then he paused an instant, after which he resumed: "I don't mean to say that I hate to see people enjoying themselves. But I hate holidays, nevertheless, because to me they are always the saddest and dreariest days of the year. I shudder at the name of holiday. I dread the approach of one, and thank heaven when it is over. I pass through, on a holiday, the most horrible sensations, the bitterest feelings, the most oppressive melancholy; in fact, I am not myself at holiday-times."

"Very strange," I ventured to interpose.

"A plague on it!" said he, almost with violence. "I'm not inhuman. I don't wish anybody harm. I'm glad people can enjoy themselves. But I hate holidays all the same. You see, this is the reason: I am a bachelor; I am without kin; I am in a place that did not know me at birth. And so, when holidays come around, there is no place anywhere for me. I have friends, of course; I don't think I've been a very sulky, shut-in, reticent fellow; and there is many a board that has a place for me—but not at Christmastime. At Christmas, the dinner is a family gathering; and I've no family. There is such a gathering of kindred on this occasion, such a reunion of family folk, that there is no place for a friend, even if the friend be liked. Christmas, with all its kindliness and charity and good-will, is, after all, deuced selfish. Each little set gathers within its own circle; and people like me, with no particular circle, are left in the lurch. So you see, on the day of all the days in the year that my heart pines for good cheer, I'm without an invitation.

"Oh, it's because I pine for good cheer," said the bachelor, sharply, interrupting my attempt to speak, "that I hate holidays. If I were an infernally selfish fellow, I wouldn't hate holidays. I'd go off and have some fun all to myself, somewhere or somehow. But, you see, I hate to be in the dark when all the rest of the world is in light. I hate holidays because I ought to be merry and happy on holidays and can't.

"Don't tell me," he cried, stopping the word that was on my lips; "I tell you, I hate holidays. The shops look merry, do they, with their bright toys and their green branches? The pantomime is crowded with merry hearts, is it? The circus and the show are brimful of fun and laughter, are they? Well, they all make me miserable. I haven't any pretty-faced girls or bright-eyed boys to take to the circus or the show, and all the nice girls and fine boys of my acquaintance have their uncles or their grand-dads or their cousins to take them to those places; so, if I go, I must go alone. But I don't go. I can't bear the chill of seeing everybody happy, and knowing myself so lonely and desolate. Confound it, sir, I've too much heart to be happy under such circumstances! I'm too humane, sir! And the result is, I hate holidays. It's miserable to be out, and yet I can't stay at home, for I get thinking of Christmases past. I can't read—the shadow of my heart makes it impossible. I can't walk—for I see nothing but pictures through the bright windows, and happy groups of pleasure-seekers. The fact is, I've nothing to do but to hate holidays. But will you not dine with me?"

Of course, I had to plead engagement with my own family circle, and I couldn't quite invite Mr. Bluff home that day, when Cousin Charles and his wife, and Sister Susan and her daughter, and three of my wife's kin had come in from the country, all to make a merry Christmas with us. I felt sorry, but it was quite impossible, so I wished Mr. Bluff a "Merry Christmas," and hurried homeward through the cold and nipping air.

I did not meet Bachelor Bluff again until a week after Christmas of the next year, when I learned some strange particulars of what occurred to him after our parting on the occasion just described. I will let Bachelor Bluff tell his adventure for himself.

"I went to church," said he, "and was as sad there as everywhere else. Of course, the evergreens were pretty, and the music fine; but all around me were happy groups of people, who could scarcely keep down merry Christmas long enough to do reverence to sacred Christmas. And nobody was alone but me. Every happy paterfamilias in his pew tantalized me, and the whole atmosphere of the place seemed so much better suited to every one else than me that I came away hating holidays worse than ever. Then I went to the play, and sat down in a box all alone by myself. Everybody seemed on the best of terms with everybody else, and jokes and banter passed from one to another with the most good-natured freedom. Everybody but me was in a little group of friends. I was the only person in the whole theatre that was alone. And then there was such clapping of hands, and roars of laughter, and shouts of delight at all the fun going on upon the stage, all of which was rendered doubly enjoyable by everybody having somebody with whom to share and interchange the pleasure, that my loneliness got simply unbearable, and I hated holidays infinitely worse than ever.

"By five o'clock the holiday became so intolerable that I said I'd go and get a dinner. The best dinner the town could provide. A sumptuous dinner for one. A dinner with many courses, with wines of the finest brands, with bright lights, with a cheerful fire, with every condition of comfort—and I'd see if I couldn't for once extract a little pleasure out of a holiday!

"The handsome dining-room at the club looked bright, but it was empty. Who dines at this club on Christmas but lonely bachelors? There was a flutter of surprise when I ordered a dinner, and the few attendants were, no doubt, glad of something to break the monotony of the hours.

"My dinner was well served. The spacious room looked lonely; but the white, snowy cloths, the rich window hangings, the warm tints of the walls, the sparkle of the fire in the steel grate, gave the room an air of elegance and cheerfulness; and then the table at which I dined was close to the window, and through the partly drawn curtains were visible centres of lonely, cold streets, with bright lights from many a window, it is true, but there was a storm, and snow began whirling through the street. I let my imagination paint the streets as cold and dreary as it would, just to extract a little pleasure by way of contrast from the brilliant room of which I was apparently sole master.

"I dined well, and recalled in fancy old, youthful Christmases, and pledged mentally many an old friend, and my melancholy was mellowing into a low, sad undertone, when, just as I was raising a glass of wine to my lips, I was startled by a picture at the windowpane. It was a pale, wild, haggard face, in a great cloud of black hair, pressed against the glass. As I looked it vanished. With a strange thrill at my heart, which my lips mocked with a derisive sneer, I finished the wine and set down the glass. It was, of course, only a beggar-girl that had crept up to the window and stole a glance at the bright scene within; but still the pale face troubled me a little, and threw a fresh shadow on my heart. I filled my glass once more with wine, and was again about to drink, when the face reappeared at the window. It was so white, so thin, with eyes so large, wild, and hungry-looking, and the black, unkempt hair, into which the snow had drifted, formed so strange and weird a frame to the picture, that I was fairly startled. Replacing, untasted, the liquor on the table, I rose and went close to the pane. The face had vanished, and I could see no object within many feet of the window. The storm had increased, and the snow was driving in wild gusts through the streets, which were empty, save here and there a hurrying wayfarer. The whole scene was cold, wild, and desolate, and I could not repress a keen thrill of sympathy for the child, whoever it was, whose only Christmas was to watch, in cold and storm, the rich banquet ungratefully enjoyed by the lonely bachelor. I resumed my place at the table; but the dinner was finished, and the wine had no further relish. I was haunted by the vision at the window, and began, with an unreasonable irritation at the interruption, to repeat with fresh warmth my detestation of holidays. One couldn't even dine alone on a holiday with any sort of comfort, I declared. On holidays one was tormented by too much pleasure on one side, and too much misery on the other. And then, I said, hunting for justification of my dislike of the day, 'How many other people are, like me, made miserable by seeing the fullness of enjoyment others possess!'

"Oh, yes, I know," sarcastically replied the bachelor to a comment of mine; "of course, all magnanimous, generous, and noble-souled people delight in seeing other people made happy, and are quite content to accept this vicarious felicity. But I, you see, and this dear little girl—"

"Dear little girl?"

"Oh, I forgot," said Bachelor Bluff, blushing a little, in spite of a desperate effort not to do so. "I didn't tell you. Well, it was so absurd! I kept thinking, thinking of the pale, haggard, lonely little girl on the cold and desolate side of the window-pane, and the over-fed, discontented, lonely old bachelor on the splendid side of the window-pane, and I didn't get much happier thinking about it, I can assure you. I drank glass after glass of the wine—not that I enjoyed its flavour any more, but mechanically, as it were, and with a sort of hope thereby to drown unpleasant reminders. I tried to attribute my annoyance in the matter to holidays, and so denounced them more vehemently than ever. I rose once in a while and went to the window, but could see no one to whom the pale face could have belonged.

"At last, in no very amiable mood, I got up, put on my wrappers, and went out; and the first thing I did was to run against a small figure crouching in the doorway. A face looked up quickly at the rough encounter, and I saw the pale features of the window-pane. I was very irritated and angry, and spoke harshly; and then, all at once, I am sure I don't know how it happened, but it flashed upon me that I, of all men, had no right to utter a harsh word to one oppressed with so wretched a Christmas as this poor creature was. I couldn't say another word, but began feeling in my pocket for some money, and then I asked a question or two, and then I don't quite know how it came about—isn't it very warm here?" exclaimed Bachelor Bluff, rising and walking about, and wiping the perspiration from his brow.

"Well, you see," he resumed nervously, "it was very absurd, but I did believe the girl's story—the old story, you know, of privation and suffering, and just thought I'd go home with the brat and see if what she said was all true. And then I remembered that all the shops were closed, and not a purchase could be made. I went back and persuaded the steward to put up for me a hamper of provisions, which the half-wild little youngster helped me carry through the snow, dancing with delight all the way. And isn't this enough?"

"Not a bit, Mr. Bluff. I must have the whole story."

"I declare," said Bachelor Bluff, "there's no whole story to tell. A widow with children in great need, that was what I found; and they had a feast that night, and a little money to buy them a load of wood and a garment or two the next day; and they were all so bright, and so merry, and so thankful, and so good, that, when I got home that night, I was mightily amazed that, instead of going to bed sour at holidays, I was in a state of great contentment in regard to holidays. In fact, I was really merry. I whistled. I sang. I do believe I cut a caper. The poor wretches I had left had been so merry over their unlooked-for Christmas banquet that their spirits infected mine.

"And then I got thinking again. Of course, holidays had been miserable to me, I said. What right had a well-to-do, lonely old bachelor hovering wistfully in the vicinity of happy circles, when all about there were so many people as lonely as he, and yet oppressed with want? 'Good gracious!' I exclaimed, 'to think of a man complaining of loneliness with thousands of wretches yearning for his help and comfort, with endless opportunities for work and company, with hundreds of pleasant and delightful things to do. Just to think of it! It put me in a great fury at myself to think of it. I tried pretty hard to escape from myself and began inventing excuses and all that sort of thing, but I rigidly forced myself to look squarely at my own conduct. And then I reconciled my confidence by declaring that, if ever after that day I hated a holiday again, might my holidays end at once and forever!

"Did I go and see my proteges again? What a question! Why—well, no matter. If the widow is comfortable now, it is because she has found a way to earn without difficulty enough for her few wants. That's no fault of mine. I would have done more for her, but she wouldn't let me. But just let me tell you about New Year's—the New-Year's day that followed the Christmas I've been describing. It was lucky for me there was another holiday only a week off. Bless you! I had so much to do that day I was completely bewildered, and the hours weren't half long enough. I did make a few social calls, but then I hurried them over; and then hastened to my little girl, whose face had already caught a touch of colour; and she, looking quite handsome in her new frock and her ribbons, took me to other poor folk, and,—well, that's about the whole story.

"Oh, as to the next Christmas. Well, I didn't dine alone, as you may guess. It was up three stairs, that's true, and there was none of that elegance that marked the dinner of the year before; but it was merry, and happy, and bright; it was a generous, honest, hearty Christmas dinner, that it was, although I do wish the widow hadn't talked so much about the mysterious way a turkey had been left at her door the night before. And

Molly—that's the little girl—and I had a rousing appetite. We went to church early; then we had been down to the Five Points to carry the poor outcasts there something for their Christmas dinner; in fact, we had done wonders of work, and Molly was in high spirits, and so the Christmas dinner was a great success.

"Dear me, sir, no! Just as you say. Holidays are not in the least wearisome any more. Plague on it! When a man tells me now that he hates holidays, I find myself getting very wroth. I pin him by the buttonhole at once, and tell him my experience. The fact is, if I were at dinner on a holiday, and anybody should ask me for a sentiment, I should say, 'God bless all holidays!'"

XXXI. MASTER SANDY'S SNAPDRAGON*

* This story was first published in Wide Awake, vol. 26.

ELDRIDGE S. BROOKS

There was just enough of December in the air and of May in the sky to make the Yuletide of the year of grace 1611 a time of pleasure and delight to every boy and girl in "Merrie England" from the princely children in stately Whitehall to the humblest pot-boy and scullery-girl in the hall of the country squire.

And in the palace at Whitehall even the cares of state gave place to the sports of this happy season. For that "Most High and Mighty Prince James, by the Grace of God King of Great Britain, France, and Ireland"— as you will find him styled in your copy of the Old Version, or what is known as "King James' Bible"—loved the Christmas festivities, cranky, crabbed, and crusty though he was. And this year he felt especially gracious. For now, first since the terror of the Guy Fawkes plot which had come to naught full seven years before, did the timid king feel secure on his throne; the translation of the Bible, on which so many learned men had been for years engaged, had just been issued from the press of Master Robert Baker; and, lastly, much profit was coming into the royal treasury from the new lands in the Indies and across the sea.

So it was to be a Merry Christmas in the palace at Whitehall. Great were the preparations for its celebration, and the Lord Henry, the handsome, wise and popular young Prince of Wales, whom men hoped some day to hail as King Henry of England, was to take part in a jolly Christmas mask, in which, too, even the little Prince Charles was to perform for the edification of the court when the mask should be shown in the new and gorgeous banqueting hall of the palace.

And to-night it was Christmas Eve. The Little Prince Charles and the Princess Elizabeth could scarcely wait for the morrow, so impatient were they to see all the grand devisings that were in store for them. So good Master Sandy, under-tutor to the Prince, proposed to wise Archie Armstrong, the King's jester, that they play at snapdragon for the children in the royal nursery.

The Prince and Princess clamoured for the promised game at once, and soon the flicker from the flaming bow lighted up the darkened nursery as, around the witchlike caldron, they watched their opportunity to snatch the lucky raisin. The room rang so loudly with fun and laughter that even the King himself, big of head and rickety of legs, shambled in good-humouredly to join in the sport that was giving so much pleasure to the royal boy he so dearly loved, and whom he always called "Baby Charles."

But what was snapdragon, you ask? A simple enough game, but dear for many and many a year to English children. A broad and shallow bowl or dish half-filled with blazing brandy, at the bottom of which lay numerous toothsome raisins—a rare tidbit in those days—and one of these, pierced with a gold button, was known as the "lucky raisin." Then, as the flaming brandy flickered and darted from the yawning bowl, even as did the flaming poison tongues of the cruel dragon that St. George of England conquered so valiantly, each one of the revellers sought to snatch a raisin from the burning bowl without singe or scar. And he who drew out the lucky raisin was winner and champion, and could claim a boon or reward for his superior skill. Rather a dangerous game, perhaps it seems, but folks were rough players in those old days and laughed at a burn or a bruise, taking them as part of the fun.

So around Master Sandy's Snapdragon danced the royal children, and even the King himself condescended to dip his royal hands in the flames, while Archie Armstrong the jester cried out: "Now fair and softly, brother

Jamie, fair and softly, man. There's ne'er a plum in all that plucking so worth the burning as there was in Signor Guy Fawkes' snapdragon when ye proved not to be his lucky raisin." For King's jesters were privileged characters in the old days, and jolly Archie Armstrong could joke with the King on this Guy Fawkes scare as none other dared.

And still no one brought out the lucky raisin, though the Princess Elizabeth's fair arm was scotched and good Master Sandy's peaked beard was singed, and my Lord Montacute had dropped his signet ring in the fiery dragon's mouth, and even His Gracious Majesty the King was nursing one of his royal fingers.

But just as through the parted arras came young Henry, Prince of Wales, little Prince Charles gave a boyish shout of triumph.

"Hey, huzzoy!" he cried, "'tis mine, 'tis mine! Look, Archie; see, dear dad; I have the lucky raisin! A boon, good folk; a boon for me!" And the excited lad held aloft the lucky raisin in which gleamed the golden button.

"Rarely caught, young York," cried Prince Henry, clapping his hands in applause. "I came in right in good time, did I not, to give you luck, little brother? And now, lad, what is the boon to be?"

And King James, greatly pleased at whatever his dear "Baby Charles" said or did, echoed his eldest son's question. "Ay lad, 'twas a rare good dip; so crave your boon. What does my bonny boy desire?"

But the boy hesitated. What was there that a royal prince, indulged as was he, could wish for or desire? He really could think of nothing, and crossing quickly to his elder brother, whom, boy-fashion, he adored, he whispered, "Ud's fish, Hal, what DO I want?"

Prince Henry placed his hand upon his brother's shoulder and looked smilingly into his questioning eyes, and all within the room glanced for a moment at the two lads standing thus.

And they were well worth looking at. Prince Henry of Wales, tall, comely, open-faced, and well-built, a noble lad of eighteen who called to men's minds, so "rare Ben Jonson" says, the memory of the hero of Agincourt, that other

> thunderbolt of war,

> Harry the Fifth, to whom in face you are

> So like, as Fate would have you so in worth;

Prince Charles, royal Duke of York, Knight of the Garter and of the Bath, fair in face and form, an active, manly, daring boy of eleven—the princely brothers made so fair a sight that the King, jealous and suspicious of Prince Henry's popularity though he was, looked now upon them both with loving eyes. But how those loving eyes would have grown dim with tears could this fickle, selfish, yet indulgent father have foreseen the sad and bitter fates of both his handsome boys.

But, fortunately, such foreknowledge is not for fathers or mothers, whatever their rank or station, and King James's only thought was one of pride in the two brave lads now whispering together in secret confidence. And into this he speedily broke.

"Come, come, Baby Charles," he cried, "stand no more parleying, but out and over with the boon ye crave as guerdon for your lucky plum. Ud's fish, lad, out with it; we'd get it for ye though it did rain jeddert staves here in Whitehall."

"So please your Grace," said the little Prince, bowing low with true courtier-like grace and suavity, "I will, with your permission, crave my boon as a Christmas favor at wassail time in to-morrow's revels."

And then he passed from the chamber arm-in-arm with his elder brother, while the King, chuckling greatly over the lad's show of courtliness and ceremony, went into a learned discussion with my lord of Montacute and Master Sandy as to the origin of the snapdragon, which he, with his customary assumption of deep learning, declared was "but a modern paraphrase, my lord, of the fable which telleth how Dan Hercules did kill the flaming dragon of Hesperia and did then, with the apple of that famous orchard, make a fiery dish of burning apple brandy which he did name 'snapdragon.'"

For King James VI of Scotland and I of England was, you see, something too much of what men call a pendant.

Christmas morning rose bright and glorious. A light hoarfrost whitened the ground and the keen December air nipped the noses as it hurried the song-notes of the score of little waifs who, gathered beneath the windows of the big palace, sung for the happy awaking of the young Prince Charles their Christmas carol and their Christmas noel:

A child this day is born,

A child of great renown;

Most worthy of a sceptre,

A sceptre and a crown.

Noel, noel, noel,

Noel sing we may

Because the King of all Kings

Was born this blessed day.

These tidings shepherds heard

In field watching their fold,

Were by an angel unto them

At night revealed and told.

Noel, noel, noel,

Noel sing we may

Because the King of all Kings

Was born this blessed day.

He brought unto them tidings

Of gladness and of mirth,

Which cometh to all people by

This holy infant's birth.

Noel, noel, noel,

Noel sing we may

Because the King of all Kings

Was born this blessed day.

The "blessed day" wore on. Gifts and sports filled the happy hours. In the royal banqueting hall the Christmas dinner was royally set and served, and King and Queen and Princes, with attendant nobles and holiday guests, partook of the strong dishes of those old days of hearty appetites.

"A shield of brawn with mustard, boyl'd capon, a chine of beef roasted, a neat's tongue roasted, a pig roasted, chewets baked, goose, swan and turkey roasted, a haunch of venison roasted, a pasty of venison, a kid stuffed with pudding, an olive-pye, capons and dowsets, sallats and fricases"—all these and much more, with strong beer and spiced ale to wash the dinner down, crowned the royal board, while the great boar's head and the Christmas pie, borne in with great parade, were placed on the table joyously decked with holly and rosemary and bay. It was a great ceremony—this bringing in of the boar's head. First came an attendant, so the old record tells us,

"attyr'd in a horseman's coat with a Boares-speare in his hande; next to him another huntsman in greene, with a bloody faulchion drawne; next to him two pages in tafatye sarcenet, each of them with a messe of mustard; next to whom came hee that carried the Boareshead, crosst with a greene silk scarfe, by which hunge the empty scabbard of the faulchion which was carried before him."

After the dinner—the boar's head having been wrestled for by some of the royal yeomen—came the wassail or health-drinking. Then the King said:

"And now, Baby Charles, let us hear the boon ye were to crave of us at wassail as the guerdon for the holder of the lucky raisin in Master Sandy's snapdragon."

And the little eleven-year-old Prince stood up before the company in all his brave attire, glanced at his brother Prince Henry, and then facing the King said boldly:

"I pray you, my father and my liege, grant me as the boon I ask—the freeing of Walter Raleigh."

At this altogether startling and unlooked-for request, amazement and consternation appeared on the faces around the royal banqueting board, and the King put down his untasted tankard of spiced ale, while surprise, doubt and anger quickly crossed the royal face. For Sir Walter Raleigh, the favourite of Queen Elizabeth, the lord-proprietor and colonizer of the American colonies, and the sworn foe to Spain, had been now close prisoner in the Tower for more than nine years, hated and yet dreaded by this fickle King James, who dared not put him to death for fear of the people to whom the name and valour of Raleigh were dear.

"Hoot, chiel!" cried the King at length, spluttering wrathfully in the broadest of his native Scotch, as was his habit when angered or surprised. "Ye reckless fou, wha hae put ye to sic a jackanape trick? Dinna ye ken that sic a boon is nae for a laddie like you to meddle wi'? Wha hae put ye to't, I say?"

But ere the young Prince could reply, the stately and solemn-faced ambassador of Spain, the Count of Gondemar, arose in the place of honour he filled as a guest of the King.

"My Lord King," he said, "I beg your majesty to bear in memory your pledge to my gracious master King Philip of Spain, that naught save grave cause should lead you to liberate from just durance that arch enemy of Spain, the Lord Raleigh."

"But you did promise me, my lord," said Prince Charles, hastily, "and you have told me that the royal pledge is not to be lightly broken."

"Ma certie, lad," said King James, "ye maunay learn that there is nae rule wi'out its aicciptions." And then he added, "A pledge to a boy in play, like to ours of yester-eve, Baby Charles, is not to be kept when matters of state conflict." Then turning to the Spanish ambassador, he said: "Rest content, my lord count. This recreant Raleigh shall not yet be loosed."

"But, my liege," still persisted the boy prince, "my brother Hal did say—"

The wrath of the King burst out afresh.

"Ay, said you so? Brother Hal, indeed!" he cried.

"I thought the wind blew from that quarter," and he angrily faced his eldest son. "So, sirrah; 'twas you that did urge this foolish boy to work your traitorous purpose in such coward guise!"

"My liege," said Prince Henry, rising in his place, "traitor and coward are words I may not calmly hear even from my father and my king. You wrong me foully when you use them thus. For though I do bethink me that the Tower is but a sorry cage in which to keep so grandly plumed a bird as my Lord of Raleigh, I did but seek—"

"Ay, you did but seek to curry favour with the craven crowd," burst out the now thoroughly angry King, always jealous of the popularity of this brave young Prince of Wales. "And am I, sirrah, to be badgered and browbeaten in my own palace by such a thriftless ne'er-do-weel as you, ungrateful boy, who seekest to gain preference with the people in this realm before your liege lord the King? Quit my presence, sirrah, and that instanter, ere that I do send you to spend your Christmas where your great-grandfather, King Henry, bade his astrologer spend his—in the Tower, there to keep company with your fitting comrade, Raleigh, the traitor!"

Without a word in reply to this outburst, with a son's submission, but with a royal dignity, Prince Henry bent his head before his father's decree and withdrew from the table, followed by the gentlemen of his household.

But ere he could reach the arrased doorway, Prince Charles sprang to his side and cried, valiantly: "Nay then, if he goes so do I! 'Twas surely but a Christmas joke and of my own devising. Spoil not our revel, my gracious liege and father, on this of all the year's red-letter days, by turning my thoughtless frolic into such bitter threatening. I did but seek to test the worth of Master Sandy's lucky raisin by asking for as wildly great a boon as might be thought upon. Brother Hal too, did but give me his advising in joke even as I did seek it. None here, my royal father, would brave your sovereign displeasure by any unknightly or unloyal scheme."

The gentle and dignified words of the young prince—for Charles Stuart, though despicable as a king, was ever loving and loyal as a friend—were as oil upon the troubled waters. The ruffled temper of the ambassador of Spain—who in after years really did work Raleigh's downfall and death—gave place to courtly bows, and the King's quick anger melted away before the dearly loved voice of his favourite son.

"Nay, resume your place, son Hal," he said, "and you, gentlemen all, resume your seats, I pray. I too did but jest as did Baby Charles here—a sad young wag, I fear me, is this same young Prince."

But as, after the wassail, came the Christmas mask, in which both Princes bore their parts, Prince Charles said to Archie Armstrong, the King's jester:

"Faith, good Archie; now is Master Sandy's snapdragon but a false beast withal, and his lucky raisin is but an evil fruit that pays not for the plucking."

And wise old Archie only wagged his head and answered, "Odd zooks, Cousin Charlie, Christmas raisins are not the only fruit that burns the fingers in the plucking, and mayhap you too may live to know that a mettlesome horse never stumbleth but when he is reined."

Poor "Cousin Charlie" did not then understand the full meaning of the wise old jester's words, but he did live to learn their full intent. For when, in after years, his people sought to curb his tyrannies with a revolt that ended only with his death upon the scaffold, outside this very banqueting house at Whitehall, Charles Stuart learned all too late that a "mettlesome horse" needed sometimes to be "reined," and heard, too late as well, the stern declaration of the Commons of England that "no chief officer might presume for the future to contrive the enslaving and destruction of the nation with impunity."

But though many a merry and many a happy day had the young Prince Charles before the dark tragedy of his sad and sorry manhood, he lost all faith in lucky raisins. Not for three years did Sir Walter Raleigh—whom both the Princes secretly admired—obtain release from the Tower, and ere three more years were past his head fell as a forfeit to the stern demands of Spain. And Prince Charles often declared that naught indeed could come from meddling with luck saving burnt fingers, "even," he said, "as came to me that profitless night when I sought a boon for snatching the lucky raisin from good Master Sandy's Christmas snapdragon."

XXXII. A CHRISTMAS FAIRY*

* Reprinted with the permission of the Henry Altemus Company.

JOHN STRANGE WINTER

It was getting very near to Christmas time, and all the boys at Miss Ware's school were talking about going home for the holidays.

"I shall go to the Christmas festival," said Bertie Fellows, "and my mother will have a party, and my Aunt will give another. Oh! I shall have a splendid time at home."

"My Uncle Bob is going to give me a pair of skates," remarked Harry Wadham.

"My father is going to give me a bicycle," put in George Alderson.

"Will you bring it back to school with you?" asked Harry.

"Oh! yes, if Miss Ware doesn't say no."

"Well, Tom," cried Bertie, "where are you going to spend your holidays?"

"I am going to stay here," answered Tom in a very forlorn voice.

"Here—at school—oh, dear! Why can't you go home?"

"I can't go home to India," answered Tom.

"Nobody said you could. But haven't you any relatives anywhere?"

Tom shook his head. "Only in India," he said sadly.

"Poor fellow! That's hard luck for you. I'll tell you what it is, boys, if I couldn't go home for the holidays, especially at Christmas—I think I would just sit down and die."

"Oh, no, you wouldn't," said Tom. "You would get ever so homesick, but you wouldn't die. You would just get through somehow, and hope something would happen before next year, or that some kind fairy would—"

"There are no fairies nowadays," said Bertie.

"See here, Tom, I'll write and ask my mother to invite you to go home with me for the holidays."

"Will you really?"

"Yes, I will. And if she says yes, we shall have such a splendid time. We live in London, you know, and have lots of parties and fun."

"Perhaps she will say no?" suggested poor little Tom.

"My mother isn't the kind that says no," Bertie declared loudly.

In a few days' time a letter arrived from Bertie's mother. The boy opened it eagerly. It said:

My own dear Bertie:

I am very sorry to tell you that little Alice is ill with scarlet fever. And so you cannot come for your holidays. I would have been glad to have you bring your little friend with you if all had been well here.

Your father and I have decided that the best thing that you can do is to stay at Miss Ware's. We shall send your Christmas present to you as well as we can.

It will not be like coming home, but I am sure you will try to be happy, and make me feel that you are helping me in this sad time.

Dear little Alice is very ill, very ill indeed. Tell Tom that I am sending you a box for both of you, with two of everything. And tell him that it makes me so much happier to know that you will not be alone.

Your own mother.

When Bertie Fellows received this letter, which ended all his Christmas hopes and joys, he hid his face upon his desk and sobbed aloud. The lonely boy from India, who sat next to him, tried to comfort his friend in every way he could think of. He patted his shoulder and whispered many kind words to him.

At last Bertie put the letter into Tom's hands. "Read it," he sobbed.

So then Tom understood the cause of Bertie's grief. "Don't fret over it," he said at last. "It might be worse. Why, your father and mother might be thousands of miles away, like mine are. When Alice is better, you will be able to go home. And it will help your mother if she thinks you are almost as happy as if you could go now."

Soon Miss Ware came to tell Bertie how sorry she was for him.

"After all," said she, smiling down on the two boys, "it is an ill wind that blows nobody good. Poor Tom has been expecting to spend his holidays alone, and now he will have a friend with him—Try to look on the bright side, Bertie, and to remember how much worse it would have been if there had been no boy to stay with you."

"I can't help being disappointed, Miss Ware," said Bertie, his eyes filling with tears.

"No; you would be a strange boy if you were not. But I want you to try to think of your poor mother, and write her as cheerfully as you can."

"Yes," answered Bertie; but his heart was too full to say more.

The last day of the term came, and one by one, or two by two, the boys went away, until only Bertie and Tom were left in the great house. It had never seemed so large to either of them before.

"It's miserable," groaned poor Bertie, as they strolled into the schoolroom. "Just think if we were on our way home now—how different."

"Just think if I had been left here by myself," said Tom.

"Yes," said Bertie, "but you know when one wants to go home he never thinks of the boys that have no home to go to."

The evening passed, and the two boys went to bed. They told stories to each other for a long time before they could go to sleep. That night they dreamed of their homes, and felt very lonely. Yet each tried to be brave, and so another day began.

This was the day before Christmas. Quite early in the morning came the great box of which Bertie's mother had spoken in her letter. Then, just as dinner had come to an end, there was a peal of the bell, and a voice was heard asking for Tom Egerton.

Tom sprang to his feet, and flew to greet a tall, handsome lady, crying, "Aunt Laura! Aunt Laura!"

And Laura explained that she and her husband had arrived in London only the day before. "I was so afraid, Tom," she said, "that we should not get here until Christmas Day was over and that you would be disappointed. So I would not let your mother write you that we were on our way home. You must get your things packed up at once, and go back with me to London. Then uncle and I will give you a splendid time."

For a minute or two Tom's face shone with delight. Then he caught sight of Bertie and turned to his aunt.

"Dear Aunt Laura," he said, "I am very sorry, but I can't go."

"Can't go? and why not?"

"Because I can't go and leave Bertie here all alone," he said stoutly. "When I was going to be alone he wrote and asked his mother to let me go home with him. She could not have either of us because Bertie's sister has scarlet fever. He has to stay here, and he has never been away from home at Christmas time before, and I can't go away and leave him by himself, Aunt Laura."

For a minute Aunt Laura looked at the boy as if she could not believe him. Then she caught him in her arms and kissed him.

"You dear little boy, you shall not leave him. You shall bring him along, and we shall all enjoy ourselves together. Bertie, my boy, you are not very old yet, but I am going to teach you a lesson as well as I can. It is that kindness is never wasted in this world."

And so Bertie and Tom found that there was such a thing as a fairy after all.

XXXIII. THE GREATEST OF THESE*

*This story was first printed in the Youth's Companion, vol. 76.

JOSEPH MILLS HANSON

The outside door swung open suddenly, letting a cloud of steam into the small, hot kitchen. Charlie Moore, a milk pail in one hand, a lantern in the other, closed the door behind him with a bang, set the pail on the table and stamped the snow from his feet.

"There's the milk, and I near froze gettin' it," said he, addressing his partner, who was chopping potatoes in a pan on the stove.

"Dose vried bodadoes vas burnt," said the other, wielding his knife vigorously.

"Are, eh? Why didn't you watch 'em instead of readin' your old Scandinavian paper?" answered Charlie, hanging his overcoat and cap behind the door and laying his mittens under the stove to dry. Then he drew up a chair and with much exertion pulled off his heavy felt boots and stood them beside his mittens.

"Why didn't you shut the gate after you came in from town? The cows got out and went up to Roney's an' I had to chase 'em; 'tain't any joke runnin' round after cows such a night as this." Having relieved his mind of its grievance, Charlie sat down before the oven door, and, opening it, laid a stick of wood along its outer edge and thrust his feet into the hot interior, propping his heels against the stick.

"Look oud for dese har biscuits!" exclaimed his partner, anxiously.

"Oh, hang the biscuits!" was Charlie's hasty answer. "I'll watch 'em. Why didn't you?"

"Ay tank Ay fergit hem."

"Well, you don't want to forget. A feller forgot his clothes once, an' he got froze."

"Ay gass dose taller vas ketch in a sbring snowstorm. Vas dose biscuits done, Sharlie?"

"You bet they are, Nels," replied Charlie, looking into the pan.

"Dan subbar vas ready. Yom on!"

Nels picked up the frying-pan and Charlie the biscuits, and set them on the oilcloth-covered table, where a plate of butter, a jar of plum jelly, and a coffee-pot were already standing.

Outside the frozen kitchen window the snow-covered fields and meadows stretched, glistening and silent, away to the dark belt of timber by the river. Along the deep-rutted road in front a belated lumber-wagon passed slowly, the wheels crunching through the packed snow with a wavering, incessant shriek.

The two men hitched their chairs up to the table, and without ceremony helped themselves liberally to the steaming food. For a few moments they seemed oblivious to everything but the demands of hunger. The potatoes and biscuits disappeared with surprising rapidity, washed down by large drafts of coffee. These men, labouring steadily through the short daylight hours in the dry, cold air of the Dakota winter, were like engines whose fires had burned low—they were taking fuel. Presently, the first keen edge of appetite satisfied, they ate more slowly, and Nels, straightening up with a sigh, spoke:

"Ay seen Seigert in town ta-day. Ha vants von hundred fifty fer dose team."

"Come down, eh?" commented Charlie. "Well, they're worth that. We'd better take 'em, Nels. We'll need 'em in the spring if we break the north forty."

"Yas, et's a nice team," agreed Nels. "Ha vas driven ham ta-day."

"Is he haulin' corn?"

"Na; he had his kids oop gettin' Christmas bresents."

"Chris—By gracious! to-morrow's Christmas!"

Nels nodded solemnly, as one possessing superior knowledge. Charlie became thoughtful.

"We'll come in sort of slim on it here, I reckon, Nels. Christmas ain't right, somehow, out here. Back in Wisconsin, where I came from, there's where you get your Christmas!" Charlie spoke with the unswerving prejudice of mankind for the land of his birth.

"Yas, dose been right. En da ol' kontry dey havin' gret times Christmas."

Their thoughts were all bent now upon the holiday scenes of the past. As they finished the meal and cleared away and washed the dishes they related incidents of their boyhood's time, compared, reiterated, and embellished. As they talked they grew jovial, and laughed often.

"The skee broke an' you went over kerplunk, hey? Haw, haw! That reminds me of one time in Wisconsin—"

Something of the joyous spirit of the Christmastide seemed to have entered into this little farmhouse set in the midst of the lonely, white fields. In the hearts of these men, moving about in their dim-lighted room, was reechoed the joyous murmur of the great world without: the gayety of the throngs in city streets, where the brilliant shop-windows, rich with holiday spoils, smile out upon the passing crowd, and the clang of street-cars and roar of traffic mingle with the cries of street-venders. The work finished, they drew their chairs to the stove, and filled their pipes, still talking.

"Well, well," said Charlie, after the laugh occasioned by one of Nels' droll stories had subsided. "It's nice to think of those old times. I'd hate to have been one of these kids that can't have any fun. Christmas or any other time."

"Ay gass dere ain't anybody much dot don'd have someding dis tams a year."

"Oh, yes, there are, Nels! You bet there are!"

Charlie nodded at his partner with serious conviction.

"Now, there's the Roneys," he waved his pipe over his shoulder. "The old man told me to-night when I was up after the cows that he's sold all the crops except what they need for feedin'—wheat, and corn, and everything, and some hogs besides—and ain't got hardly enough now for feed and clothes for all that family. The rent and the lumber he had to buy to build the new barn after the old one burnt ate up the money like fury. He kind of laughed, and said he guessed the children wouldn't get much Christmas this year. I didn't think about it's being so close when he told me."

"No Christmas!" Nels' round eyes widened with astonishment. "Ay tank dose been pooty bad!" He studied the subject for a few moments, his stolid face suddenly grown thoughtful. Charlie stared at the stove. Far away by the river a lonely coyote set up his quick, howling yelp.

"Dere's been seven kids oop dere," said Nels at last, glancing up as it for corroboration.

"Yes, seven," agreed Charlie.

"Say, do ve need Seigert's team very pad?"

"Well, now that depends," said Charlie. "Why not?"

"Nothin', only Ay vas tankin' ve might tak' some a das veat we vas goin' to sell and—and—"

"Yep, what?"

"And dumb it on Roney's granary floor to-night after dere been asleeb."

Charlie stared at his companion for a moment in silence. Then he rose, and, approaching Nels, examined his partner's face with solemn scrutiny.

"By the great horn spoon," he announced, finally, "you've got a head on you like a balloon, my boy! Keep on gettin' ideas like that, and you'll land in Congress or the poor-farm before many years!"

Then, abandoning his pretense of gravity, he slapped the other on the back.

"Why didn't I think of that? It's the best yet. Seigert's team? Oh, hang Seigert's team. We don't need it. We'll have a little merry Christmas out of this yet. Only they mustn't know where it came from. I'll write a note and stick it under the door, 'You'll find some merry wheat—'No, that ain't it. 'You'll find some wheat in the granary to give the kids a merry Christmas with,' signed, 'Santa Claus.'"

He wrote out the message in the air with a pointing forefinger. He had entered into the spirit of the thing eagerly.

"It's half-past nine now," he went on, looking at the clock. "It'll be eleven time we get the stuff loaded and hauled up there. Let's go out and get at it. Lucky the bobs are on the wagon; they don't make such a racket as wheels."

He took the lantern from its nail behind the door and lighted it, after which he put on his boots, cap, and mittens, and flung his overcoat across his shoulders. Nels, meanwhile, had put on his outer garments, also.

"Shut up the stove, Nels." Charlie blew out the light and opened the door. "There, hang it!" he exclaimed, turning back. "I forgot the note. Ought to be in ink, I suppose. Well, never mind now; we won't put on any style about it."

He took down a pencil from the shelf, and, extracting a bit of wrapping paper from a bundle behind the woodbox, wrote the note by the light of the lantern.

"There, I guess that will do," he said, finally. "Come on!"

Outside, the night air was cold and bracing, and in the black vault of the sky the winter constellations flashed and throbbed. The shadows of the two men, thrown by the lantern, bobbed huge and grotesque across the snow and among the bare branches of the cottonwoods, as they moved toward the barn.

"Ay tank ve put on dose extra side poards and make her an even fifty pushel," said Nels, after they had backed the wagon up to the granary door. "Ve might as vell do it oop right, skence ve're at it."

Having carried out this suggestion, the two shovelled steadily, with short intervals of rest, for three quarters of an hour, the dark pile of grain in the wagon-box rising gradually until it stood flush with the top.

Good it was to look upon, cold and soft and yielding to the touch, this heaped-up wealth from the inexhaustible treasure-house of the mighty West. Charlie and Nels felt something of this as they viewed the results of their labours for a moment before hitching up the team.

"It's A number one hard," said Charlie, picking up a handful and sifting it slowly through his fingers, "and it'll fetch seventy-four cents. But you can't raise any worse on this old farm of ours if you try," he added, a little proudly. "Nor anywhere else in the Jim River Valley, for that matter."

As they approached the Roney place, looking dim and indistinct in the darkness, their voices hushed apprehensively, and the noise of the sled-runners slipping through the snow seemed to them to increase from a purr to a roar.

"Here, stob a minute!" whispered Nels, in agony of discovery. "Ve're magin' an awful noise. Ay'll go und take a beek."

He slipped away and cautiously approached the house. "Et's all right," he whispered, hoarsely, returning after a moment; "dere all asleeb. But go easy; Ay tank ve pest go easy." They seemed burdened all at once with the consciences of criminals, and went forward with almost guilty timidity.

"Thunder, dere's a bump! Vy don'd you drive garefuller, Sharlie?"

"Drive yourself, if you think you can do any better!" As they came into the yard a dog suddenly ran out from the barn, barking furiously. Charlie reined up with an ejaculation of despair; "Look there, the dog! We're done for now, sure! Stop him, Nels! Throw somethin' at 'im!"

The noise seemed to their excited ears louder than the crash of artillery. Nels threw a piece of snow crust. The dog ran back a few steps, but his barking did not diminish.

"Here, hold the lines. I'll try to catch 'im." Charlie jumped from the wagon and approached the dog with coaxing words: "Come, doggie, good doggie, nice boy, come!"

His manoeuvre, however, merely served to increase the animal's frenzy. As Charlie approached the dog retired slowly toward the house, his head thrown back, and his rapid barking increased to a long-drawn howl.

"Good boy, come! Bother the brute! He'll wake up the whole household! Nice doggie! Phe-e—"

The noise, however, had no apparent effect upon the occupants of the house. All remained as dark and silent as ever.

"Sharlie, Sharlie, let him go!" cried Nels, in a voice smothered with laughter. "Ay go in dose parn; maype ha'll chase me."

His hope was well founded. The dog, observing this treacherous occupation by the enemy of his last harbour of refuge, gave pursuit and disappeared within the door, which Charlie, hard behind him, closed with a bang. There was the sound of a hurried scuffle within. The dog's barking gave place to terrified whinings, which in turn were suddenly quenched to a choking murmur.

"Gome in, Sharlie, kvick!"

"You got him?" queried Charlie, opening the door cautiously. "Did he bite you?"

"Na, yust ma mitten. Gat a sack or someding da die him oop in."

A sack was procured from somewhere, into which the dog, now silenced from sheer exhaustion and fright, was unceremoniously thrust, after which the sack was tied and flung into the wagon. This formidable obstacle overcome and the Roneys still slumbering peacefully, the rest was easy. The granary door was pried open and the wheat shovelled hurriedly in upon the empty floor. Charlie then crept up to the house and slipped his note under the door.

The sack was lifted from the now empty wagon and opened before the barn, whereupon its occupant slipped meekly out and retreated at once to a far corner, seemingly too much incensed at his discourteous treatment even to fling a volley of farewell barks at his departing captors.

"Vell," remarked Nels, with a sigh of relief as they gained the road, "Ay tank dose Roneys pelieve en Santa Claus now. Dose peen funny vay fer Santa Claus to coom."

Charlie's laugh was good to hear. "He didn't exactly come down the chimney, that's a fact, but it'll do at a pinch. We ought to have told them to get a present for the dog—collar and chain. I reckon he wouldn't hardly be thankful for it, though, eh?"

"Ay gass not. Ha liges ta haf hes nights ta hemself."

"Well, we had our fun, anyway. Sort of puts me in mind of old Wisconsin, somehow."

From far off over the valley, with its dismantled cornfields and snow-covered haystacks, beyond the ice-bound river, floated slow, and sonorous, the mellow clanging of church bells. They were ushering in the Christmas morn. Overhead the starlit heavens glistened, brooding and mysterious, looking down with luminous, loving eyes upon these humble sons of men doing a good deed, from the impulse of simple, generous hearts, as upon that other Christmas morning, long ago, when the Jewish shepherds, guarding their flocks by night, read in their shining depths that in Bethlehem of Judea the Christ-Child was born.

The rising sun was touching the higher hilltops with a faint rush of crimson the next morning when the back door of the Roney house opened with a creak, and Mr. Roney, still heavy-eyed with sleep, stumbled out upon the porch, stretched his arms above his head, yawned, blinked at the dazzling snow, and then shambled off toward the barn. As he approached, the dog ran eagerly out, gambolled meekly around his feet and caressed his boots. The man patted him kindly.

"Hello, old boy! What were you yappin' around so for last night, huh? Grain-thieves? You needn't worry about them. There ain't nothin' left for them to steal. No, sir! If they got into that granary they'd have to take a lantern along to find a pint of wheat. I don't suppose," he added, reflectively, "that I could scrape up enough to feed the chickens this mornin', but I guess I might's well see."

He passed over to the little building. What he saw when he looked within seemed for a moment to produce no impression upon him whatever. He stared at the hillock of grain in motionless silence. Finally Mr. Roney gave utterance to a single word, "Geewhilikins!" and started for the house on a run. Into the kitchen, where his wife was just starting the fire, the excited man burst like a whirlwind.

"Come out here, Mary!" he cried. "Come out here, quick!"

The worthy woman, unaccustomed to such demonstrations, looked at him in amazement.

"For goodness sake, what's come over you, Peter Roney?" she exclaimed. "Are you daft? Don't make such a noise! You'll wake the young ones, and I don't want them waked till need be, with no Christmas for 'em, poor little things!"

"Never mind the young 'uns," he replied. "Come on!"

As they passed out he noticed the slip of paper under the door and picked it up, but without comment.

He charged down upon the granary, his wife, with a shawl over her head, close behind.

She peered in, apprehensively at first, then with eyes of widening wonder.

"Why, Peter!" she said, turning to him. "Why, Peter! What does—I thought—"

"You thought!" he broke in. "Me, too. But it ain't so. It means that we've got some of the best neighbours that ever was, a thinkin' of our young 'uns this way! Read that!" and he thrust the paper into her hand.

"Why, Peter!" she ejaculated again, weakly. Then suddenly she turned, and laying her head on his shoulder, began to sob softly.

"There, there," he said, patting her arm awkwardly.

"Don't you go and cry now. Let's just be thankful to the good Lord for puttin' such fellers into the world as them fellers down the road. And now you run in and hurry up breakfast while I do up the chores. Then we'll hitch up and get into town 'fore the stores close. Tell the young 'uns Santy didn't get round last night with their things, but we've got word to meet him in town. Hey? Yes, I saw just the kind of sled Pete wants when I was up yesterday, and that china doll for Mollie. Yes, tell 'em anything you want. Twon't be too big. Santy Claus has come to Roney's ranch this year, sure!"

XXXIV. LITTLE GRETCHEN AND THE WOODEN SHOE*

* From "Christmastide," published by the Chicago Kindergarten College, copyright 1902.

ELIZABETH HARRISON

The following story is one of many which has drifted down to us from the story-loving nurseries and hearthstones of Germany. I cannot recall when I first had it told to me as a child, varied, of course, by different tellers, but always leaving that sweet, tender impression of God's loving care for the least of his children. I have since read different versions of it in at least a half-dozen story books for children.

Once upon a time, a long time ago, far away across the great ocean, in a country called Germany, there could be seen a small log hut on the edge of a great forest, whose fir-trees extended for miles and miles to the north. This little house, made of heavy hewn logs, had but one room in it. A rough pine door gave entrance to this room, and a small square window admitted the light. At the back of the house was built an old-fashioned stone chimney, out of which in winter usually curled a thin, blue smoke, showing that there was not very much fire within.

Small as the house was, it was large enough for the two people who lived in it. I want to tell you a story to-day about these two people. One was an old, gray-haired woman, so old that the little children of the village, nearly half a mile away, often wondered whether she had come into the world with the huge mountains, and the great fir-trees, which stood like giants back of her small hut. Her face was wrinkled all over with deep lines, which, if the children could only have read aright, would have told them of many years of cheerful, happy, self-sacrifice, of loving, anxious watching beside sick-beds, of quiet endurance of pain, of many a day of hunger and cold, and of a thousand deeds of unselfish love for other people; but, of course, they could not read this strange handwriting. They only knew that she was old and wrinkled, and that she stooped as she walked. None of them seemed to fear her, for her smile was always cheerful, and she had a kindly word for each of them if they chanced to meet her on her way to and from the village. With this old, old woman lived a very little girl. So bright and happy was she that the travellers who passed by the lonesome little house on the edge of the forest often thought of a sunbeam as they saw her. These two people were known in the village as Granny Goodyear and Little Gretchen.

The winter had come and the frost had snapped off many of the smaller branches from the pine-trees in the forest. Gretchen and her Granny were up by daybreak each morning. After their simple breakfast of oatmeal, Gretchen would run to the little closet and fetch Granny's old woollen shawl, which seemed almost as old as Granny herself. Gretchen always claimed the right to put the shawl over her Granny's head, even though she had to climb onto the wooden bench to do it. After carefully pinning it under Granny's chin, she gave her a good-bye kiss, and Granny started out for her morning's work in the forest. This work was nothing more nor less than the gathering up of the twigs and branches which the autumn winds and winter frosts had thrown upon the ground. These were carefully gathered into a large bundle which Granny tied together with a strong linen band. She then managed to lift the bundle to her shoulder and trudged off to the village with it. Here she sold the fagots for kindling wood to the people of the village. Sometimes she would get only a few pence each day, and sometimes a dozen or more, but on this money little Gretchen and she managed to live; they had their home, and the forest kindly furnished the wood for the fire which kept them warm in cold weather.

In the summer time Granny had a little garden at the back of the hut where she raised, with little Gretchen's help, a few potatoes and turnips and onions. These she carefully stored away for winter use. To this meagre supply, the pennies, gained by selling the twigs from the forest, added the oatmeal for Gretchen and a little black coffee for Granny. Meat was a thing they never thought of having. It cost too much money. Still, Granny and Gretchen were very happy, because they loved each other dearly. Sometimes Gretchen would be left alone all day long in the hut, because Granny would have some work to do in the village after selling her bundle of sticks and twigs. It was during these long days that little Gretchen had taught herself to sing the song which the wind sang to the pine branches. In the summer time she learned the chirp and twitter of the birds, until her voice might almost be mistaken for a bird's voice; she learned to dance as the swaying shadows did, and even to talk to the stars which shone through the little square window when Granny came home too late or too tired to talk.

Sometimes, when the weather was fine, or her Granny had an extra bundle of newly knitted stockings to take to the village, she would let little Gretchen go along with her. It chanced that one of these trips to the town came just the week before Christmas, and Gretchen's eyes were delighted by the sight of the lovely Christmas-trees which stood in the window of the village store. It seemed to her that she would never tire of looking at the knit dolls, the woolly lambs, the little wooden shops with their queer, painted men and women in them, and all the other fine things. She had never owned a plaything in her whole life; therefore, toys which you and I would not think much of, seemed to her to be very beautiful.

That night, after their supper of baked potatoes was over, and little Gretchen had cleared away the dishes and swept up the hearth, because Granny dear was so tired, she brought her own small wooden stool and placed it very near Granny's feet and sat down upon it, folding her hands on her lap. Granny knew that this meant she wanted to talk about something, so she smilingly laid away the large Bible which she had been reading, and took up her knitting, which was as much as to say: "Well, Gretchen, dear, Granny is ready to listen."

"Granny," said Gretchen slowly, "it's almost Christmas time, isn't it?"

"Yes, dearie," said Granny, "only five more days now," and then she sighed, but little Gretchen was so happy that she did not notice Granny's sigh.

"What do you think, Granny, I'll get this Christmas?" said she, looking up eagerly into Granny's face.

"Ah, child, child," said Granny, shaking her head, "you'll have no Christmas this year. We are too poor for that."

"Oh, but, Granny," interrupted little Gretchen, "think of all the beautiful toys we saw in the village to-day. Surely Santa Claus has sent enough for every little child."

"Ah, dearie," said Granny, "those toys are for people who can pay money for them, and we have no money to spend for Christmas toys."

"Well, Granny," said Gretchen, "perhaps some of the little children who live in the great house on the hill at the other end of the village will be willing to share some of their toys with me. They will be so glad to give some to a little girl who has none."

"Dear child, dear child," said Granny, leaning forward and stroking the soft, shiny hair of the little girl, "your heart is full of love. You would be glad to bring a Christmas to every child; but their heads are so full of what they are going to get that they forget all about anybody else but themselves." Then she sighed and shook her head.

"Well, Granny," said Gretchen, her bright, happy tone of voice growing a little less joyous, "perhaps the dear Santa Claus will show some of the village children how to make presents that do not cost money, and some of them may surprise me Christmas morning with a present. And, Granny, dear," added she, springing up from her low stool, "can't I gather some of the pine branches and take them to the old sick man who lives in the house by the mill, so that he can have the sweet smell of our pine forest in his room all Christmas day?"

"Yes, dearie," said Granny, "you may do what you can to make the Christmas bright and happy, but you must not expect any present yourself."

"Oh, but, Granny," said little Gretchen, her face brightening, "you forget all about the shining Christmas angels, who came down to earth and sang their wonderful song the night the beautiful Christ-Child was born! They are so loving and good that they will not forget any little child. I shall ask my dear stars to-night to tell them of us. You know," she added, with a look of relief, "the stars are so very high that they must know the angels quite well, as they come and go with their messages from the loving God."

Granny sighed, as she half whispered, "Poor child, poor child!" but Gretchen threw her arm around Granny's neck and gave her a hearty kiss, saying as she did so: "Oh, Granny, Granny, you don't talk to the stars often enough, else you wouldn't be sad at Christmas time." Then she danced all around the room, whirling her little skirts about her to show Granny how the wind had made the snow dance that day. She looked so droll and funny that Granny forgot her cares and worries and laughed with little Gretchen over her new snow-dance. The days passed on, and the morning before Christmas Eve came. Gretchen having tidied up the little room—for Granny had taught her to be a careful little housewife—was off to the forest, singing a birdlike song, almost as happy and free as the birds themselves. She was very busy that day, preparing a surprise for Granny. First, however, she gathered the most beautiful of the fir branches within her reach to take the next morning to the old sick man who lived by the mill. The day was all too short for the happy little girl. When Granny came trudging wearily home that night, she found the frame of the doorway covered with green pine branches.

"It's to welcome you, Granny! It's to welcome you!" cried Gretchen; "our old dear home wanted to give you a Christmas welcome. Don't you see, the branches of evergreen make it look as if it were smiling all over, and it is trying to say, 'A happy Christmas' to you, Granny!"

Granny laughed and kissed the little girl, as they opened the door and went in together. Here was a new surprise for Granny. The four posts of the wooden bed, which stood in one corner of the room, had been trimmed by the busy little fingers, with smaller and more flexible branches of the pine-trees. A small bouquet of red mountain-ash berries stood at each side of the fireplace, and these, together with the trimmed posts of the bed, gave the plain old room quite a festival look. Gretchen laughed and clapped her hands and danced about until the house seemed full of music to poor, tired Granny, whose heart had been sad as she turned toward their home that night, thinking of the disappointment which must come to loving little Gretchen the next morning.

After supper was over little Gretchen drew her stool up to Granny's side, and laying her soft, little hands on Granny's knee, asked to be told once again the story of the coming of the Christ-Child; how the night that he was born the beautiful angels had sung their wonderful song, and how the whole sky had become bright with a strange and glorious light, never seen by the people of earth before. Gretchen had heard the story many, many times before, but she never grew tired of it, and now that Christmas Eve had come again, the happy little child wanted to hear it once more.

When Granny had finished telling it the two sat quiet and silent for a little while thinking it over; then Granny rose and said that it was time for them to go to bed. She slowly took off her heavy wooden shoes, such as are worn in that country, and placed them beside the hearth. Gretchen looked thoughtfully at them for a minute or two, and then she said, "Granny, don't you think that somebody in all this wide world will think of us to-night?"

"Nay, Gretchen," said Granny, "I don't think any one will."

"Well, then, Granny," said Gretchen, "the Christmas angels will, I know; so I am going to take one of your wooden shoes, and put it on the windowsill outside, so that they may see it as they pass by. I am sure the stars will tell the Christmas angels where the shoe is."

"Ah, you foolish, foolish child," said Granny, "you are only getting ready for a disappointment To-morrow morning there will be nothing whatever in the shoe. I can tell you that now."

But little Gretchen would not listen. She only shook her head and cried out: "Ah, Granny, you don't talk enough to the stars." With this she seized the shoe, and, opening the door, hurried out to place it on the windowsill. It was very dark without, and something soft and cold seemed to gently kiss her hair and face. Gretchen knew by this that it was snowing, and she looked up to the sky, anxious to see if the stars were in sight, but a strong wind was tumbling the dark, heavy snow-clouds about and had shut away all else.

"Never mind," said Gretchen softly to herself, "the stars are up there, even if I can't see them, and the Christmas angels do not mind snowstorms."

Just then a rough wind went sweeping by the little girl, whispering something to her which she could not understand, and then it made a sudden rush up to the snow-clouds and parted them, so that the deep, mysterious sky appeared beyond, and shining down out of the midst of it was Gretchen's favourite star.

"Ah, little star, little star!" said the child, laughing aloud, "I knew you were there, though I couldn't see you. Will you whisper to the Christmas angels as they come by that little Gretchen wants so very much to have a Christmas gift to-morrow morning, if they have one to spare, and that she has put one of Granny's shoes upon the windowsill ready for it?"

A moment more and the little girl, standing on tiptoe, had reached the windowsill and placed the shoe upon it, and was back again in the house beside Granny and the warm fire.

The two went quietly to bed, and that night as little Gretchen knelt to pray to the Heavenly Father, she thanked him for having sent the Christ-Child into the world to teach all mankind how to be loving and unselfish, and in a few moments she was quietly sleeping, dreaming of the Christmas angels.

The next morning, very early, even before the sun was up, little Gretchen was awakened by the sound of sweet music coming from the village. She listened for a moment and then she knew that the choir-boys were singing the Christmas carols in the open air of the village street. She sprang up out of bed and began to dress herself as quickly as possible, singing as she dressed. While Granny was slowly putting on her clothes, little Gretchen, having finished dressing herself, unfastened the door and hurried out to see what the Christmas angels had left in the old wooden shoe.

The white snow covered everything—trees, stumps, roads, and pastures—until the whole world looked like fairyland. Gretchen climbed up on a large stone which was beneath the window and carefully lifted down the wooden shoe. The snow tumbled off of it in a shower over the little girl's hands, but she did not heed that; she ran hurriedly back into the house, putting her hand into the toe of the shoe as she ran.

"Oh, Granny! Oh, Granny!" she exclaimed, "you didn't believe the Christmas angels would think about us, but see, they have, they have! Here is a dear little bird nestled down in the toe of your shoe! Oh, isn't he beautiful?"

Granny came forward and looked at what the child was holding lovingly in her hand. There she saw a tiny chick-a-dee, whose wing was evidently broken by the rough and boisterous winds of the night before, and who had taken shelter in the safe, dry toe of the old wooden shoe. She gently took the little bird out of Gretchen's hands, and skilfully bound his broken wing to his side, so that he need not hurt himself by trying to fly with it. Then she showed Gretchen how to make a nice warm nest for the little stranger, close beside the fire, and when their breakfast was ready she let Gretchen feed the little bird with a few moist crumbs.

Later in the day Gretchen carried the fresh, green boughs to the old sick man by the mill, and on her way home stopped to see and enjoy the Christmas toys of some other children whom she knew, never once wishing that they were hers. When she reached home she found that the little bird had gone to sleep. Soon, however, he opened his eyes and stretched his head up, saying just as plain as a bird could say, "Now, my new friends, I want you to give me something more to eat." Gretchen gladly fed him again, and then, holding him in her lap, she softly and gently stroked his gray feathers until the little creature seemed to lose all fear of her. That evening Granny taught her a Christmas hymn and told her another beautiful Christmas story. Then Gretchen made up a funny little story to tell to the birdie. He winked his eyes and turned his head from side to side in such a droll fashion that Gretchen laughed until the tears came.

As Granny and she got ready for bed that night, Gretchen put her arms softly around Granny's neck, and whispered: "What a beautiful Christmas we have had to-day, Granny! Is there anything in the world more lovely than Christmas?"

"Nay, child, nay," said Granny, "not to such loving hearts as yours."

XXXV. CHRISTMAS ON BIG RATTLE*

* This story was first printed in the Youth's Companion, Dec. 14, 1905.

THEODORE GOODRIDGE ROBERTS

Archer sat by the rude hearth of his Big Rattle camp, brooding in a sort of tired contentment over the spitting fagots of var and glowing coals of birch.

It was Christmas Eve. He had been out on his snowshoes all that day, and all the day before, springing his traps along the streams and putting his deadfalls out of commission—rather queer work for a trapper to be about.

But Archer, despite all his gloomy manner, was really a sentimentalist, who practised what he felt.

"Christmas is a season of peace on earth," he had told himself, while demolishing the logs of a sinister deadfall with his axe; and now the remembrance of his quixotic deed added a brightness to the fire and to the rough, undecorated walls of the camp.

Outside, the wind ran high in the forest, breaking and sweeping tidelike over the reefs of treetops. The air was bitterly cold. Another voice, almost as fitful as the sough of the wind, sounded across the night. It was the waters of Stone Arrow Falls, above Big Rattle.

The frosts had drawn their bonds of ice and blankets of silencing snow over all the rest of the stream, but the white and black face of the falls still flashed from a window in the great house of crystal, and threw out a voice of desolation.

Sacobie Bear, a full-blooded Micmac, uttered a grunt of relief when his ears caught the bellow of Stone Arrow Falls. He stood still, and turned his head from side to side, questioningly.

"Good!" he said. "Big Rattle off there, Archer's camp over there. I go there. Good 'nough!"

He hitched his old smooth-bore rifle higher under his arm and continued his journey. Sacobie had tramped many miles—all the way from ice-imprisoned Fox Harbor. His papoose was sick. His squaw was hungry. Sacobie's belt was drawn tight.

During all that weary journey his old rifle had not banged once, although few eyes save those of timberwolf and lynx were sharper in the hunt than Sacobie's. The Indian was reeling with hunger and weakness, but he held bravely on.

A white man, no matter how courageous and sinewy, would have been prone in the snow by that time.

But Sacobie, with his head down and his round snowshoes padding! padding! like the feet of a frightened duck, raced with death toward the haven of Archer's cabin.

Archer was dreaming of a Christmas-time in a great faraway city when he was startled by a rattle of snowshoes at his threshold and a soft beating on his door, like weak blows from mittened hands. He sprang across the cabin and pulled open the door.

A short, stooping figure shuffled in and reeled against him. A rifle in a woollen case clattered at his feet.

"Mer' Christmas! How-do?" said a weary voice.

"Merry Christmas, brother!" replied Archer. Then, "Bless me, but it's Sacobie Bear! Why, what's the matter, Sacobie?"

"Heap tired! Heap hungry!" replied the Micmac, sinking to the floor.

Archer lifted the Indian and carried him over to the bunk at the further end of the room. He filled his iron-pot spoon with brandy, and inserted the point of it between Sacobie's unresisting jaws. Then he loosened the Micmac's coat and shirt and belt.

He removed his moccasins and stockings and rubbed the straight thin feet with brandy.

After a while Sacobie Bear opened his eyes and gazed up at Archer.

"Good!" he said. "John Archer, he heap fine man, anyhow. Mighty good to poor Injun Sacobie, too. Plenty tobac, I s'pose. Plenty rum, too."

"No more rum, my son," replied Archer, tossing what was left in the mug against the log wall, and corking the bottle, "and no smoke until you have had a feed. What do you say to bacon and tea! Or would tinned beef suit you better?"

"Bacum," replied Sacobie.

He hoisted himself to his elbow, and wistfully sniffed the fumes of brandy that came from the direction of his bare feet. "Heap waste of good rum, me t'ink," he said.

"You ungratefu' little beggar!" laughed Archer, as he pulled a frying pan from under the bunk.

By the time the bacon was fried and the tea steeped, Sacobie was sufficiently revived to leave the bunk and take a seat by the fire.

He ate as all hungry Indians do; and Archer looked on in wonder and whimsical regret, remembering the miles and miles he had tramped with that bacon on his back.

"Sacobie, you will kill yourself!" he protested.

"Sacobie no kill himself now," replied the Micmac, as he bolted a brown slice and a mouthful of hard bread. "Sacobie more like to kill himself when he empty. Want to live when he chock-full. Good fun. T'ank you for more tea."

Archer filled the extended mug and poured in the molasses—"long sweet'nin'" they call it in that region.

"What brings you so far from Fox Harbor this time of year?" inquired Archer.

"Squaw sick. Papoose sick. Bote empty. Wan' good bacum to eat."

Archer smiled at the fire. "Any luck trapping?" he asked.

His guest shook his head and hid his face behind the upturned mug.

"Not much," he replied, presently.

He drew his sleeve across his mouth, and then produced a clay pipe from a pocket in his shirt.

"Tobac?" he inquired.

Archer passed him a dark and heavy plug of tobacco.

"Knife?" queried Sacobie.

"Try your own knife on it," answered Archer, grinning.

With a sigh Sacobie produced his sheath-knife.

"You t'ink Sacobie heap big t'ief," he said, accusingly.

"Knives are easily lost—in people's pockets," replied Archer.

The two men talked for hours. Sacobie Bear was a great gossip for one of his race. In fact, he had a Micmac nickname which, translated, meant "the man who deafens his friends with much talk." Archer, however, was pleased with his ready chatter and unforced humour.

But at last they both began to nod. The white man made up a bed on the floor for Sacobie with a couple of caribou skins and a heavy blanket. Then he gathered together a few plugs of tobacco, some tea, flour, and dried fish.

Sacobie watched him with freshly aroused interest.

"More tobac, please," he said. "Squaw, he smoke, too."

Archer added a couple of sticks of the black leaf to the pile.

"Bacum, too," said the Micmac. "Bacum better nor fish, anyhow."

Archer shook his head.

"You'll have to do with the fish," he replied; "but I'll give you a tin of condensed milk for the papoose."

"Ah, ah! Him good stuff!" exclaimed Sacobie.

Archer considered the provisions for a second or two. Then, going over to a dunnage bag near his bunk, he pulled its contents about until he found a bright red silk handkerchief and a red flannel shirt. Their colour was too gaudy for his taste. "These things are for your squaw," he said.

Sacobie was delighted. Archer tied the articles into a neat pack and stood it in the corner, beside his guest's rifle.

"Now you had better turn in," he said, and blew out the light.

In ten minutes both men slept the sleep of the weary. The fire, a great mass of red coals, faded and flushed like some fabulous jewel. The wind washed over the cabin and fingered the eaves, and brushed furtive hands against the door.

It was dawn when Archer awoke. He sat up in his bunk and looked about the quiet, gray-lighted room. Sacobie Bear was nowhere to be seen.

He glanced at the corner by the door. Rifle and pack were both gone. He looked up at the rafter where his slab of bacon was always hung. It, too, was gone.

He jumped out of his bunk and ran to the door. Opening it, he looked out. Not a breath of air stirred. In the east, saffron and scarlet, broke the Christmas morning, and blue on the white surface of the world lay the imprints of Sacobie's round snowshoes.

For a long time the trapper stood in the doorway in silence, looking out at the stillness and beauty.

"Poor Sacobie!" he said, after a while. "Well, he's welcome to the bacon, even if it is all I had."

He turned to light the fire and prepare breakfast. Something at the foot of his bunk caught his eye. He went over and took it up. It was a cured skin—a beautiful specimen of fox. He turned it over, and on the white hide an uncultured hand had written, with a charred stick, "Archer."

"Well, bless that old red-skin!" exclaimed the trapper, huskily. "Bless his puckered eyes! Who'd have thought that I should get a Christmas present?"

The End

www.ingramcontent.com/pod-product-compliance
Lightning Source LLC
Chambersburg PA
CBHW070630290526
45790CB00001B/70